WOMEN SCHOLARS

Navigating the Doctoral Journey

WOMEN SCHOLARS

Navigating the Doctoral Journey

Edited by
Jelane A. Kennedy, EdD
Beverly A. Burnell, PhD

AAP APPLE
ACADEMIC
PRESS

Apple Academic Press Inc.
3333 Mistwell Crescent
Oakville, ON L6L 0A2 Canada

Apple Academic Press Inc.
9 Spinnaker Way
Waretown, NJ 08758 USA

Library and Archives Canada Cataloguing in Publication

Women scholars : navigating the doctoral journey / edited by Jelane A. Kennedy, EdD, Beverly A. Burnell, PhD.
Includes bibliographical references and index.
Issued in print and electronic formats.
ISBN 978-1-77188-678-9 (hardcover).--ISBN 978-1-351-20263-3 (PDF)
   1. Doctor of philosophy degree--Case studies. 2. Women--Education (Graduate)--Case studies. 3. Women doctoral students--Case studies. 4. Women scholars--Case studies. 5. Universities and colleges—Graduate work--Case studies. 6. Case studies. I. Burnell, Beverly A., editor II. Kennedy, Jelane A., editor

LB2386.W66 2018	378.2	C2018-905579-0	C2018-905580-4

Library of Congress Cataloging-in-Publication Data

Names: Kennedy, Jelane A., editor.
Title: Women scholars : navigating the doctoral journey / editors, Jelane A. Kennedy, EdD., Beverly A. Burnell, PhD.
Description: New Jersey : Apple Academic Press Toronto, [2018] | Includes bibliographical references and index.
Identifiers: LCCN 2018044890 (print) | LCCN 2018047026 (ebook) | ISBN 9781351202633 (ebook) | ISBN 9781771886789 (hardcover : alk. paper)
Subjects: LCSH: Women doctoral students--United States--Case studies.
Classification: LCC LB2386 (ebook) | LCC LB2386+ (print) | DDC 378.0082--dc23
LC record available at https://lccn.loc.gov/2018044890

Apple Academic Press also publishes its books in a variety of electronic formats. Some content that appears in print may not be available in electronic format. For information about Apple Academic Press products, visit our website at **www.appleacademicpress.com** and the CRC Press website at **www.crcpress.com**

DEDICATION

In memory of Mary L. Roark, EdD, who fought her way through the male-dominated academy, persevering with dignity and profession-alism, and paving the way for the rest of us. Mary always provided just the right blend of challenge, support, love, and inspiration that her graduate students needed to succeed in their academic endeavors and to fully develop themselves as counselors, educators, and scholars. She would have loved this book!

—Beverly A. Burnell, PhD

ABOUT THE EDITORS

Jelane A. Kennedy, EdD, is Program Coordinator and Associate Professor in the Student Development and Higher Education Program, Counselor Education and Family Therapy Department, Central Connecticut State University, New Britain, CT, USA. She was previously a full professor in the Counseling and College Student Services Department at The College of Saint Rose. She teaches graduate students in both Counseling and Student Development in Higher Education. At The College of Saint Rose, she had been the program coordinator of College Student Services for more than 20 years. Some of her areas of professional focus have been career development, cultural competency, and ethical practices. She has worked with numerous students completing their thesis and has coached doctoral students from other colleges as they have worked to complete their programs. She has also mentored master's level students entering doctoral programs. Dr. Jelane A. Kennedy began her career working in student affairs primarily in the area of career services.

Beverly A. Burnell, PhD, Professor Ementa at the State University of New York (SUNY) at Plattsburgh, and also served as the Employee Assistance Program Coordinator for the campus. She taught graduate students in the department's nationally accredited Clinical Mental Health Counseling program and the program in Student Affairs and Higher Education. Some of her areas of professional focus have been career development, counselor professional roles and identity, ethical practice, cultural competence, and transition processes for students with disabilities. Dr. Burnell has been an active contributor to the design of nationally accredited graduate programs in Teacher Education and Counselor Education and has coordinated the accreditation process for the Counselor Education Department. Dr. Burnell began her education career as a secondary mathematics teacher and has been a college career counselor, academic advisor, and personal counselor.

CONTENTS

LIST OF CONTRIBUTORS

Kit Anderson, PhD
Senior Lecturer (Retired), Environmental Sciences, University of Vermont, Burlington, VT, USA

Sherlene Ayala, MS
Doctoral Candidate, Clinical Specialist and Graduate Program Coordinator, Counseling and Educational Leadership, Montclair State University, Montclair, NJ, USA

Michelle C. Sterk Barrett, PhD
Director, Donelan Office of Community-Based Learning, College of the Holy Cross, Worcester, MA, USA

Jennifer A. Brown, PhD
Retired, Former Director of Institutional Research and Policy Studies, University of Massachusetts, Boston, Boston, MA, USA

Beverly A. Burnell, PhD
Professor Emerita, State University of New York at Plattsburgh, Plattsburgh, NY, USA

Hillary Hurst Bush, PhD
Postdoctoral Fellow, Department of Psychiatry, Massachusetts General Hospital, Boston, MA, USA

Eileen Cecilione, PT, DPT
Physical Therapist, C. O. R. E. Physical Therapy, Albany, NY, USA

Susannah C. Coaston, EdD
Assistant Professor, Counselor Education, Northern Kentucky University, Newport, KY, USA

Nancy L. Elwess, PhD
Distinguished Teaching Professor, Biological Sciences, State University of New York at Plattsburgh, Plattsburgh, NY, USA

Jody J. Fiorini, PhD
Department Head, Counseling, Educational Leadership, Educational andSchool Psychology Department, Wichita State University, Wichita, KS, USA

Tammy Lynn Garren, PhD
Instructional Designer, Center for Innovative Learning, Albany College of Pharmacy and Health Sciences, Albany, NY, USA

Kim R. Harris, PhD
Visiting Professor, Theological Studies, Loyola Marymount University in Los Angeles, CA, USA

Allison M. Hrovat, MEd
Human Services Faculty, Program Coordinator, Holyoke Community College, Holyoke, MA, USA

Patrice Jenkins, PhD
Self-employed, Catskill, NY, USA

Nadja C. Johnson, PhD
Assistant Dean of Students, Clark University, Worcester, MA, USA

Signe M. Kastberg, PhD

Private Therapist; Retired Associate Professor and Director of the M.S. Program in Mental Health Counseling, St. John Fisher College in Rochester, NY, USA

Jelane A. Kennedy, EdD
Associate Professor and Program Coordinator, Student Development and Higher Education Program, Counselor Education and Family Therapy, Central Connecticut State University, New Britain, CT, USA

Cherie L. King, ScD
Associate Professor, Program Coordinator, Clinical Professional Counseling Program, and Chair of the Department of Counselor Education and Family Therapy, Central Connecticut State University, New Britain, CT, USA

Aja E. LaDuke, PhD
Assistant Professor, Literacy Studies and Elementary Education, Sonoma State University, Rohnert Park, CA, USA

Delmy M. Lendof, EdD
Director for Residential Staff and Programs, New York University, New York City, NY, USA and Adjunct Assistant Professor, Higher and Postsecondary Education Program, New York University and Teachers College Columbia University, New York City, NY, USA

Margaret Leone, PhD
Lecturer, Department of Foreign Languages, State University of New York at Plattsburgh, Plattsburgh, NY, USA

Melissa Luke, PhD
Dean's Professor in Counseling and Human Services and Associate Dean for Research in School of Education, Syracuse University, Syracuse, NY, USA

Karen L. Mackie, PhD
Clinical Associate Professor of Counseling and Human Development, Mental Health Counseling Program, Counseling and Human Development, Warner School of Education, Rochester University, Rochester, NY, USA

Yettieve A. Marquez-Santana, EdD
Assistant Director, Office of Residence Life and Housing Services, New York University, New York City, NY, USA

Kate Bresonis McKee, MAT, MSEd
Doctoral Candidate, Assistant Dean, School of Arts and Sciences, Massachusetts College of Pharmacy and Health Sciences, Boston, MA, USA

Silvia Mejía, PhD
Associate Professor, Spanish and Latin American Literature and Film, The College of Saint Rose, Albany, NY, USA

Markesha Miller, PhD
Clinical Coordinator, Clinical Mental Health Counseling, South University, Savannah, GA, USA; Owner and Director of Holistic Psychological Associates in Columbia, SC, USA

Wanda I. Montañez EdD
Director of College Success for the Massachusetts Charter Public School Association, Hudson, MA, USA

Anna W. Nolan, PhD
2016 Doctoral Graduate and current stay-at-home mom with three children, Menands, NY, USA

Cinzia Pica-Smith, EdD

Associate Professor of Human Services and Rehabilitation Studies, Assumption College, Worcester, MA, USA

Emily Phillips, PhD
Adjunct Lecturer and Retired Professor, Educational Psychology, Counseling, and Special Education, State University of New York at Oneonta, Oneonta, NY, USA

Seema Rivera, PhD
Assistant Professor, STEM Education, Clarkson University, Capital Region Campus, Schenectady, NY, USA

Anne Toolan Rowley, PhD
Associate Professor, Communication Sciences and Disorders, The College of Saint Rose, Albany, NY, USA

Deborah J. Smith, EdD
Professor, Health Sciences, Empire State College, Saratoga Springs, NY, USA

Maureen E. Squires, EdD
Associate Professor and Program Coordinator, M.S.Ed. Program, Teacher Education, State University of New York at Plattsburgh, Plattsburgh, NY, USA

Jamie S. Switzer, EdD
Associate Professor, Department of Journalism and Technical Communication, Colorado State University, Fort Collins, CO, USA

Liza A. Talusan, PhD
Educational Consultant and Speaker, Brockton, MA, USA

Ying Tang, PhD
Associate Professor, School Counseling, State University of New York at Oneonta, Oneonta, NY, USA

Terri Ward, EdD
Associate Professor, Special Education, The College of Saint Rose, Albany, NY, USA

Wendy Neifeld Wheeler, PhD
Dean of Students, Albany College of Pharmacy and Health Sciences, Albany, NY, USA

ACKNOWLEDGEMENTS

First, I want to acknowledge the women who were brave enough to offer their stories to be a part of the collection that you are about to read. They have inspired me. I am awed by their willingness to be authentically themselves and to share that with others. If only we could find this in our everyday lives.

I also need to acknowledge the women scholars who have come before me and helped pave my way. When NAWE (formerly National Association of Women Deans, Administrators, and Counselors) still existed, I found support and many important women role models at the annual conferences I attended as a young student affairs professional. For 15 years, these women showed me the way as a first-generation, working-class new professional in the academy. I am indebted to the women whose shoulders I have had the opportunity to stand on. They helped me believe I could go for my doctorate.

In this vein, I also need to thank the ACES Women's Retreat that held me up through the years after the close of NAWE, when I struggled in my life as an academic. When I was just about ready to leave the field, I landed at the retreat because my advisor from my doctoral program, Dr. Kathy Evans, encouraged me to meet her there, and again I found the sisters I needed to carry on.

I also need to acknowledge Marion Roach Smith who, through her teaching of personal essay/memoir classes I have taken over the years, helped me find my voice and confidence as a writer. I must also give a nod to the women of the Women's Writing Retreat at Pyramid Lake in Paradox Lake, NY, for their loving encouragement throughout the years.

Last, but not least, the loving support of my partner, Eileen, has made all things possible. She believes in me as an artist and writer, supports my academic work, and reminds me to take life more lightly! She always reminds me that working together, the load is easier. Without her wonderful meals, fun, laughter, and support, I could not do half of what I do—thank you!

—**Jelane A. Kennedy, EdD**

PREFACE

The idea for this book arose for me, Jelane, within the first six years after I had completed my doctoral degree. As a first-generation student always feeling caught in limbo between my working-class background and life in the academy, I wondered if others felt the same way. Having read about strong women and their strategies and experiences in other areas, such as leadership, I was provided good guidance, inspiration, and motivation for my life as a new professional. So, I always felt there should be something for women traversing the doctoral process. Twenty years later, there is still nothing. Jelane's perspective resonated with me, Bev, and we decided to collaborate. Thus, this book was born.

The editors, Dr. Jelane A. Kennedy and Dr. Beverly A. Burnell, have both been "doctors" for many years, having acquired their doctoral degrees in the 1990s. As the 2016 major motion picture "Hidden Figures" revealed, much of the intellectual acumen and accomplishments of women, and particularly of women of color, is hidden, unknown, and, in fact, deliberately concealed when honorifics such as "Dr." were reserved for men only. We are familiar with experiences of other women with doctorates, and each of us has experienced situations such as the following: a group of people with doctorates is being introduced and those with doctorates who are men are referred to as "Dr.," and those with doctorates who are women are referred to by their first names such as "Jelane" and "Bev."

The dichotomy in which men are identified by their scholarly accomplishments and women are identified by first names, which reveal nothing of their scholarly accomplishments, is an underlying reason why we wanted to develop this book. We hope that our readers will find helpful information, motivation, inspiration, and strategies for navigating the doctoral process in these pages.

REFERENCE

Williams, P.; & Melfi, T. (Director); Gigliotti, D.; Chernin, P.; & Topping, J. (Producers); Melfi, T. (2016). *Hidden Figures* [Motion Picture]. United States: 20th Century Fox.

INTRODUCTION

Statistics on doctoral degree attainment demonstrates that women have earned the majority of doctoral degrees for seven consecutive years, at 51.8% in 2014–2015, the most recent year for which data are available (Okahana, Feaster, & Allum, 2016). More women than men are first-time enrollees in master's degree and certificate programs (58.2%) and doctoral programs (51.3%). However, data have also consistently shown that approximately 50% of students who enroll in doctoral programs drop out before completion (Ali and Kohun, 2007; Cassuto, 2013; Walker, Golde, Jones, Bueschel, & Hutchings, 2008). Thus, out of the 134,335 first-time doctoral program enrollees in 2014–2015 (Okahana, et al., 2016), 50% attrition rate amounts to the loss of more than 67,000 students. These numbers are staggering.

Social isolation and stress are the main causes of such failure (Ali & Kohun, 2006; Lovitts, 2001). Ali & Kohun note that social isolation and stress are typically considered attributes of students themselves, rather than embedded within the culture of doctoral programs, or possibly some combination of program culture and individuals' circumstances. Emotional exhaustion occurs when work demands exceed resources, resulting in depletion of emotional energy (Hunter & Devine, 2016). Emotional exhaustion also contributes to attrition of students from doctoral programs, though perceived socio-emotional support from the department and/or faculty and high-quality relationships with one's doctoral advisor have been found to significantly reduce emotional exhaustion. Students who are older (Hunter & Devine, 2016) or more socially competent (Ali & Kohun, 2007) fare better, but some level of social isolation and stress is inherent in a culture in which individual effort and competition are most prized and where attending to academic commitments and completion of the degree over other more personal responsibilities is expected. Women, particularly, experience stress when faced with choices that bring about strong contradictory emotions, such as "feelings of guilt and frustration about the high cost of the doctoral study in terms of lost time, opportunities, and relationships alongside feelings of intellectual satisfaction and pleasure in their scholarly work," (Aitchison & Mowbray, 2013, p. 861).

A recent study from New Zealand indicated that women's experiences of the doctoral process are nuanced by gender. Carter, Blumenstein, & Cook

(2013) found recurring counseling themes, over a ten-year time period, of women needing to manage family commitments (i.e., children, partner relationship, elder care, etc.), relationship issues (i.e., children, partner, etc.), time commitments, female identity issues, and personal trauma history. Women who choose to do doctoral work are often confronted with challenges to identity, life roles, and the "legitimacy" of their simultaneous engagement in doctoral studies and personal relationships (Carter et al., 2013, p. 348). This corresponds with a study from the south of England that underscored being a mother, domestic responsibilities, and balancing home and academic lives added to women's stress while working on the doctoral degree (Brown and Watson, 2010). In the United States, Kurtz-Costes, Helmke, & Ulku-Steiner (2006) also found that women had concerns related to family and personal life, and Onwuegbuzie, Rosli, Ingram, & Frels (2014) identified similar themes related to the challenges of "dual roles (i.e., as doctoral students and wives/mothers or as doctoral students and professionals) or triple roles (i.e., as doctoral students, wives/mothers, and professionals)" (p. 1).

Women report that having a female mentor is beneficial, especially since the mentor may be interested in supporting other women to become scholars (Kurtz-Costes, et al., 2006). Although there has been progress in the numbers of women completing doctoral degrees, there is still a lag in the number of women among faculty, especially at the higher ranks. Women are not always present to serve as role models on campus and in academic departments. Women students, and especially women of color, need to see themselves in other women who fulfill meaningful roles in higher education (Aryan & Guzman, 2010).

These factors, collectively, offered us, the editors, compelling reasons to create an ethnographic book by women about their doctoral developmental experiences. Women anticipating and entering the life of academia can benefit from the voices and experiences of other women scholars. Research that has examined bibliotherapy supports the idea that reading about others' experiences can be therapeutic in coping with stress, anxiety, and depression (Bowman, Scogin, & Lyrene, 1995; Evans, 2015; Jeffcoat & Hayes, 2012). In her work with Black women, Evans (2015) emphasized the value of literary mentoring as a potent method for empowering women. This work is in that same spirit; stories from a variety of women who have been through or who are in the midst of the doctoral journey can serve as valuable guides for those contemplating setting out on that journey for themselves.

Utilizing Ali & Kohun's four stages of doctoral study (2006, 2007), the essay writers in this volume offer an examination of critical incidents in their doctoral experiences and offer strategies they have found helpful in managing those incidents. We, the editors, added a fifth "stage" for contributors to address as well, as we are aware that the transition from doctoral study to postdoctoral employment also has its challenges. Thus, writers were asked to present one or more incidents from one of five points along the doctoral path.

Stage 1: Preadmission to Enrollment: This is the period of inquiry and research into potential doctoral programs and may include campus visits and/or interviews, the application process, and orientation; this stage also includes the students' experiences during the early days of enrollment into the program (Ali & Kohun, 2007).

Stage 2: First Year of the Program: This first year includes coursework related to the students' field of study but is most notable for the processes of socialization to the culture of the doctoral program, identity as a scholar, and an educational environment and expectations that differ greatly from previous experiences (Ali & Kohun, 2007).

Stage 3: Second Year through Candidacy: This is the period after completion of the first year of study until attainment of candidacy, signified by successful completion of the comprehensive or qualifying exams. During this time, the student continues with coursework, completes the comprehensive or qualifying exam, selects a dissertation advisor and committee, and prepares and defends a dissertation proposal (Ali & Kohun, 2007).

Stage 4: The Dissertation Stage: During this stage, coursework has been completed and the focus is on independent research guided by the dissertation advisor (and, perhaps, committee). The increased independence of this stage is generally characterized by less structure and more pressure. This stage culminates in the successful defense of the dissertation research (Ali & Kohun, 2007).

Completion and Transition to Employment: This stage focuses on transition into employment in the academy or other venues related to the student's field of study and includes a further acculturation period as the individual learns, for example, firsthand about the hierarchy within academic departments, as well as the relative emphasis on the three pillars of academic life—research, teaching, and service.

In this volume, we present 46 essays from 40 women representing a range of ages, ethnicities, academic disciplines, sexual orientations, family circumstances, and family educational histories. Nine women share stories from Stage 1, fourteen write about experiences in Stage 2, nine writers address the challenges of Stage 3, ten essays address the dissertation processes of Stage 4, and five contributors write from the perspective of completion and transition into employment. Two women wrote essays for each of four stages, and one woman wrote essays for two stages. Their stories are stories of empowerment, of pitfalls and overcoming barriers, of successful negotiations of the graduate school process, of the joys and challenges of scholarly pursuits, of positive help-seeking behaviors and strategies, and of life after the dissertation is completed.

The final sections of the book include brief biographies of the 40 essay contributors and a glossary of terms. The glossary reflects the fact that the world of doctoral study has its own culture and language with which many readers may be unfamiliar.

We are deeply indebted to the women who contributed to this volume and were willing to dig deep and share critical incidents from their doctoral journeys: incidents of inspiration, vulnerability, joy, confusion, disillusionment, intellectual challenge, intimacy, and accomplishment. It is our hope that this collection of the voices of women sharing their experiences and lessons learned will empower, support, and inspire you, dear reader, to approach your own doctoral studies armed with knowledge attained from others who came before you; that you will *know* that doctoral education and completion are possible, and that grasping the outstretched hands of those who have been there and succeeded will help you succeed.

REFERENCES

Ali, S., & Kohun, F. (2006). Dealing with isolation feelings at IS doctoral programs. *International Journal of Doctoral Studies, 1,* 21–33. Available at: http://ijds.org/Volume1/IJDSv1p021-033Ali13.pdf.

Ali, A.; & Kohun, F. (2007). Dealing with social isolation to minimize doctoral attrition—a four stage framework. *International Journal of Doctoral Studies, 2,* 33–49. Retrieved from: http://www.informingscience.org/Journals/IJDS/Articles?Volume=2–2007&Search.

Aryan, B.; & Guzman, F. (2010). Women of color and the PhD: Experiences in formal graduate support programs. *Journal of Business Studies Quarterly, 1*(4), 69–77. http://jbsq.org/.

Atchison, C.; & Mowbray, S. (2013). Doctoral women: Managing emotions, managing doctoral studies. *Teaching in Higher Education, 18,* 859–870.http://dx.doi.org/10.1080/13562517.2013.827642.

Bowman, D.; Scogin, F.; & Lyrene, B. (1995). The efficacy of self-examination therapy and cognitive bibliotherapy in the treatment of mild to moderate depression. *Psychotherapy Researcher, 5*(2) 131–140. DOI: 10.1080/10503309512331331256.

Brown, L.; & Watson, P. (2010). Understanding the experiences of female doctoral students. *Journal of Further Higher Education, 34*(3), 385–404. DOI:10.1080/0309877X.2010.484056.

Carter, S.; Blumenstein, M.; & Cook, C. (2013). Different for women? The challenges of doctoral studies. *Teaching in Higher Education, 18*(4), 339–351. DOI: 10.1080/13562517.2012.719159.

Cassuto, L. (2013). Attrition: How much is too much? *Chronicle of Higher Education*, July 1, 2013. http://chronicle.com/article/PhD-Attrition-How-Much-Is/140045/.

Castro, V.; Garcia, E. E.; Cavazos Jr., J.; & Castro, A. Y. (2011). The road to doctoral success and beyond. *International Journal of Doctoral Studies*, *6*, 51–77.

Evans, S. Y. (2015). Healing traditions in Black women's writing: Resources for poetry therapy. *Journal of Poetry Therapy*, *28*(3), 165–178. DOI: 10.1080/08893675.2015.1051286.

Hunter, K. H.; & Devine, K. (2016). Doctoral students' emotional exhaustion and intentions to leave academia. *International Journal of Doctoral Studies*, *11*, 35–61. Retrieved from http://ijds.org/Volume11/IJDSv11p035-061Hunter2198.pdf.

Jeffcoat, T.; & Hayes, S.C. (2012). A randomized trial of ACT Bibliotherapy on the mental health of K-12 teachers and staff. *Behavioral Research and Therapy*, *50*, 571–579. Retrieved from http://www.elsevier.com/locate/brat.

Kurtz-Costes, B., Helmke, L. A.; & Ulku-Steiner, B. (2006). Gender and doctoral studies: The perceptions of PhD students in an American university. *Gender and Education*, *18*(2), 137–155. DOI: 10.1080/09540250500380513.

Lovitts, B. E. (2001). *Leaving the ivory tower: The causes and consequences of departure from doctoral study.* Lanham, MD: Rowman & Littlefield.

Okahana, H., Feaster, K.; & Allum, J. (2016). *Graduate enrollment and degrees, 2005 to 2015.* Washington, DC: Council of Graduate Schools.

Onwuegbuzie, A. J., Rosli, R., Ingram, J. M.; & Frels, R. K. (2014). A critical dialectical pluralistic examination of the lived experience of select women doctoral students. *Qualitative Report 19* (Article 5), 1–35. Retrieved from: http://www.nova.edu/ssss/QR/QR19/onwuegbuzie5.pdf

Walker, G., Golde, C. M., Jones, L., Bueschel, A. C.; & Hutchings, P. (2008). *The formation of scholars: Rethinking doctoral education for the twenty-first century.* Stanford, CA: Jossey-Bass.

PART I:
Stage 1: From Preadmission to Enrollment

This stage is the period of inquiry and research into potential doctoral programs, which usually includes campus visits and/or interviews, the application process, and orientation. This stage also includes students' experiences during the early days of enrollment in the program (Ali & Kohun, 2007).

PREADMISSION RESEARCH

Research into doctoral programs includes evaluation of several factors, such as (a) faculty members' areas of research and records of scholarship, (b) the program's history of doctoral completion, (c) potential for the program to provide experiences consistent with the applicant's goals, (d) potential for funding via scholarships, fellowships, grants, and/or research assistantships, teaching assistantships, or other graduate assistantships (e.g., administrative), (e) program accreditation, if applicable to the discipline, (f) expectations and requirements (e.g., number of credits required and number of credits allowed for previous graduate-level work, time to completion, relevant resources and facilities), and (g) experiences of current or recent students—best obtained via a campus visit. It is worth noting that the campus visit helps in providing a prospective student with a sense of the program/department culture, and particularly to gauge whether the climate is welcoming to diverse students.

THE APPLICATION PROCESS

Completion of the application process requires several tasks, as follows:

- Completion of the application form,
- Paying the application fee,
- Official transcripts from previous educational experiences,
- Letters of recommendation (from former faculty or supervisors; these should address your potential to complete doctoral work),

- A personal statement,
- Official test scores (e.g., GRE, TOEFL),
- A resume,
- A portfolio,
- A writing sample, and
- An interview (a campus visit is recommended with an opportunity to meet students and faculty).

Deadlines for submission of the above application materials are generally 9–12 months before the semester when the applicant hopes to begin study, so one's research on potential programs begins even earlier. For information on researching graduate programs, please see the Peterson's Graduate Education Directory: https://www.petersons.com/graduate-schools.aspx.

GRADUATE SCHOOL IS NOT AN ADD-ON

It is important to consider how to make space and what modifications will be required in your life to find the time required to do graduate-level work. Graduate school is considered a gift of professional development. Choose wisely a program that you feel will be professionally good for you, a good fit, and that you are able to make room for within your life. Then honor that choice by making time to get the most from your studies. Consider what is right for you: Going part-time? Being full-time, but taking only the minimum number of courses required for full-time status? Taking an absolute full-time load of courses? How many credits will fit your lifestyle? Do not stress yourself out with too many classes at once. The doctorate is a marathon, not a sprint.

PREPARE TO WRITE

You will write a lot. Work on keyboarding. If you have not learned to keyboard, sign up to take a class. Typing with two fingers will become impractical in no time. Learning to compose at the keyboard will also save you valuable time. This does not mean that there is no need for you to write longhand, but exercising your brain in multiple ways will help your work. Writing letters to friends and family via e-mail is a good way of practicing. This will help you take the exercise seriously.

STAGE 1 NARRATIVES

In this section, nine women share their experiences from the germination of desire to obtain a doctoral degree to the early days of actually beginning a degree program. As is true throughout this book, the women contributors are a diverse group—some are married/partnered/have children, while others are not; some work part-time, others are full-time; some were first-generation students as undergraduates; some are women of color, others are not; some are heterosexual, others are not; some entered their doctoral programs straight out of undergraduate school and some have years of professional experience before beginning doctoral studies.

The essays from the authors in this section echo the observations of Ali and Kohun (2006, 2007) that successful completion of prior college experiences (i.e., bachelor's or master's degrees) does not fully prepare one for the reality of the doctoral experience. The authors also subtly, and sometimes not so subtly, remind us that they are fully aware of the fact that the transitions they are about to make will potentially cause identity challenges and disruptions in their lives, as well as open new opportunities for employment and professional accomplishments.

REFERENCES

Ali, A.: & Kohun, F. (2006). Dealing with isolation feelings in IS doctoral programs. *International Journal of Doctoral Studies, 1,* 21–22. Retrieved from: http://www.informingscience. org/Journals/IJDS/Articles?Volume=1–2006 &Search.

Ali, A.; & Kohun, F. (2007). Dealing with social isolation to minimize doctoral attrition—a four stage framework. *International Journal of Doctoral Studies, 2,* 33–49. Retrieved from: http://www.informingscience.org/Journals/IJDS/Articles?Volume=2–2007&Search.

CHAPTER 1

FROM THE CONCRETE WALLS OF SPANISH HARLEM TO THE MOSAIC TILES OF ACADEMIA

SHERLENE AYALA, MS, Doctoral Candidate

Clinical Specialist and Graduate Program Coordinator, Counseling and Educational Leadership, Montclair State University, Montclair, NJ, USA

It was a Friday evening around 5:00 pm. I had left work and was standing at a bus stop in Newark, NJ. It was the first of April, so it was dark outside, cool and raining. It was the type of rain that combined with wind somehow finds its way under one's umbrella. My bus always ran late, so I usually spent my time scrolling through social media or texting friends, but this time, I left my phone in my bag untouched.

Earlier that week, I had attended an all-day interview for consideration for admission into the PhD Counselor Education program at a local university. I had reached the point in my professional career where the idea of being a doctor was attractive, yet seemed to be so farfetched because people who look like me were often displayed in positions as nannies, housekeepers, cafeteria workers, or medical assistants. I wasn't quite sure what I'd do with the degree; however, I knew that I wanted to add those special letters after my name with hopes and dreams of being a role model for other people of color to follow.

According to Yosso (2006), the Chicano and Chicana educational pipeline suggests that, of the 100 students who start out in elementary school, only .2% go on to pursue and persist in a doctoral program. Overcrowded classrooms, lack of resources, lack of afterschool programs, and children who have to work in order to contribute to their families are some of the factors that impact the path that the students choose in their education. As a first-generation college student, I could empathize with the lack of resources as my high school had one guidance counselor for a population of 500 students. Pursuit of higher education was not something my family was well versed on. While we knew that it was important, we didn't quite understand how to utilize the system to help us get there. My lack of social capital meant that, as a first-year undergraduate, I showed up at a college which I had never visited with one suitcase and a pillow. I had enough money to make a phone call using a payphone and enough clothing to make it through a month. I was fortunate enough to be taken in by the Educational Opportunity Program (EOP) at a SUNY (State University of New York) school. The staff mentored me, academically; however, I lacked an understanding of the nuances of university culture and politics and lacked awareness of funding opportunities such as student employment that would help me pay for things. I didn't understand the importance of developing my co-curricular resume, nor did I know whom to speak with to discuss my feelings of isolation at this Predominantly White University. I was unprepared.

And now, here I was, several years post-college graduation in the same unfamiliar territory. It was times like these when I wished I had a mentor in the field who could provide me with guidance and support. It just seemed unfair that I always had to roll up my sleeves and do this hard investigative work. It seemed as if I never got a break. To learn about doctoral programs, I scanned blogs that were written by White men and women who completed their doctoral degrees. They emphasized Western individualistic values that celebrated autonomy and hard work. To persist in a doctoral program, they suggest you toughen up and pull yourself up by the bootstraps, create timelines, focus on school work, and cut everything and everyone else out of your life for the next five to seven years. I struggled with this narrative, as it was a voice of privilege and dominance that did not embody my intersecting identities and lived experiences as a first-generation woman of color. I valued a collectivist approach and saw my journey to be one of collaboration with my cohort, my family, and my advisors.

So here I was, days after my interview, standing at the bus stop for quite some time. After looking at my watch, I realized that my bus was late, as usual. I paced back and forth, leaning over the curb to see if I could spot my bus in the far distance among the slow-moving traffic. Suddenly, I saw it emerging. I sprinted to the curb flagging it down while closing my wet umbrella. As I showed my bus pass to the driver and walked toward the back of the bus looking around at the other familiar black and brown folks, I thought to myself, "My life is about to change." There was a sense of pride that I had made it to the next level of academia, and yet there was an immense sense of loss because I knew my privileged identity would make me an "other" in my own community. My rank in society would advance me to a different level of socioeconomic status, and perhaps I would be surrounded by others who would invalidate my experiences and struggles. The idea of leaving my people behind didn't feel too good, as I was proud to be from Spanish Harlem and was also proud of the struggles that I success-fully endured to get into the position where I am today. I was unsure how I would make sense of my new positionality in the world.

As I shuffled through the bus to find a seat, I felt my cell phone vibrate in my purse. My heart raced and my breathing shortened as I saw an unfamiliar number. I knew this would be the call that would determine whether I would be able to join elite academia in pursuit of a doctoral degree. I answered the call, and it was the Department Chair from the program. There was a small talk that I don't quite remember. I nervously smiled to calm my nerves; however, deep down inside, I was scared and doubted my academic abilities to be accepted in this doctoral program. I'm a product of the public school system. Yes, I was an outstanding student leader on a college campus, and yes I founded a chapter of a Latina sorority, but I never published anything nor did I do research with any faculty. And, yes, I had ten years of profes-sional experience in higher education, I am a midlevel administrator in higher educaiton, and I still had a lot to learn. Those who achieved doctoral degrees came from institutions such as Yale, Harvard, and Columbia. What did I know? I really didn't hear anything that the Department Chair said; instead, I found that my thoughts kept drifting away. I had this feeling that she was calling to share the bad news. I feared that she would say something along the lines that the committee had decided to choose other students and only she wanted to thank me for my time. I imagined this uncomfortable moment and the uncomfortable moment and that we'd both be polite as the call would end.

As the bus swayed from side to side trying to avoid the large potholes, I pressed the phone closer to my ear so that I would not miss any words from this conversation. I held my breath for what felt like days. My eyes widened as I looked around nervously as if everyone on the bus could hear our conversation. Could they also hear the voices in my head saying, "You are out of your league" ? I was ready for rejection, but instead I heard, "Sher-lene, congratulations! We'd like to invite you to join our doctoral program." My mouth opened but words did not come through. "Wait, what? Are you sure? Me?" I remember saying that out loud as if she had made a mistake. I cheered with happiness over the phone. I thanked her for the personalized phone call and we hung up shortly afterwards.

As I looked up from the phone, I made a mental note of where I was and knew I had just a few more stops before I was home. I fumbled with my phone in my hands. I opened Facebook scanned status updates from friends, many of whom were celebrating the end-of-the-work week and others who were dreading the rainy weather. I closed the application and stared out the window; however, because of the dark sky, all I could see was my reflection in the glass. I saw a different me; a look of excitement yet pensiveness as if I had made a mistake. I was going to be the "other" within my family and friends, and although the idea of being a doctor was attractive, would this role and status ostracize me? Is this what I really wanted? Did I need a doctoral degree to be successful? Or had I internalized Western ideas of what success meant, and not realized the cultural wealth within my own community that made each and every one of us successful in our own way? Would I be able to handle this new role in my life?

Statistically, I wasn't meant to make it out of Spanish Harlem. The academic system was designed so I would remain in my place and allow those with privileged identities to make decisions for me and for my community. I was meant to remain in a position where my voice would be missing from the narrative, and the media would continue to portray brown folks as lazy, unmotivated, and not interested in education. However, because of my achievement, I would be tokenized and used as an example of the model minority. Comments and thoughts such as "Well if she made it, then why couldn't you?" would be made to place blame on racial and ethnic minorities. I was uncomfortable being a token; however, I knew that this opportunity would give me a seat at the table that so many did not have access to.

The crowded bus came to a stop, and I squeezed through the back door. The rain had slowed down, so I tucked my umbrella in my bag and grabbed my cell phone. I pondered who I would share this significant moment with, but without thinking too much into it, I dialed a very familiar number. The phone rang a few times, and finally a voice on the other end,

Her: "Hello, *Muneca*, how are you doing? Is it raining over there?"

Me: "Hi, *Abuela*. It was raining, but now it has slowed down. I am just getting home from work, and I am calling because I have some news."

A very uneasy and dragged-out "okay" came over the phone. I took a deep breath.

Me: "Okay, so I did something crazy."

Her: [silence] "*Muneca*, what did you do?"

Here it goes—deep breath and a huge exhale as I put it out in the universe.

Me: "I applied for graduate school."

Her: "But you already went to school. You're going back?"

Me: "Well this is different. I applied to a PhD program, and today I was accepted. They think I have what it takes to be a doctor. I am going to be a doctor, *Abuela*. I'm going to be a *doctor*."

I heard a loud shout of delight and joy on the other end of the phone.

Her: "Ay, *mi Muneca*, I am so proud of you."

The tears roll off my cheeks and onto my coat. I cling onto my phone wishing she was there to embrace and hold. Who would have thought that the girl from Spanish Harlem was going to become a doctor?

REFERENCES

Yosso, T. J. (2006). *Critical race counterstories along the Chicana/Chicano educational pipeline*. New York: Routledge.

CHAPTER 2

DO I REALLY WANT OR NEED A DOCTORATE, AND HOW DO I CHOOSE THE RIGHT PROGRAM FOR ME?

DELMY M. LENDOF, EdD

New York University and Teachers College, Columbia University, New York City, NY, USA

During my last year in my master's program, the Assistant Vice President for Student Affairs said to me, "Kid, you are really bright but if you want to move up to be a Vice President or higher, you will need to get a doctorate." I was 22 years old and did not have full-time work experience. However, I knew I did not want an employer to rule me out as a candidate because I did not have a degree. I knew that at some point, I would need to go back to school and get a doctorate, but I had a long road ahead to figure out what, where, when, and how.

As a first-generation college student whose parents had a fifth-grade education, I did not understand the difference between associate, bachelor, master, or doctoral degrees. However, my parents had raised me with an understanding that the more education I received, the better my life and future would be. To this date, even though they don't understand the challenges of my educational journey or the meaning of any of my credentials, they have always been on my side, providing the support and encouragement that took me from application to degree completion. While they can't explain my degrees, they proudly share with family and friends that I have a doctorate and work at a university.

From the time I began my doctoral work in the fall of 2000, I have been asked hundreds of times about the process of applying for graduate school and the journey of completing the program. For the last 16 years,

I have mentored, and provided guidance and assistance to a number of friends, colleagues, direct reports, and mentees on the graduate application process. While I don't track the individuals I have assisted, I am happy to share that most of the people I have assisted have either completed their programs or are currently enrolled and making progress toward program completion. Furthermore, as I worked on writing this chapter, I provided assistance to a direct report and two mentees applying for admissions to doctoral programs for the 2017 academic year. I am also mentoring/ supporting six current students enrolled in doctoral programs. Finally, my teaching experience in two well-established higher education programs, my involvement in national higher education associations, combined with a strong network of faculty members teaching in doctoral programs around the country have greatly influenced my ability to understand the doctoral application process.

2.1   DO I NEED A DOCTORATE? DO I WANT A DOCTORATE?

These are often the first two questions I am asked by people exploring doctoral programs. As I help them answer these questions, I am reminded of my own journey in answering them. For years, my answers to these questions changed based on whom I was speaking with or how I felt about the work I was doing. I tried to convince myself that I did not want a doctorate, that I did not need one, and every so often I would think that maybe I did want it. I can't remember if these thoughts were the result of my personal insecurities, fear of the unknown, or both, but these feelings were very real and I am sure that other people thinking of applying may share similar fears as well.

I am now forty-four years old and three years after completing my EdD. I am here to tell those asking these questions that whether you think you want it or need it, you do want it and you do need it. You need it for your career advancement, but I need you to do it because it will impact generations of women and students of color and their ability to see the possibility of a doctorate in a person they can identify with and will help them see possibilities beyond their reach. I hope that these three paragraphs have inspired you to consider getting a doctorate and that the information below will be helpful in getting started with the process. The section below is structured around the following themes: what, where, when, and how?

2.2   WHICH DEGREE (PhD OR EdD), AND IN WHAT?

One of the most influential women in my journey, Joan Carbone, used to say, "You don't let a higher education professional pull your teeth or do dental work on you, so why would you trust someone without a higher education degree to care for the development of your college student?" While this example is a little extreme, I think it is important that you pursue a degree in an area relevant to the work you hope to be doing. While most disciplines and careers have transferable skills, there are a few professions that look for a doctorate in a specific area. However, I believe that in most areas of higher education and areas related to social services, EdD or PhD completion, followed by experience in that area, is more important than the area of study. I also believe that in most programs, you will have flexibility with regard to the topic you focus on and you will be allowed to do research on topics that are important to you. I strongly believe that what is most important is that you find a program that will support you and that has a good retention and completion record.

2.2.1   PhD VERSUS EdD

- PhD: Historically known for those interested in research and teaching. Often heavier on the number of required research courses.
- EdD: Historically known to be more focused on practice, application of theory, and policy.
- PhD and EdD requirements (as they pertain to a number of credits and research/dissertation expectations) vary from one institution to the next, so make sure to do your research.
- PhD: Was historically viewed more positively in tenure-track teaching roles and university president roles, but that has been and continues to change. *In recent years there has been an increase in college presidents with EdDs.*
- If your goal is to land a tenure-track teaching role or become a college president, regardless of the program you choose—EdD or PhD—you need to make sure you are doing research and publishing.
- *Finally, both PhD and EdD graduates wear almost identical, great looking caps and gowns, formally known as regalia.*

2.3   WHAT TO RESEARCH?

There are people who prolong applying to a program because they feel they need to have a research topic before applying to a program. This is not a requirement for most programs. If you have a research topic, that is great; however, if you don't, that is OK. We all have areas of interest and passions, and your courses and faculty interactions will help you identify new areas of interest that you may want to explore. A good way to explore topics is to read the research done by the faculty members in the programs you are interested in, to research dissertations sponsored by some of those faculty members, and to read journals in your areas of interest.

2.4   WHERE?

There are hundreds of institutional and program options to consider, and as such, it is essential that you take the time to research the institution and program that would work best for you.

- If you are working in a higher education institution or corporation that will pay for your education, I say it is an opportunity worth exploring as it will reduce the amount of loan funding you will have to obtain. Although working while going to school may prolong the process to degree completion, the financial savings may make it worth while for you.
- Do you want to stay in your current state or region or are you willing to explore relocating? The more open you are to relocating, the more options for programs you will have and the more likely you are to find programs that provide funding.
- Can you afford an executive program? Executive programs that are accredited are becoming more and more popular for those working full-time and managing multiple priorities. These programs often entail a combination of online courses and a few weeks per year. However, these programs often can be cost prohibitive for some as the cost can be close to or over $100,000; they provide little, if any, financial aid, and most employers don't provide funding or tuition remission for them.
- Are you open to online programs? While I am personally not a fan of online programs, you will want to do your research before investing

in one. You want to look at completion rates, what graduates from the program are doing for employment postgraduation, and, of course, cost.

2.5 WHEN?

There is no right time for starting a doctoral program; there is *YOUR* time. Your time is always the right time. Because there is NO right time for starting a program, it means that when you decide on the time, there will still be fear, insecurities, anxiety, and a number of things you will need to work on to prepare for the journey. The process is never problem or stress-free, but don't let these things keep you from getting started. I guarantee you it is doable. The points below, I hope, will help you work on a plan to determine when the time is right for you.

- *Work Experience:* While some people argue that you should get professional experience before applying for a doctoral program, and many people do, there are those who go directly from a master's program to a doctoral program. Either way, I think it is important that you are able to answer these questions: What degree do I want? Why do I want that degree? Am I ready to make the commitment?
- *Part-Time versus Full-Time:* At the time I applied to doctoral programs, I felt part-time was the only option mainly because I was worried about the cost and ability to pay my bills. While part-time was a great option for me, I realized that colleagues attending full-time were often highly or fully funded and as a result able to move faster through the program, graduate sooner, and engage more actively in research and student teaching than I was able to.
- *Family:* There are those who believe in getting it done before making significant life-changing commitments, such as marriage or having children, and there is nothing wrong with that. However, there are those who are married and have children and go back to work on the degree, and in these cases, it is important to make sure that you have a discussion with your partner, children, and family members about the journey you will be going on and the fact that you will need their support.

2.6 HOW?

How do you get started? The starting process can be overwhelming but it is all about research and having a plan. I suggest using a computer program to track the above-mentioned information and to create folders or notes to keep information organized. I personally use Excel™ and Google Drive™ for most of my work. Once you have answers to the questions above, you will want to develop an action plan. While some people can work on applying to programs and get it all done in six months to a year, others take from one to three years in the planning process. Develop a plan. Begin with the end in mind. Decide when you think you want to begin your doctoral program and let that drive the timeline you create. I hope the suggestions below will be of assistance in getting started.

- Researching programs and faculty (focus on program [does not have to be higher education] what is the faculty interested in). Make sure to research program completion rates.
- Researching institutions (the place where you work, the place where you want to work, the place close to you, and the places you are willing to relocate to). Make sure the program is accredited.
- Researching requirements (GRE required, or not, writing sample, work experience, recommendations). Some programs take applications every two years, rather than every year.
- Researching cost (part-time versus full-time, scholarships and grants, do you qualify for loans?).
- Attend open houses. If you are able to attend in person that is great, but there are programs that offer webinars and have online videos as well.
- Research recent graduates from the program and look at what they are doing, post- graduation.
- Apply … apply … apply … apply to a minimum of 3–5 programs. Make sure your list of schools includes safe schools—those whose requirements you meet—but don't be afraid to try for your dream school. Finally, don't let the fear of getting a NO keep you from applying. You have heard NO many times in your life, and you are still alive and breathing. My hope is that you will be accepted in all the programs to which you apply, but if you don't, remember you can apply again, and NO is most often a reflection of the applicant pool and number of spaces available in the program and not about you as a person.

Whether you think you want it or need it, get it done! As you get started, take some time to reflect on your life goals and priorities. Communicate with and engage family, friends, and loved ones in the process. Let them know how important this is to you, that this journey will impact how visible you will be for a few years. Tell them you need them on your side, supporting you and cheering you on, and they will be there because they love you. If for some reason they are not able to be there for you, find a community that will support you, that could be your cohort, your church, or a good mentor.

I look forward to soon calling you Doctor_____.

*A few things from my personal experience: My first son was born on December 12, 2000. I was working full-time and that was my first semester in my doctoral program. I was taking three courses (nine credits). In August 2001, I moved from NYC to NJ but remained a student at Teachers College while working full-time at Rutgers University. In December 2001, my son began having seizures, and seizures became a part of life until 2008. During this time, I took four years off from school to focus on my son while still working full-time. In 2005, my husband moved out and in 2006, I went through a divorce. For some time, I was a single parent with an ill child and believed to be on the road to ABD (All But Dissertation). I married again in 2009, changed jobs in 2011 (moved back to NYC), defended in December 2012 and walked in May 2013. I then had my second child in February 2014. I share this to say that while you can plan a number of things, the unexpected will still happen and as long as you are patient with yourself and allow others to help you and support you, you WILL finish. I had faith that I would finish but my son was always my top priority.

CHAPTER 3

YOU CAN'T DO THAT![1]

CHERIE L. KING, ScD

Central Connecticut State University, New Britain, CT, USA

E-mail: kingche@ccsu.edu

In 2001, I was a self-employed rehabilitation counselor and consultant with 16 years of private rehabilitation and counseling experience, a wife, and a mother of three children (an eight-year-old daughter and four-year-old twin boys, including one with sensory and learning disabilities). Attempting to balance family and work was the groove of my life. After the bus picked up my daughter and the boys were off to preschool, I would sit in my home office and daydream in between phone calls, report writing, grocery shopping, and loads of laundry. I was always a career woman: productive, motivated, focused, and effective. However, something big was missing; I was burnt out, a little apathetic, sad, and had a huge hole in my heart. My daydreams included web surfing for ideas and inspiration. Nothing was filling the deep yearning I had for "something." Since I had always received satisfaction from my work, I thought that this was where the answers lay. But this hole was different; it was one of those "dark night of the soul" kind of existential crises that would not go away. I loved my kids and family life, but it did not sustain the longing for something that I could deeply connect with in terms of purpose. Consequently, I also had tremendous "mom" guilt about wanting something more for myself not connected to my marriage or family. Something that was truly mine. I asked myself: How would I be viewed by others? How would I be judged? Would I damage my kids? Could my marriage sustain a change in me? Would making a change for me put my kids in therapy when they were teens? Could I still be a dedicated mom and still have my own dream? Was I being selfish?

---

[1]Dr. King's doctoral journey is told in four parts, from preadmission through the dissertation stage.

I was active as a leader in my professional association. I had built a terrific network of colleagues and friends. I was highly sought out as a consultant to work difficult cases, provide expert opinions, and testify as an expert witness in cases related to disability and employment. I was also a good counselor. In addition, as part of my work as a counselor and consultant, I was hired a lot by companies to train and provide clinical supervision to other rehabilitation counselors. I would supervise counselors for certification. At the time, expanding my skills into teacher and supervisor roles was what kept me engaged in my profession. After training a small group of rehabilitation counselors, a long-time colleague complimented me and told me that I was a good teacher. I was good at it and it made me happy. This was when the first seed was planted for my journey to academia.

I approached my research into a doctoral degree with the same gusto and enthusiasm I used to have for my work. My initial consideration about going back school started with reaching out to people I knew in academia. I was active in my professional association, where I had developed close relationships with colleagues who were educators. My first contact was with a colleague. I discovered that to teach full-time in a master's program, I needed to have a doctorate. I also discovered that there was a need for experienced professionals with clinical expertise in the field of Counselor Education. I also knew my life with a young family was going to be a significant consideration in pursuing an advanced degree. Fortunately, I knew a few women who were mothers and educators in the midst of pursuing doctoral degrees. I reached out to these women for their stories and advice. These women were honest about the challenges, demands, and rewards, and were incredibly supportive.

I had several criteria as I started my doctoral program research and was very specific about my concentration for a doctoral program in Rehabilitation Counselor Education. The focus on rehabilitation counseling was limited to about a dozen programs. I also needed to secure funding. We could not afford a full doctoral program and a reduced income. As a master's student in rehabilitation counseling, I had received a scholarship under a unique long-term training grant from the United States Department of Education's Rehabilitation Services Administration (RSA). One of the criteria for my program search was to secure an RSA doctoral grant. Another essential criterion was the location of the program. At the time of my exploration, my husband was willing to relocate, but we needed to focus on locations where he could transfer with his company. As senior staff, he needed to stay with his company and maintain his salary and benefits for our family while I was in school.

There were four program options for me. I contacted each program's doctoral program director to discuss their program, structures, expectations, and admissions requirements. I was also able to talk to current students and recent graduates. This is when I recognized I was going to be a different doctoral candidate. Most students I spoke to were single, no kids, and had minimal to no professional experience. I realized I was interviewing the program as much as they would interview me. One particularly distressing conversation I had with a current student warned me that if were accepted into their program, there would be pressure to show that the program was my priority above my family. Or in the words of the student, "You will need to pretend you don't have kids." I immediately marked this program off my list.

Admission processes were simple: GRE scores, application, telephone interviews, and references. My mind freaked "Oh no! GRE?!" It had been over 25 years since I had taken a standardized test. It had been 25 years since I had done an algebra problem! It had been at least 20 years since I had seen or needed to use any statistical data. Off to the Barnes and Noble to buy GRE for Dummies! I was terrified of the quantitative reasoning portion. I was terrible at mathematics and while in high school had to take summer school mathematics courses. In my mind, this was the opening of an old wound: my academic self-doubt. Could I do this? Was I smart enough to do this? At 37, I had built a lot of professional confidence but was so surprised at the effects of this limiting belief about myself. It took me six months to schedule the test. In the meantime, I confronted my mathematics demons and hired a friend's husband, a high school mathematics teacher, to tutor me. I found I understood it now. What happened to me between 16 and 37? How come this made sense to me this time around? It was a great confidence booster!

I applied to three programs and was accepted to all, but in the same timeframe, my husband had been offered a partnership with his company. The caveat—he would need to stay in Hartford (Connecticut). Transfer was not an option. This was a great accomplishment for my husband but where did that leave my goals? We struggled to come up with a solution that was best for everyone. The kids were young, we were committed to raising them together under the same roof, and we could not imagine living apart even for short periods of time. He had worked very hard for the partnership, and it was important for our family's financial stability and future. I rejected the offers from all three programs and considered my options. I had initially considered a program in my region (about a 90-minute drive) but dismissed it because I wanted a larger program. On a whim, I contacted the Director at Boston University, whom I had met several years before at a professional conference. He remembered me and welcomed my application.

I did something different in my application essay that I had not disclosed in my other applications. I wrote about my experiences as a counselor and advocate for people with disabilities and how my personal and professional views had changed as a mother of a child with disabilities.

I was interviewed within two weeks by the program faculty. The program was small and accepted only one doctoral student per year. Most of its doctoral students were working full-time and had families. It felt right. I went home and waited for word on their decision. I was in the minivan with the kids in car seats when the Director called me about a week later, invited me to the program, and offered me a full RSA doctoral scholarship. He was taking me on as his student and was to be my mentor. After thanking him, I started to cry and I took the kids out for ice cream to celebrate. In preparation for starting the program, I was anxious about taking a doctoral-level statistics course. The summer before I started classes, and in between taking kids to camp and the beach, I went to my local community college and registered for an intermediate statistics course. It was the best decision I ever made, and my confidence was boosted. I was ready.

About three weeks before classes were to start, I was in the children's section of our town library with my kids. Seeing other moms after a busy summer, we talked about the upcoming school year, starting kindergarten, and back to school year routines. One mom I had been friendly with asked what I was planning on now that the kids would be in school full time. I replied, "I'm going back to school" (without mention of a doctoral program). Without missing a beat, the mom said, "You can't do that! Who's going to take care of the kids? Why would you want to do that?" My worst fears had come true. I was judged and I was a selfish mom. I watched myself spitting out rationalizations such as "My husband is a great help," "I have found a great college student to get the kids off the bus," and "My mother-in-law is going to help." The more I tried to assure her everyone would be OK, the voice in my head said, "What the hell are you doing? Why are you defending your choice to her?" I spent the weekend vacillating between doubting my decision and making up awful comebacks to put that mom in her place. I would wrestle with this dilemma of family and fulfilling my dream for a long time.

CHAPTER 4

"GOOD MOMS DON'T GO TO DOCTORAL PROGRAMS"

JODY J. FIORINI, PhD

Wichita State University, Wichita, KS, USA

E-mail: jody.fiorini@wichita.edu

I began my doctoral journey as the result of a paradoxical intervention prescribed by my therapist. I had been toying with the idea of applying to several doctoral programs back in the mid-nineties. I had gathered the materials but somehow could just not bring myself to fill them out; after all, I already had a perfect life—a house, two kids, two cats, good jobs with nice salaries. It would be selfish of me to go back to school, wouldn't it? I brought it up to my counselor, and she said, "That would be incredibly selfish. I think you should go home right now and tear up those applications." I left furious. Who was she to tell me to give up my dream? So I went right home and filled out those applications. A couple of months later, I sat on the living room couch crying, tears splattering on all three letters of acceptance, as my husband walked in the door from work. He asked why I was crying and I said, "I got into all three with a full ride. It's nice that they want me but we both know I can't go. I can't uproot our lives here." He smiled and sat next to me. "Of course we can go. I don't want you to look back and have regrets about what might have been. Let's start a new adventure."

With that, we went and toured, University of Connecticut and Syracuse University (SU), which were my top choices. I had been working in disability services at the higher education level and as a disability advocate for most of my adult career. SU had a rehabilitation counseling program so I decided that in going there, I had an opportunity to pursue courses in both areas. My third option was a clinical psychology program, but that just did not fit my professional identity in the least, so I opted out of that program.

SU also held a dear place in my heart. I had grown up about two hours from there, and I remembered my father taking me to a football game at the

Carrier Dome. I must have been nine or ten years old. I remembered being in awe of the old ivied buildings and Latin words etched into granite blocks. One building looked just like a castle; I know now that it was the Crouse School of Music. I was holding my father's hand as we walked, and I asked, "Dad, what is the biggest degree you can get?" My father, son of immigrant parents from Italy and Slovakia, beamed at me. "A PhD is the highest degree you can get," he said. "Do they have those here?" I asked, looking up at him. "Yes, they do," he replied. "Well I want to go here and get one of those," I responded. "You can do anything you put your mind to," he said. I believed him and I never forgot that exchange as I returned to SU for concerts and games for many years to come. Each time thinking, someday.

My husband and I met at Binghamton University and eloped when I was a junior and he was a sophomore. We were dirt poor and struggled to get by and finish our degrees, but we eventually did and worked our way into positions that gave us a good standard of living. We owned our first home in Oneonta, NY, USA, where I had completed my master's degree in school counseling. My eldest daughter was in kindergarten and the younger one was due to start school the following year. This was the backdrop of my transition to doctoral study. When you are the child of depression-era parents who work paycheck to paycheck, you never quite feel financially secure. I was literally scared to death that I was dragging my family into poverty by going back to college. I knew my husband was right, however, and I knew that I would always regret not going, so we packed up our lives and went on a new adventure.

No one would rent to us when we tried to find a place to live in Syracuse because we did not have employment. So, my advisor, Dr. Alan Goldberg, wrote a letter to my prospective landlord stating that I had student loans and an assistantship stipend to live on. With that, we unknowingly moved into an apartment next to a crack house on the north side of Syracuse in an Italian neighborhood where the rents were cheap. Although the neighborhood was sketchy, the drug-selling neighbors in the house next door took a protective stance toward my children, and I remember them helping us plant flowers in our yard one afternoon. I enrolled my children in kindergarten and first grade at an elementary school in the Syracuse City School District and went on a search to find affordable and flexible after school child care. Having just come from a relatively affluent suburban elementary school district, the Syracuse City Schools with their limited resources were a rude awakening from the privilege I was used to. Classrooms didn't have enough books for every child, so they had to share. It was an entirely different world and incredibly diverse. My children made friends with children from every conceivable ethnic and racial group. In their five years in the Syracuse City Schools, they were in the minority as White students. Even at the time, I felt that this was a gift to them that they would come to know more than the comfortable White world of suburbia.

Meanwhile, my husband surprised me one morning. He had no job but had an interview with one company. He was a healthcare administrator. I woke up one morning to him kissing me goodbye, dressed in a suit, and carrying his briefcase. "Where are you going?" I asked. "To work," he replied. "But you don't have a job," I said incredulously. He looked down at me with a crooked smile. "Well, I look at this way. They have an opening so I am going to just show up and go to work. Most people cannot deal with conflict, so I doubt they will ask me to leave." He did and he was hired for that job, and eight months later, he became the President of the Homecare Division of Community General Hospital.

His having a job was a relief as I began my doctoral studies. I was awarded a departmental assistantship, so I began my duties when the semester began. I was a bit taken aback to realize that there was no status in being a doctoral student. I had a tremendous amount of responsibility thrust upon me from learning the routine of the office, answering the phones and running errands, clinically supervising six master's-level students (and had no training in supervision), and co-teaching courses in counseling techniques and group counseling. I was also taking three courses. Themes of sexism ran throughout my experiences in my doctoral program. There seemed to be a trend that female graduate assistants were the workhorses—expected to give more than their 20-hour obligation, going above and beyond, while our male counterparts were given far fewer tasks. I loved my doctoral program, do not get me wrong. I soaked up so much of the accumulated wisdom of my peers and professors, but there was an undercurrent of a chilly climate in a department that, in 1996, had just hired its first female professor in its 90-year history.

I was not used to the small seminar-style classes, and it soon became apparent I had better come prepared, having read every ounce of material and ready to defend my stance on issues discussed. It did not take long for me to adjust and thrive in the academic rigor of the classroom, and my "imposter syndrome" almost disappeared when I met with practicum students and realized that I did indeed have wisdom to share with them.

The day finally came when I had to send my children to their first day of school. My eldest was excited. She adapted easily and was anxious to meet her new teacher and new friends. My younger daughter, however, had always been more cautious; she was brave but a little teary when I took her to school. I gave the teacher the note of instructions for the bus driver to take her from half-day kindergarten to her daycare provider a few blocks away. Emily was only four, as a November birthday baby, and I was nervous about the whole adventure, but I was reassured by both the transportation office and the teacher that Emily was all set to be delivered safely to her daycare at noon.

I was in class when the secretary brought in the note. This predates cell phones, at least for most of us; they were a luxury I could not afford. The note read, "Your sitter called and wants to know where Emily is." I looked at the clock. It was 12:30 and all the blood drained from my body. I shared the note with the class, and the professor was annoyed that I had interrupted the course. He sighed and suggested a break. I was new, remember, so I was embarrassed and still trying to impress, but my child was lost in a still-unfamiliar city somewhere. I used the office phone to call the school and spoke with the teacher. I had already confirmed with my daycare provider that she had never arrived. The teacher said she handed the bus driver the note with the instructions and address, but she did not speak directly to him as she put Emily on the bus. I was increasingly frantic as I asked where she could be. The teacher responded with "I don't know, Mrs. Fiorini. This is why I stayed home with my children. Good mothers do not go to doctoral programs until their children are grown." I was both furious and afraid and already guilt-ridden. I actually considered her words for a moment. This was my fault. My child was lost or abducted and it was my fault. I made many more phone calls until I reached the bus dispatcher who said that Emily was at the bus garage as the driver had attempted to drop her off at our apartment and she refused to get off because she knew no one was home. I had had no luck getting in touch with my husband because he was on the road, and besides, it was my job as a mother to take care of these things, wasn't it? Events like this rarely reflect on the father; only the mother is blamed for her negligence. I had no idea where the district bus garage was, and the directions did not help because I was so unfamiliar with Syracuse (pre-GPS). The dispatcher and I agreed the easiest thing to do was for them to deliver Emily to her daycare provider's address, and I could pick her up when her sister, Samantha, got there. Then I worried that the same thing would happen with Sam and that the nightmare would repeat when she got out of school, but the dispatcher assured me that there would be no more mistakes. I went back to my class a mess and wanted only to go get my baby. When I told everyone what had happened, all of my female classmates were appalled, particularly by the teacher's comments. "How dare she blame you for her incompetence!" My professor was not sympathetic. He did not understand why I was still upset when the situation was resolved. I would continue with class and the class following, and their father would pick them up from daycare after work. And I stayed, for both classes, as I was afraid not to. I was afraid that I had already established a negative impression in my professor's mind. I have never quite forgiven myself for that.

This story came immediately to mind when I was asked to contribute to this book about women's voices. There were many times when I felt guilt from a society that purports to value women in education but does not always provide support or encouragement. My advice to those of you who are mothers, who are considering doctoral study, or are already pursuing it, is to persevere. My children grew up on campus. They attended classes with me, hung out with the professors while I worked, watched me study and get hooded, and walk across that stage. I think it is no coincidence that they both have graduate degrees (one from Syracuse). They are bright, articulate, politically aware, social justice advocates, and diehard Syracuse Orange fans. Best of all, my father can now say that his little girl is a doctor—and trust me, he does it every chance he gets.

CHAPTER 5

FIRST STEPS

MARGARET LEONE, PhD

State University of New York at Plattsburgh, Plattsburgh, NY, USA

E-mail: margaret.leone719@gmail.com

Public high schools need to supply a safe haven for teachers who actually enjoy their jobs. It is indeed harmful to enter the common faculty lounge, caught in a crossfire between the venomous comments regarding students or administration hurled about and the waves of whining and moaning of those once-enthusiastic, burned-out teachers, who are counting the days (or even years!) before they are able to retire. After having worked as a French teacher in a middle/high school for 14 years, I still enjoyed being in the classroom, challenging as it was at times. But I was convinced that down the road, that disgruntled employee who dreaded going to work would be me. It seemed to happen to the best of teachers who had devoted so much of their time and energy to help the kids. They were tired.

I was not going to get tired. There was too much left to learn. Although this atmosphere still greatly contributed to my knowledge about education and people, I kept imagining the eventuality that I would not escape becoming a fossilized professional. I decided that the best way to avoid this fate was to change my surroundings before they became too familiar. Moving was out of the question because I needed to stay put until my children graduated from high school due to a joint custody agreement. In addition, I couldn't afford to lose my pension, as I was already vested in the state retirement system. After some soul searching and reading Spencer Johnson's Who Moved My Cheese, I decided that I would take a year sabbatical to see if I had the grit to work toward a PhD in second language education.

Living in northern New York State, I did not have the luxury of choosing between many programs; however, I was extremely fortunate. The nearest and most convenient university for me to attend happened to staff an award-winning research faculty in my chosen field of study. I do not know how I mustered up the courage or confidence at age 41 to believe that I could be accepted, let alone survive, in such a high-profile graduate program.

Contrary to my belief that the most difficult leg of this new adventure would actually be attending courses and writing research papers after such a lengthy hiatus, obtaining the paperwork to study in Canada, and in the province of Quebec as well, proved much more demanding of my time and patience. This process was certainly not intended for the faint of heart. Even though I am bilingual in French and English, I felt as if people didn't speak my language at all, and that the bureaucracy ritual tested my stamina as if I had been asked to repeatedly take off my shoes and put them back on as my "baggage" was inspected. I had the false impression that as an American student, completing paperwork for a Canadian student visa and a Quebec study permit would be quite painless. But I suppose that being a middle-aged woman who was commuting back and forth three times a week to Montreal fit the profile of a person capable of hiding great illicit activity.

These suspicions harbored by authority figures did not stop at the border. Each term that I attended classes, from 2001 to 2008, I was subjected to the same request from the young man behind the desk at the graduate administration office—to provide a handwritten copy of why I did not live in Canada during my studies. I just took it for granted that after writing one letter, it would remain on file for the subsequent terms. *Mais non!* Each term I had to rewrite a letter, while the young man waited to tell me, "Too short" or "Too long" "Too much unnecessary information" or "Not enough necessary information." A copy of the previous letter was not acceptable. Nor was the copy of my insurance card from the previous year. Each term I had to return to the International Student Office to remove student insurance fees from my bill by producing the same insurance card as the first visit.

The odyssey of completing paperwork, of paying my tuition bill only when the bank was open, and of paying off several city parking tickets at the same bank (because the meter only ran for two hours and my courses lasted three), taught me that I had a lot to learn as an international student in my own North America.

I spent a year taking graduate classes to qualify for the PhD program and explore my areas of research interest. I enrolled in three courses per term, commuting three hours for three-hour evening classes three times a week while teaching two French courses as a university adjunct instructor and working part time at the county housing association. Thankfully, I had a great deal of support from my cooperative children and partner. I was accepted into the program.

Life was good as things fell into place. I continued the rhythm of teaching my university classes, now as a full-time lecturer, taking courses, and attending research groups consisting of the best and the brightest students of all ages and nationalities. Although sometimes I felt quite disconnected from the others because I went to the city only for academic reasons and not to socialize, they were always encouraging and supportive of my work.

When this journey began, I was entering the unknown. I got scared, I cried, and I fell down a lot. So, I ask myself, "Was it all worth it?" At times, when I get tired of repaying student loans, when it hits me that I had given up time with my family, my tenure, and a solid salary to embark on this new adventure, I think not. But then I think about what was gained.

My children learned how to be self-sufficient. They also learned that it is okay to take risks and that things turn out if one is strong, patient, and persistent. After I graduated in 2013, students new to the PhD program at my alma mater were the first to fall under new and updated dissertation regulations that I had vehemently fought for as a student. The college students in my classroom are receiving a better education because I continually aspire to incorporate the best techniques possible in my lessons and continue to learn from my colleagues in the field.

As for me, it is not always clear to me what I have gained from the experience. Financially, I have just this year attained the same salary that I worked for 17 years ago when I left my position as a high school teacher. My hopes of getting a tenure-track position at my university were shattered when two full-time professors in the French section left but were not replaced due to budget cuts. As job stability is certainly not a guarantee, I wavered between leaving my lectureship three years before retirement to pursue a new job elsewhere, thus leaving my home and family behind, and staying in my current position, holding on to the possibility of my subsequent one-year contract being renewed. Decisions such as these are never easy, especially when one is very close to the end of a career.

Was pursuing a PhD in middle age worth it? If I let my ego guide my answer, I would say, "Yes." I like having the title "Dr." on my office door and sharing my conquest on social media. I also admit that I enjoyed rubbing elbows with the scholars whose research I had read, and I proudly share these experiences with my colleagues and students. However, I still honestly cannot commit to a definitive, single answer to that question. As a doctoral student, the only future that I thought about was the day that I would finally defend my dissertation. I thought everything else would magically fall into place. Although that did not happen, and I cannot say what the future holds for me, I do know that I am not among those educators who have lost their passion and energy, counting down the hours until they receive their last paycheck.

REFERENCE

Johnson, S. (1998). *Who Moved My Cheese? New York, NY:* Putnam.

CHAPTER 6

MAKING THE PhD HAPPEN: STAGE 1—PREADMISSION TO ENROLLMENT[1]

ANNE TOOLAN ROWLEY, PhD

The College of Saint Rose, Albany, NY, USA

As I reflected on my doctoral journey, many memories surfaced when I tried to identify the points of excitement, challenge, frustration, and accomplishment. With a review of Ali and Kohun's (2007) work addressing social isolation as it is related to doctoral attrition, I found myself noting periods during my doctoral journey that are related to their four stages in the process of completing the degree. Thinking back now to my program and those of colleagues and friends who did or didn't complete their degree, stages of social isolation as described by the authors become apparent to me.

My desire to complete a PhD degree was an ambition for many years. Life factors, such as full-time work, family needs, finance, location, and time, played a role in the decision. As a speech-language pathologist, I thought that a degree in reading would provide a desirable academic bridge between language and literacy. With this in mind, I began to research programs that offered this connection.

I began with an online search for colleges that had doctoral programs and a review of the specific coursework, comprehensive exams, and dissertation requirements. An overall search is suggested to get a feel of the academic demands that are prescriptive in most programs. A detail worth exploring is the possibility that an admissions committee for a doctoral program often considers some of the credits from an individual's master's program, if the topics are related. I was fortunate that the admissions committee reviewed my master's work favorably and accepted 21 credits toward the initial 66

---

[1]Dr. Rowley's doctoral journey is told in four parts, from preadmission through the dissertation stage.

credit degree requirement that is completed prior to the comprehensive exam stage.

The next challenge was to determine a location relative to my home. Since it was necessary for me to maintain a full-time employment status, the doctoral program needed to be local with in-class and online course components. In my case, I was able to identify a state campus within driving distance of home and work that required both in-class and online courses. With this factor identified, the amount of time for completion was the next area of concern.

The time required for degree completion is determined by the department with regard to part-time or full-time status. The website review revealed two options for enrollment. The full-time program required a minimum of a three-year commitment with completion in approximately seven years. A part-time program was described by the number of credits per semester, usually six, in order to remain active in the program. Moreover, a ten-year maximum time to completion was generally noted. These were serious concerns as I planned balancing my need for full-time employment, part-time coursework, and financial support for the endeavor. The availability of financial support was the next factor to consider.

A full-time commitment of three or more years would have neces-sitated me to resign from my position in an academic setting. Since this was not an option based on my family situation, part-time enrollment was my only choice. I explored the world of academic loans awarded based on need and financial status. However, part-time enrolled students are more challenged because paying per credit can be more costly than paying for a full-time semester load. Moreover, one needs to explore the additional fees that seem to be never ending, as they are introduced on a semester basis. Trying to navigate various websites and hoping that my questions would be addressed in the "frequently asked questions" sections was frustrating and time consuming. At this point in the preadmission process, I felt socially isolated as I assumed that some type of informational event would be avail-able where I could meet with doctoral faculty, learn firsthand about the program and its requirements, and chat with current students. When this was not scheduled, I sought an interview with the department chair, who described the program and answered my questions. The admissions process was described as the submission of four essays related to my background, my purpose in achieving a doctoral degree, and my perspective on beginning academic study in a new field different from, but related to, my current work. With my initial questions answered and the application process begun, the next step was the waiting process, hoping to be admitted. When admission to the doctoral program was announced, other concerns arose related to my family and educational financial needs.

When I was accepted to the doctoral program, I had one child in college. Each year that a child attends college, the family is required to submit the Free Application for Federal Student Aid (FAFSA) financial form to determine eligibility for financial support. All family members taking college credits are added to the financial mix to determine the family's needs. My frustration increased during the second year of my child's FAFSA submission, when the government decided to eliminate any parental course work in the equation. This decreased our overall financial eligibility.

With regard to available funding, some institutions offer small honorary scholarships that are limited in quantity and value. Usually, part-time study does not yield financial support from the institution. On occasion, a prospective student might be able to secure some funding from a current employer through their human resources department since the employee's future potential can enhance the current work. If the employer is an academic site, one might be able to take related courses while employed and transfer the credits to the doctoral institution. Although this was not possible in my case, I did hear of other students who were able to successfully transfer related coursework to a doctoral program. When taking all of these factors into consideration, the plan being considered would not be complete without looking at family and lifestyle needs.

As Beeler (1991) says, "unconscious incompetence" (p. 164) is the stage where one is making decisions without really knowing what one "is getting into." If one's spouse or partner makes up the nucleus of the family, planning together requires an open discussion on everyday routine changes, adherence to an academic calendar, stress, and financial issues. If the family includes children and/or extended family ties, such as senior or ill family members, the changes and stress of the new lifestyle can be challenging. Most in-class doctoral courses are held in the early- to late-evening time slots. Online courses have time frames in which class discussion takes place, often with a time limit on the individual module. Mealtimes, children's extracurricular activities, and one's study time are critical issues in need of review. Mason-Williams and Wasburn-Moses (2016) suggest considering carefully one's organization and time management skills, study habits, and needed space for working and thinking in order to meet the challenges ahead.

"Time for me" took on many definitions. It referred to my class time on campus or designated to an online course. It meant a commitment to employment, family, and daily routines. It also meant that I needed opportunities to complete homework, prepare individual and group projects, and try to include "down" time to relax. Time commitments were modified as the program demands fluctuated during the semesters leading to the dissertation.

All of these factors came into play for me. Even with open discussions regarding the impact that my potential studies would have on my work, my family responsibilities, my husband and three children, and personal commitments, I still did not realize "what I was getting into" for the next nine years! Walking into my first course on a Tuesday evening was the beginning of a journey that the best-made plans could not have predicted.

REFERENCES

Ali, A.; Kohun, F. (2006). Dealing with isolation feelings in IS doctoral programs. *International Journal of Doctoral Studies, 1*, 21–22. Retrieved from: http://www.informingscience. org/Journals/IJDS/Articles?Volume=1–2006&Search.

Beeler, K. D. (1991). Graduate student adjustment to academic life: A four-stage framework. *NASPA Journal. 28*(2), 163–171.

Mason-Williams, L.; Wasburn-Moses, L. (2016). Considering a doctoral degree? Everything you need to know. *Teaching Exceptional Children, 49*(1), 74–81.

CHAPTER 7

THE OVERNIGHT PSYCHOLOGIST

HILLARY HURST BUSH, PhD

Massachusetts General Hospital, Boston, MA, USA

E-mail: hillary.hurst.bush@gmail.com

When people ask me how I decided to become a clinical psychologist, I joke that I simply woke up one day wanting to be one. In the spring of 2007, I was one year out of college, where I had majored in American Studies and Spanish. Through my liberal arts training, I felt simultaneously prepared to do anything … and nothing at all. I was working as a marketing assistant at a downtown Boston law firm, but it had not taken long for me to figure out that corporate life was not right for me. Yet, I was intrigued by the psychology that infused my marketing work. I also reflected on how much I had enjoyed studying different cultures through my undergraduate majors, and how energized I felt in high school while working at a fast-food restaurant and volunteering with adults with intellectual disabilities—positions that heavily involved interacting with diverse people, sometimes seeing them at their very best and at their very worst. Suddenly and subconsciously, I put these experiences together and found myself consumed with a burning desire to become a clinical psychologist. The only problem was that I had not taken a single psychology course in college. I had not conducted psychological research—in fact, I had not even participated in a research study. I had only a working understanding of what clinical psychologists did and what their training looked like. I had no concept yet of what it took to be admitted to a doctoral program. And yet, I could not imagine anything that I wanted more than to be a clinical psychologist. I had my work cut out for me.

After realizing my new goal, one of the first steps I took was to enroll in college-level psychology classes. I figured that taking classes would be an easy way of testing my hypothesis that I just *had* to become a clinical psychologist. Living with my family in the suburbs and working a full-time entry-level job, I was looking for classes that were inexpensive and conducted only on nights and weekends. Being in the Greater Boston area, I fortunately had many schools to choose from. It was sheer luck, however, that led me to the University of Massachusetts (UMass) Boston's continuing education program. I was fortunate because UMass Boston had a PhD program in clinical psychology, and advanced graduate students—who were incredibly generous with their time and mentorship—taught many of the continuing education courses. In the summer of 2007, I enrolled in two introductory psychology courses at UMass Boston and enjoyed them just as much as I had hoped. As soon as I received "A"s in those two courses, I began mentally preparing my PhD program applications. I could not wait to get started!

What I did not realize—and thankfully, what my graduate student instructors gently but very clearly informed me—was that I was nowhere near ready to apply to clinical psychology PhD programs. I learned that traditional applicants to these programs generally have majored in psychology and have joined a research team on campus. Many have completed an honors thesis or other research projects during their undergraduate careers. After graduating, many work for several years in full-time psychological research positions and have conference presentations, if not peer-reviewed publications, to show for their efforts. This information stung—not because it felt impossible, but because I understood just how long the path to admission would be.

An important next step in getting ready for graduate school was finding a new job. Understanding that most successful applicants to clinical psychology programs work in full-time research positions beforehand, I submitted a slew of applications to universities and hospitals in the Boston area. However, finding a research job was challenging too, as the same lack of experience that kept me from being a competitive graduate school applicant also kept me from being a competitive research assistant applicant. In fact, I did not get a single callback. This certainly would have been the time to feel discouraged—and I did—but I decided to change gears and pursue clinical jobs. In a stroke of good fortune, in late summer 2007, I got a full-time position at the nonprofit agency where I had volunteered in high school. For nearly three years, I worked as a direct support provider for adults with intellectual disabilities. My job entailed teaching our clients a wide range of skills, including cooking, budgeting, household management, safety, social, and job skills. I also helped our clients to access the community and pursue leisure activities, and later, I served on the agency's human rights committee. Working in the human services field prepared me well for the intense clinical experiences that I would have in graduate school at diverse sites, including a university counseling center, a community health center, and a children's psychiatric hospital. Moreover, working in this field afforded me with income and somewhat flexible hours such that I could continue taking education classes at UMass Boston and following the long path to graduate school admission.

As I started my new job in the nonprofit world, I continued to take one or two psychology courses per semester. In time, this resulted in about the equivalent of an undergraduate psychology major, including courses in social psychology, personality, adolescence, developmental psychopathology, and statistics. Taking these classes also exposed me to new graduate student instructors, one of whom was incredibly supportive of my desire to prepare for graduate school and introduced me to his research mentor. After meeting with her and explaining my plan to attend graduate school but lacking critical research experience, I was offered the opportunity to join her research team on a part-time, volunteer basis in the spring of 2008. While her research program focused on research involving adolescence and emerging adulthood, and I suspected that I wanted to study disabilities, I realized that this invitation was nothing short of a huge break. By joining the lab—even in a small capacity—and attending weekly lab meetings and working closely with graduate students on data analysis and conference posters, I finally understood what being a graduate student would entail. Although far less glamorous than I had envisioned, I still wanted this path every bit as much as I had before.

I was actively volunteering in this lab in early 2009 when a paid part-time research coordinator position was posted for a different psychology lab at UMass Boston. This lab, headed by a junior faculty member, studied early childhood development as well as developmental disabilities. With the support of my research mentor, I applied for the job, and I got it! Upon receiving the offer, I was able to scale back my hours at the nonprofit agency and work part-time there, too. I did not realize it then, but working two part-time jobs—one research, one clinic—was excellent practice and training for balancing the multiple demands of my clinical psychology program. This position also provided me with the valuable opportunity to explore my disability interests, as well as to gain more experience with different aspects of the research process, including study administration, data collection, coordinating research team members, and getting a new research study up and running. While volunteering in the first lab gave me confidence that I could navigate being a graduate student, working in this second lab cultivated my passion for research and the activities of a clinical psychologist beyond graduate school, and, most importantly, it exposed me to the brilliant, warm, kind, and utterly supportive faculty member who would become my faculty mentor and research advisor in graduate school.

In late 2009, I finally had the coursework, research experience, and clinical experience to apply to graduate school. Seeing that doctoral programs in clinical psychology accept, on average, only 8% of their applicants (Stamm et al., 2016), I was encouraged to apply to many different programs and not to restrict myself geographically. This was very good advice yet emotionally and financially draining to follow, because after more than two years of preparation, I knew how much I wanted to attend UMass Boston and what a good fit it would be. Fortunately, in the spring of 2010, I was offered one of eight positions in the incoming cohort that fall. I can still remember where I was (with clients at the nonprofit agency, where I was still working part-time), what I was doing (waiting anxiously for a phone call), and the feeling in my chest (like my heart would explode), when I received the phone call with the offer. I accepted on the spot; I did not have to think twice. When I matriculated at UMass Boston in the fall of 2010, it was the culmination of more than three years of patience, planning, reaching inside and finding the strength to keep working even when I felt tired or discouraged, and building and nurturing relationships, both with colleagues and with the friends and family who had seen me through the process to admission. Interestingly enough, it was exactly these skills and experiences that propelled me through the following six years in graduate school.

Looking back, I remember feeling frustrated—not about having to do the legwork to prepare for graduate school, but about how *long* it took to get ready to apply. Ever since that day that I "woke up" wanting to be a clinical psychologist, I had known that this was the path that I wanted to follow. And although it looks somewhat unusual, I appreciate my path to clinical psychology. I also feel grateful for all of the good things—learning to cook, running a half-marathon, traveling to South America, spending valuable time with my grandmother, and meeting the person who would become my spouse—that occurred in the in-between space when I was getting ready to apply. Seeing how demanding graduate school was, it frightens me that I may not have had the time or space to experience these things if I had taken a more traditional route. While it felt frustrating at the time to wait, the years I spent preparing to apply were just as valid as those that I later spent as a graduate student, and my development as a clinical psychologist started well before I entered graduate school.

REFERENCE

Stamm, K.; Michalski, D.; Cope, C.; Fowler, G.; Christidis, P.; Lin, L. (2016). Datapoint: What are the acceptance rates for graduate psychology programs? *Monitor on Psychology, 47*(2), 16.

CHAPTER 8

NOT ALL WHO WANDER ARE LOST

BEVERLY A. BURNELL, PhD

State University of New York at Plattsburgh, Plattsburgh, NY, USA

E-mail: burnelb@plattsburgh.edu

My experiences leading up to entering my doctoral program were filled with excitement and energy. The *excitement* came from knowing that becoming a counselor educator was the next step I wanted to take on my professional journey and that this degree was what I needed to be able to take that step. I was *energized* when visualizing the intellectual environment into which I intended to fully immerse myself, the smart and thoughtful colleagues I imagined I would encounter, and the new learning adventures and opportunities I vowed I would take full advantage of. I am grateful to be able to say that *all* of that came to fruition during my program at Syracuse University (SU), though not without some bumps and bruises along the way.

When I was nine or ten years old, I wanted to become a college professor, although I had no idea what that meant. I thought I knew what it meant to be a teacher, and "college professor" sounded like a teacher who would be highly respected and valued. My siblings and I, cousins, and neighbor kids often played "school," and I was always the teacher. I have always loved school, have worked in education settings most of my life, and for me, the year starts in September rather than January. Though no one in my family had ever gone to college, and most had not graduated high school, I learned from them that education was important. Graduating high school was never a question for my siblings and me. I thought going on to college was also without question. I was lockstep with all the students in high school who were going on to college—I thought.

I applied, was accepted, and then learned that my family had no resources to send me to college. I had no "plan B," though I knew that those in my extended family expected I would just "go to work" as everyone else in my family had done. I'm not sure how she knew my family's circumstances, but my guidance counselor applied on my behalf for the inaugural four-year scholarship from a local paper mill, and I got it! That, along with another scholarship from my mother's employer and a state regent's scholarship, allowed me to go to our local state teachers college while living at home and earn my B.S. in Secondary Mathematics Education.

As the first person in my extended family to go on to college, I had no information about what college life and academic success entailed. My undergraduate years started out as a time of utter bewilderment, accompanied by sheer delight and excitement that I was entering this world of *higher learning* that I had wanted all my life. Thankfully, I was invited into a National Science Foundation program for science and mathematics educators (Undergraduate Pre-Service Teacher Education Program). The UPSTEP Project included having two faculty advisors, a built-in peer group of other UPSTEP participants, early and ongoing student teaching placement in local schools, regular attendance at mathematics colloquia (who knew what a colloquium was!), and a space to hang out (the Dean's conference room), which was essential for me, a commuting student, to feel like I belonged and had a place at the table.

My pursuit of mathematics is another story. I earned that degree, qualifying me to teach secondary mathematics, but found that I didn't want to teach secondary mathematics. I loved mathematics, teaching, and the students; I did not like the "system." I applied for a few mathematics teaching jobs, but my heart was never in it. Though I interviewed for each job for which I had applied, I received no job offers. I was relieved.

I floundered for a while. I applied for and was accepted into the VISTA (Volunteers in Service to America) program, and moved to Brooklyn, NY, to serve as a volunteer working out of a storefront providing social service advocacy for non-English-speaking Italian immigrants. I am an introvert from a very rural region of northern New York State (way beyond "upstate"), and I did not like who I was becoming living in the big city. I enjoyed my advocacy work, the community members with whom I was working, and appreciated being introduced to human services work. I didn't like that I was becoming "hardened" by the constant verbal and nonverbal assaults from men that come with being a young woman simply going about her day-to-day life, nor was I comfortable with the competitive environment of the sponsoring agency for which I worked. I finished my one-year commitment and went back home, thinking I would go back to school and get a master's degree in Education and get back to teaching mathematics. Makes no sense now, nor did it then, really.

Still floundering, and while working as a supermarket checker, I followed up on a newspaper advertisement calling for volunteers for a training program at a crisis center. I went through 30 hours of training, became a volunteer, became a senior volunteer, became a trainer of volunteers, and joined the board of directors of the agency, all within an 18-month period. I was in consideration for the paid position as volunteer coordinator when I was contacted by the Peace Corps. My time at the crisis center had introduced me to a potential career in counseling, a professional field I had known nothing about prior to my experiences at the crisis center. But I knew I could not pass up the Peace Corps opportunity. I had applied to the Peace Corps as a college sophomore but had been advised at that time to complete my degree because they needed mathematics teachers.

Just about everyone I knew said some version of the following to me: "How can you interrupt your career to go in the Peace Corps?" Ha. It's not just a slogan; the Peace Corps really is "the toughest job you'll ever love." That is also another story, but I would never characterize my Peace Corps experience as an "interruption." I may still have been floundering, may have "known" at the time that I wanted to pursue counseling as a career, but I wasn't really interrupting anything. I thought it entirely possible that this experience could open new doors, just as my crisis center experience had. I joined the Peace Corps and served as a mathematics and English teacher for two years in Sierra Leone, West Africa.

When I returned to the United States, I did complete a master's program in counseling and then worked for nine years as a college career counselor, eight of them in Wisconsin. I loved this work and, loved being back in the higher education setting, and when I took on supervision of master's coun-seling internship students, I knew I had to eventually get my doctorate so I could teach in a graduate counseling program.

I did my research—on programs, accreditation, institutions, financial support, GREs, everything. I had stayed informed and had been doing workshops on this stuff for nine years. I was ready. I studied for the GREs, even the mathematics portion. Nerd that I am, I actually enjoyed challenging myself with the mathematics problems in my ETS (Educational Testing Service) practice exam book! I visited the two universities I was most inter-ested in, spending most of a day at one and barely an hour at the other. At SU, I was warmly welcomed by three different faculty members and spent about an hour each with two of them. The chairperson had also arranged to have a first-year doctoral student show me around, and this student had made arrangements for me to join her for lunch with several other students. I saw the full campus, the main library, the student center, and the streets nearby where students eat and have coffee. I heard the good, the bad, and the ugly. Most of it was good and exciting! The secretary was a hoot, and we connected immediately. I had a great visit and felt my goals and what the program could offer were almost perfectly aligned.

At the other institution, I only met the one faculty member I had been in contact with to set up the visit, and he was late, he was not interested in me or my goals even though his research was in career development, and he only talked about his many publications. I had arrived early, hoping to see students. Though I spent almost an hour in the doctoral student lounge, I never saw any students there or anywhere. I asked the faculty member if he knew of students I might speak with, and he had no idea. Later, when I sent in my application to this program, I received a reply that said they did not have my program. I was clearly not welcome at this institution! In my view, your "fit" with your program matters to your success. I know that there are online video tours available and that applicants can interview via Skype™. But my experience leads me to recommend that applicants should visit in person and meet as many people connected to their intended program as possible.

As part of my preparation for entry into a doctoral program, I considered the financial aspects, of course, and I started planning how to manage financially a couple of years before I even applied for admission. At the time, I had only myself to consider. While I was still working full-time, and in preparation for financing a doctoral program, I paid off a car loan early, paid off credit cards, cashed in savings bonds that had matured, saved as much as I could while still working in Wisconsin, and, later, arranged to have loan payments from my master's degree deferred. I also initially thought I would continue working full-time while going to school part-time. Online courses were not readily available at that time, so I applied for career development positions in colleges that were located reasonably near the universities with programs I was most interested in. While applying for admission to SU, I also applied for graduate assistantships, knowing they were very competitive and that I probably had little likelihood of landing one. Almost simultaneously, however, I was offered a full-time professional position at a college about an hour from Syracuse and a graduate assistantship within my department at SU. The assistantship lured me with many benefits: helping the department work on their self-study required for national accreditation, co-teaching and supervising master's-level counseling students (my ultimate goal), and providing counseling services, including career counseling to SU undergraduates. In short, I would be getting direct experience with the reality of being a college professor. Oh, and I would receive full tuition remission and a stipend! I would also not have to commute an hour each way from a demanding full-time job. I chose the privilege of becoming a full-time student with a graduate assistantship.

Finding a place to live was challenging, as I could not afford much but felt my "home" needed to be a place where I felt safe and comfortable, and could both work and relax. I wanted to be able to do laundry while doing schoolwork, rather than trekking to a laundromat. I wanted a place where I could play my piano. I wanted a place where I could go outside my door and take a long walk. I wanted a community with easy access to services—bank, grocery, drugstore, good restaurants, etc. I didn't intend to sacrifice those aspects of lifestyle for my doctorate. I spent the entire summer prior to my first semester looking at apartments in the greater Syracuse area. Each time I made the trek to Syracuse to hunt for apartments, I stayed at a KOA (Kampgrounds of America) campground, which turned out to be where I lived for the first two weeks of my first semester, after living in a disgusting dorm room for a week during my teaching assistant training. I finally found a fantastic affordable apartment that met all my requirements, but the current tenant had just bought a house that was not yet move-in ready. When she learned from the landlord that I was camping, she invited me over for spaghetti and offered to let me stay with her in the second bedroom for the last two weeks she would be there. The day she moved out, she left me with kitchen utensils and dishes to use while I waited for my other belongings to be delivered from storage. Once I was able to set up my office, I was finally able to purchase my first desktop computer and printer, for $3000—outrageous now but a bargain at the time!

Though there were many ups and downs throughout my program at SU, I thrived because I was welcome, I felt I belonged, and the program—faculty, secretarial staff, doctoral students, and master's students—was a community. I entered in a cohort of four doctoral students. Ahead of us, there were two. The six of us got tight almost immediately and carried each other through, bringing other new doctoral students into the group in subsequent cohorts. This social and academic support group was essential for each of us. E-mail and internet were still fairly new, and I recall one classmate, who lived an hour away, and I reveling in being able to do our statistics homework "together" in this virtual environment while being able to stay in our respective homes in our pajamas. Most students in the doctoral program were those smart and thoughtful colleagues I had imagined, but a few pushed ethical boundaries. From my idealistic stance as a predoctoral person, I had expected that those at this lofty level of professionalism would have higher ethical expectations. But, just as in any setting, there were those who chose to do the bare minimum and were constantly looking for "work-arounds" to get by with as little work as possible. One of these individuals, who entered in my cohort, was to become part of the 50% who do not complete the doctorate.

Some of the "downs" (i.e., frustrations), such as communication, advising, and mentorship, were sketchy; doctoral students with graduate assistantships were cheap labor for the department while master's students were the "cash cows," and all of the faculty members were older White men who had been on the faculty for 20 years or more. These men were kind and decent and knowledgeable and paternalistic. For example, in my prior professional life, I had done many presentations at professional conferences. And, by the end of my second year in the doctoral program, I had been a presenter six times at professional conferences, twice as co-presenter with my advisor. Yet, when I told my advisor that I had submitted a proposal for an upcoming regional conference, I was admonished and told I should "start out" presenting with other doctoral students and I should not be surprised if my proposal was not accepted. My proposal was accepted, my session was well attended, and I received very positive evaluations and feedback.

The academic environment was definitely intellectually rigorous, and also scary. In order to do well in my work, I had always been very thorough and conscientious, but I had never been the top student in a class or the one who didn't have to work hard for grades. I was in the big leagues now and found I had to up my game even more than I had expected. I had to go beyond being thoroughly prepared; I had to read everything about a topic and then read some more, and I was expected to express, both in writing and orally, a solid and well-constructed grasp of whatever concepts were in consideration. I quickly became aware of "deficits" in my master's preparation, which I later understood to not be deficits but, rather, differences in curricular focus and priorities. During my first semester, when a key theorist whom I had never heard of was the topic of discussion in our Advanced Theories of Counseling class, I despaired, thinking my master's program had neglected to prepare me properly for this! It was humiliating to admit I had never even heard this person's name. I was experiencing what I later learned was well known as the "imposter syndrome," or intellectual self-doubt: "People like me don't belong in doctoral programs."

On the other hand, my master's program had required that I complete a thesis, not a common occurrence in other programs. My research topic— dating violence—was controversial for the time, 1983, and required that I defend my proposal before the entire Institutional Review Board, a group of about a dozen faculty members, none of whom were in my discipline. Not only was my topic controversial, the population from whom I wanted to gather data consisted mostly of minors—high school seniors. My thesis advisor was a woman of compassion and extremely high academic standards, so I learned the process thoroughly and felt confident of my ability to defend the need for my study and to complete my thesis. Thankfully, I carried this confidence and knowledge of the process into my doctoral program as I did not receive similar preparation or support for completion of my dissertation from my doctoral advisor.

Through my graduate assistantship, I was able to apply my prior experiences and skills to address some of the frustrations related to the organization of an academic department. I helped plan the new student orientation, I developed the student handbook which addressed many of the advisement concerns I and my peers had, and I helped gather and analyze data for accreditation. And, I had opportunities to teach! The academy is most effective in preparing future scholars; surprisingly to me at the time, most college faculty members are not taught to teach, though that is perceived as their primary job. So when I was offered the opportunity to participate in the graduate school's new Future Professoriate Program, a program for preparing future professors to actually teach, I accepted and taught or co-taught a variety of courses in the master's programs in my department. In these and other ways, I was able to apply my past personal and professional experiences to the new culture and expectations of doctoral study, and to create opportunities for myself beyond the scripted curriculum.

CHAPTER 9

THE TICKET TO THE DANCE

EMILY PHILLIPS, PhD

State University of New York at Oneonta, Oneonta, NY, USA

I had reached my goals in setting up two school districts with comprehensive school counseling programs at the elementary level. This was a pretty novel approach in the early 80s. Over the course of 11 years as a school counselor, I became more involved with the state school counselor organizations, presenting at conferences, creating activity guides that matched lessons to the then national standards from American School Counselor Association. The school I was in wasn't ideal. Our goals did not match. I figured my main option was to look for another elementary school counselor position and start a whole new program.

I had begun adjunct teaching at the college from which I graduated and enjoyed that immensely. The director at the time suggested I consider a doctorate. The closest place to do this was over two hours away; I had one child entering his senior year of high school, a husband five years into sobriety, and I was 44 years old and afraid of driving in the snow. A spark happened. The leadership of the school I worked in made it clear they really wanted an assistant principal of discipline. I was place-bound, and the idea of choosing another district and starting up a third program seemed repetitive and unappealing. I loved teaching counselor education. I decided to investigate doctoral programs and options. I did not believe going to Syracuse University (SU) would be an option for me, but it was the only one I could manage by living a few days a week in Syracuse near campus and a few days a week back home, just over two hours away. I did not believe it would work out. But it did.

I went up for an interview, not believing I was smart enough and well-educated enough to make it at Syracuse, and assuming I would be found out to be an impostor! Well, the head of the department was so open and kind and took to me right away. He had lots of empathy for my background but also great admiration for my skills and recommendations. He really wanted ME and offered me the graduate assistantship during my time there, if admitted. This would pay my tuition. I couldn't believe it. Everyone I met was warm and welcoming. I had the wonderful opportunity to meet and train under Dr. Paul Peterson, a multicultural guru. He and I had an excellent talk about this impostor syndrome, and he advised me to never underestimate all the other riches I possessed besides money. I never forgot what he told me.

My advisor clucked at me when he met me and made it clear they were taking a chance on me because I have what is probably a learning disability in mathematics, and my GRE scores were so low on that area. I assured him I would do whatever it took to pass the two required statistics courses. Then he softened and said as long as I could find a way to work the department database and assure him I would not do a totally quantitative dissertation, he was behind me. We ended up becoming quite good friends. When I was feeling overwhelmed by my multiple lives, he told me to keep my eye on the prize and that this doctorate was "the ticket to the dance" if I wanted to teach in counselor education. Yes, when statistics time came, I hired a mathematics major at Syracuse and a retired mathematics professor at home to tutor me and also met several times with the statistics professor. My home tutor said to me after the first session, "My, there are some pretty big black holes up there!" Yep! So I began by being up front, telling students I supervised to double-check me, had someone double-check all my mathematics, and hired a graduate student in computer science to come in on a weekend and set up the department database. "Where there is a will, there is a way," is my motto.

The next step was to meet with the current graduate assistant so she could assess my fit for the program, provide feedback to the department regarding me, and orient me to the responsibilities so that I could make an informed decision. I drove up again and met with the graduate assistant, one of the editors of this book, Dr. Beverly Burnell. She was warm and caring, supportive, and positive. She told me honestly about her experience of the various department members and the system and was very complete in descriptions of what might be expected of me and what kind of commitment I'd need to make.

It was clear that I would have to stay from Monday until Thursday morning, then drive home and adjunct a 5 pm class, stay home for the weekend, and commute back Monday morning. I did that for two years and some of one summer. There were a couple of weekends a semester I had to be in Syracuse for the weekend as well. My college back home worked with me as well to cover any adjunct responsibilities. I had the career center staff visit my class, I arranged for other guest speakers, I did whatever it took to work it out. I was told up front I'd have to be the one to travel to the furthest sites in the snow belt to do practicum school counseling field placement visits, coordinate in-service training for the host counselors, teach a section of internship, supervise a number of master's-level techniques students and keep this database of time spent in the field, etc. up to date at the end of every semester. In my third year, after my assistantship was over, I had to go to Syracuse once a month while working with my dissertation chair and committee. I had a lot of responsibilities in both locations.

I could never have done this without the total support of my husband (he has since died). We were at the best point ever in our then 25-year marriage. He was willing to find a better paying job, have our income drop 60%, become a virtual single parent of a high school senior with attention deficit disorder and a learning disability, and hold down the home fort while I lived in two cities, got up at 5 am to type for hours, and ranted and raved at the archaic doctoral system.

I left out that at this point in time, around 1994, e-mail was new, and even owning a personal computer was not commonplace. So I also had to learn how to make a cursor move and how to do e-mail and how to work a laptop. But I was smart and resourceful, which you must be. You need to find a way to make your strengths work and your weaker areas not so important.

How did I do that? What advice can I offer? First and foremost, be yourself. There has to be a good fit. It is a tough process no matter what, and if there are dissension and tension, it will make getting a doctorate even more challenging. Focus on what you CAN offer. Learn about their system. Bev gave me such good insider information that, I believe, was the main thing that made me accept SU's offer.

In the letter I received, there was a handwritten note from the chair that said, in effect, "I know you will do whatever it takes." I did. You must. Some of us will have to do more in certain areas. I had to learn to ask for help. I had never heard of APA-style (American Psychological Association) writing. I had to learn fast enough to be a successful student and also to grade student work. I also need to add that when I graduated, I got another handwritten note from the chair, which I hung for 20 years or more in my office while I was a counselor educator. It said, in effect, that nothing made him more proud than to see me walk down that aisle and that he knows how much I sacrificed to get there.

It is good to be where you are appreciated! So choose carefully. Think outside the box. I went and researched odd funding sources: because my mother was Jewish, because I was left-handed, because I was female, and because I was older. It turned out a local branch of a national organization was looking for a female over 35 who decided to return for training. I interviewed and attended a few meetings and luncheons, and they supported me so I could afford a room near the campus. They even sent a Christmas card with a $25 personal check in it just to be nice. I joined that organization eventually for a while and helped get scholarships for other nontraditional students in this area interested in the master's in the school counseling program where I was employed. I also had to accept that I needed the money from teaching one course a semester to pay for living in two places and buying a laptop. I only took out $5000 in loans for my doctorate.

Other advice is to ask for help. Whether it's the person for whom you might be taking over as graduate assistant or needing a mathematics tutor, (or THREE!) I asked for proofreaders until I felt I was on solid ground. It is essential to put yourself out there in the early days. I am an only child. It makes it hard for me to meet new people. But it is essential to push. The doctorate is a time to be known. I remained friends with Bev, who even proofread my dissertation before defense and sat there through my defense, making strong and positive eye contact. Make sure to connect, join in, get to know people, and open up yourself to the professors.

Lastly, think of it as a great adventure. Change is your friend. Lean into it and drink it all in. It is a time of great learning about not just the field, but yourself. Enjoy the ride.

PART II:
Stage 2: First Year of the Program

The first year of doctoral work includes coursework related to the student's field of study but is most notable for the processes of socialization to the culture of the doctoral program, development of one's identity as a scholar, and the recognition that the educational environment and expectations differ greatly from previous experiences (Ali & Kohun, 2007).

DEVELOPING YOUR SUPPORT SYSTEM IS CRITICAL

As has been noted throughout this volume, social isolation and stress are often simply inherent in the doctoral journey, but you can take steps to minimize the effects of these factors on you. Further, the first year is the time to develop your support system—*before* the challenges of the comprehensive or qualifying exams and the dissertation. Your support system should consist of those who are outside of your friends and family and particularly should include those in your doctoral program who are living the doctoral experience concurrently with you. This part of your support system will become those with whom you study, commiserate, and who will encourage and motivate you to continue when the work feels overwhelming. This part of your support system may also serve as social outlets as well as your future professional network. As you identify new supports, consider whom you trust, who inspires you, who motivates you, and who energizes you (rather than those who deplete your energy).

DEVELOPING BALANCE

You will need to learn to adjust anew so that you are accounting for work, life responsibilities (including family and relationships), self-care, and now the demands of schoolwork—scheduled classes as well as time for reading, writing, research, and cognitive integration of new learning and previous understandings. You may find yourself needing to redefine "work" and "making money," as you may be working several jobs, your workday may not be the typical 9–5, or the work you may be expected to do as a teaching or research assistant will require both "on-site" and "after-hours" commitments, as well as learning new skills as a teacher or researcher. These new roles, as unfamiliar as they may be to you, will be mysteries to your friends and family. You will likely need to explain what you are doing, both as a student and as a worker with new expectations, and set new boundaries that accommodate these roles.

BEGINNING TO ESTABLISH YOUR IDENTITY AS A SCHOLAR

In the first year of doctoral study, you will be faced with an academic environment that challenges your perception of what it means to be a student. You will need to re-familiarize yourself with academic writing (and perhaps learn new forms of academic writing), integrate previous professional experiences with the scholarship you are now being exposed to, and begin to develop the professional identity expected of scholars in your discipline. Becoming a scholar will require that you hone your use of Internet search engines and professional databases so that you are employing professional sources and drawing from and expanding upon the work of other scholars. You probably will not have a secretary, of course, so you will also need to do all of your own keyboarding and document formatting.

WHAT IS THE WRITING STYLE REQUIRED FOR YOUR DEGREE?

Do they use APA (American Psychological Association), MLA (Modern Language Association), or Chicago style? Find out. Attend a workshop at the college writing center or see if there is an online tutorial available. Purchase the writing style manual. If you are concerned about your writing, remember it is a skill, and in order to get better you must write. Don't shy away from classes early on that are writing intensive; dive in and start immediately to become a better writer. Don't be afraid to go to the writing center on your campus, if they have one. Find a reader to help you develop clarity and improve your writing. Many graduate students struggle with writing.

SCHEDULE TIME FOR SELF-CARE

Take a yoga class, go to the gym, meditate. Play with your dog. Play with the kids. It is important to schedule fun time to rejuvenate yourself. Moving to a new city, making new friends, finding your way around is stressful. There may be times when you struggle with feelings of loneliness, sadness, or grief, even when you are doing something as exciting as learning new things. Being out of your comfort zone can bring on these feelings. Take care of yourself, every day.

STAGE 2 NARRATIVES

The essays in this section tell stories of women immersing themselves in and adjusting to this unfamiliar culture of doctoral study. The authors reveal challenges and vulnerabilities, share strategies and tips, and reinforce what is already known (Hunter and Devine, 2016) about the sustaining value of caring, healthy support and mentorship from doctoral peers, family, friends, and program faculty. Authors address the development of one's identity as a scholar; threats to and advocacy of one's identity as a professional or as a person; the process of developing new supports; making decisions about who to trust and who not to; and learning to write as a scholar. A key task in this stage is navigating relationships with faculty and your new set of colleagues. The section closes with an abbreviated mentoring dialogue that was undertaken via e-mail by a doctoral student and her faculty advisor; the dialogue illustrates these two women negotiating their relationship while each one reflects on her own process of identity development as a scholar.

REFERENCES

Ali, A.; Kohun, F. (2007). Dealing with social isolation to minimize doctoral attrition—a four stage framework. *International Journal of Doctoral Studies, 2*, 33–49. Retrieved from: http://www.informingscience.org/Journals/IJDS/Articles?Volume=2–2007&Search.

Hunter, K. H.; Devine, K. (2016). Doctoral students' emotional exhaustion and intentions to leave academia. *International Journal of Doctoral Studies, 11*, 35–61. Retrieved from: http://ijds.org/Volume11/IJDSv11p035–061Hunter2198.pdf.

CHAPTER 10

THE IMPORTANCE OF A SUCCESSFUL PEER SUPPORT GROUP

ANNA W. NOLAN, PhD

Menands, NY, USA

I truly believe the only way I made it through my doctoral program was through the creation of my successful peer support group. This was an unofficial group of friends that I cobbled together to help inspire, motivate, and support me through my doctoral journey. In return, I hoped to provide them with the same care.

10.1 INCEPTION

My successful peer support group came together in a class that all Educational Theory and Practice students are required to take early on in their coursework. The professor grouped the four of us by alphabetical order. There was Wanda* who was a generation older than me, married with children, and already working in higher college administration. Emre was a brilliant, younger student from Turkey who was working at the university while pursuing her degree. Tammy was about my age, quick-witted, and also a teacher at a local middle school. I was in my late twenties, working in teacher staff development, and new to the area. As the course progressed, our conversations moved from being class-based to personal. We started meeting off campus to work on assigned group projects but quickly found ourselves spending a lot of the time laughing and commiserating. Later in my studies, I met Saanyi, another student who was a new mother, as I had just become, and a real go-getter. We quickly became friends, and she also was added to my peer support group. I never said to each and every woman that they were part of my support group, but that is exactly what they were to me.

10.2 MEMBER QUALITIES

Each member was, of course, first and foremost, a friend. My perception of them as "successful" led to their designation as part of my support group. My definition of successful was a student who was ambitious, had great study habits, and who I could just tell she was on her way to greater things. I knew from life experience, and research has seconded, that there are benefits to surrounding oneself with positive, supportive, and forward-minded people (Bandura, 1977; Catalano and Hawkins, 1996; Suls, 1982). Crucial to their inclusion in my group was that each woman had a collaborative and caring nature. We would listen to each other and give advice when needed. As a perk of her university-based job, Emre often had the scoop on pertinent program gossip. Wanda was further along in her studies and would let me know what was coming down the road. Tammy and I were at the same point in our studies with similar struggles. Saanyi could understand the insanity of pursuing a doctoral degree while having a young family. I believed that birds of a feather really do flock together, and I wanted to be successful in my doctoral program. With this in mind, I looked for my flock. I met a lot of really nice people in the pursuit of my doctorate, but only a few made it into my successful peer support group.

10.3 BENEFITS PROVIDED

There is a clear hierarchy of power that exists within doctoral programs. At times, doctoral students can uniquely feel their lower designation if their attempts to seek support or guidance from an administration are unsuccessful. These negative student–administration interactions are stressful and can lead to student disillusionment and stifle creativity (Walker, Golde, Jones, Bueschel, & Hutchings, 2012). In my successful peer support group, there was great freedom that we were all equals as peers. As a student-based group, we attempted to lessen the pressure of being part of this greater doctoral hierarchy. As friends, we were kind to each other and often shared opportunities that arose. Emre started a research group and invited me to join. Wanda invited me to guest lecture at a course she was teaching. I shared the resources I was privy to from my job. Doctoral programs can be isolating, and some students may be unduly competitive (Golde, 2005). This sharing of tips, resources, and opportunities allowed us to create our own opportunities to advance our academic careers.

Another great benefit of creating your own successful peer support group is finding people with whom to celebrate your minor victories. Getting a doctorate is a very long and arduous undertaking (Gardner & Mendoza, 2010; Kiley, 2009). Frankly, only those who are in the process of or have gotten the degree can understand that. The little triumphs that I would celebrate with my group helped propel me to my next goal.

10.4   MEETINGS

Fate brought us together, but a concerted effort to keep the friendships alive sustained the relationships. During the semesters in which I did not have classes with my successful peer support group members, I would make sure we still got together for lunch or emailed frequently. As time went on, the relationships grew stronger. Emre, Wanda, and Tammy were all at my wedding. Saanyi and I had children around the same age who also became friends. We had many more things to talk about besides our academic responsibilities. Yet at the core of the relationship was our first bond: when we were students. Having this base allowed me to, at any time, email one of my peer support members with an academia-related question without having to explain the backstory. We spoke the same language because we learned to speak it at the same time. Now that I have earned my doctorate, my successful peer support group is still greatly valued. We are still listening, advising, and celebrating each other as we have embarked on our careers in academia.

10.5   ADVICE FOR CREATING YOUR OWN SUCCESSFUL PEER SUPPORT GROUP

If you would like to create a peer support group that will help you get through your doctoral program, there is no point in including students who you think will not be successful. Keep them as friends, but don't look to them for guidance and support in regard to your academic career. Toward the end of my doctoral studies, Tammy dropped out. We remained friends, but the focus of our discussions changed. Fortunately, my peer support group did not consist of one member, otherwise I would have felt very isolated. It is important to create a group that consists of a handful of diverse students from your program.

Look for members who appear open and willing to collaborate. Find peers who inspire you and are keen on sharing the "hows" and "whys" of their success. It would be frustrating and perhaps demoralizing to surround yourself with inspirational peers who wouldn't share some of their magic. With that in mind, be willing to share your own successful strategies, resources, and academic opportunities. Never forget that this is a mutually beneficial relationship.

*Names have been changed.

REFERENCES

Bandura, A. (1977). *Social learning theory.* Englewood Cliff, NJ: Prentice-Hall.

Catalano, R. F., & Hawkins, J. D. (1996).The social development model: A theory of antisocial behavior. In J. D. Hawkins (Ed.). *Delinquency and crime: Current theories* (pp 149–197). New York: Cambridge University Press.

Gardner, S. K., & Mendoza, P. (2010). *On becoming a scholar: Socialization and development in doctoral education.* Sterling, VA: Stylus.

Golde, C. M. (2005). The role of the department and discipline in doctoral student attrition: Lessons from four departments. *The Journal of Higher Education, 76,* 669–700.

Kiley, M. (2009). Identifying threshold concepts and proposing strategies to support doctoral candidates. *Innovations in Education and Teaching International, 46*(3), 293–304. DOI: 10.1080/14703290903069001.

Suls, J. (1982). Social support, interpersonal relations, and health: Benefits and liabilities. In G. Sanders & J. Suls (Eds.), *Social Psychology of Health and Illness;* (pp 255–277). Hillsdale, NJ: Lawrence Erlbaum Associates.

Walker, G. E., Golde, C. M., Jones, L., Bueschel, A. C., & Hutchings, P. (2012). *The formation of scholars: Rethinking doctoral education for the twenty-first century* (Vol. 11, Jossey-Bass/Carnegie Foundaiton for the Advancement of Teaching). San Francisco, CA: Jossey-Bass.

CHAPTER 11

THE LANGUAGE OF THE ACADEMY: AN ENGLISH LANGUAGE LEARNER IN A DOCTORAL PROGRAM

CINZIA PICA-SMITH, EdD

Assumption College, Worcester, MA, USA

I was born and raised in Napoli, in the South of Italy, in a mixed class family with a strong political working-class identity. My father was an outspoken Italian communist, a political organizer, who influenced my critical world-view and commitment to social justice. I was considered a precocious child, a "mature" child, and was deeply interested in social and political ideas from a young age. In particular, as a young girl, I most notably experienced and understood injustices based on gender and language oppression.

At the age of 12, when I was in the sixth grade, my parents thought they might move the family to the United States and sent me and my sister to an English-speaking American school (there are many such American schools in Italy) so that we could learn English. I entered the school speaking English but could neither read nor write in English. I could neither understand the teacher nor follow the lessons. An excellent student just a year before, I sat in this new classroom without the skills to comprehend or participate. The teachers, all White U.S. Americans, seemed cold and uninterested in me and what I could bring to the classroom, a stark contrast from my loving teachers in my Italian public school. Every day, I was pulled out by an ESL (English-as-a-Second-Language) teacher and brought to the library for small group instruction. The experience felt humiliating. My classmates teased and snickered at my inability to read in English or answer my teacher's questions. I never saw a teacher interrupting that behavior or comforting me for experiencing it. The kids also said terrible things about Italians, the most offensive of all for my twelve-year-old self were "Italians are stupid," "Italians stink," and/or "Italians are not clean." I felt like a smart girl trapped in a place where no one acknowledged this fact, and, to the contrary, thought I was inferior. I felt deeply that I didn't belong, and I was mad at these presumptuous and mean American kids and teachers. These circumstances angered me deeply and also urgently motivated me to learn English, as I was intent on proving to those American kids and teachers that I was smarter than they are! However, I also internalized some of that oppression and came to often doubt my abilities, capacity, and intelligence. Like all things, this experience and the learning from it are complex. On the one hand, I became somewhat insecure about my abilities, skills, and knowledge, and on the other hand, an indignant rebellious spirit and fire sparked within me to fight the erroneous perceptions of my intellectual inferiority.

Two years after beginning my schooling in English, I was reading on grade level and earning high marks again. Again, the feelings I had about this "success" were layered and complex. I was proud of my accomplishment but felt sad and inauthentic expressing myself in a language that was not my native one. I felt that the person I had to be at school was foreign, even to me.

Decades later, in graduate school, this familiar dynamic reverberated in my experiences, first as a master's student in an Ivy League university, and then as a doctoral student at another research-focused institution. As I traveled through the classroom spaces of the academy, I experienced the all-too-familiar complex, layered, and confusing feeling of dissonance around belonging and not belonging, being competent enough and not, having the "right" language or not understanding it at all. Of course, at the start of my doctoral experience, I could not have identified, conceptualized, or verbalized this feeling, but it was with me all the time, a heavy blanket of insecurity and resentment. I often walked around holding the two conflicting thoughts and feelings related to both "not belonging" and deeply knowing that I had an important way of knowing, one that was directly related to my position at the margins as a working-class girl growing up in Italy and as a bilingual child in an American school. In time, I came to realize that this was an asset, a way of knowing and seeing that was most important in my personal, political, and academic paths. This way of knowing helped me to critically identify injustice and imagine a more socially just classroom space. It helped me to understand that academia, like most institutions, reproduces racism, classism, heterosexism, sexism, language oppression, and many other systems of oppression even while understanding itself as progressive and evolved. The alienating experience of "not belonging" was being lived by so many of us, who were often isolated and imagined it to be an individual ailment, rather than a systemic problem. As I spoke to other students (mostly working-class women and people of color), I realized that we were experiencing similar things. And, the more we talked, we felt more connected, less isolated, and more like we belonged. We realized there wasn't a problem of "fit," but there was a problem of an institution built in classist, sexist, and racist notions of intelligence, in which "intelligent" or "intellectual" meant a specific classed, raced, and gendered language experience we did not share. It was by participating in mixed-race, mixed-class women's support groups, co-counseling workshops, and co-creating a bi-weekly women's writing group that we came to understand the problematic dynamics of academia and how to successfully navigate the process.

I wish I had figured this all out before entering the doctoral program (but how could I have done that?). I wish I had figured it all out before the beginning of my Early Childhood Education course in my first year of studies. In this course, we read and analyzed much research on English Language Learners (ELL). One week our assignment was to read two articles by a distinguished professor and researcher who then visited our class to participate in a discussion. This research examined a classroom community of ELL and their families and their engagement in the educational process. The most humbling aspect of this experience was that after reading the articles several times, I still had a very difficult time understanding the content as well as the implications. This experience engendered both feelings of insecurity (what is wrong with me that I don't understand this? Am I not intellectual enough to engage in this work? I must be a fraudulent doctoral student) and anger (research should be written in a way that is accessible to all—especially to those ELL students and families who volunteered their time to participate—how can the writing be so inaccessible that a doctoral-level student cannot understand it! This is unacceptable! This is academic elitism! This is using language to assert and reassert power and position! I cannot stand for this!). Again, a new language, in this case academic language, was creating contradictory, complicated, and layered emotional reactions for me: it fueled both deep insecurity and social-political consciousness.

While this experience of not understanding (and many others like this one) was confusing and trying in my process of adjusting to the doctoral program, I am grateful that I experienced it. Let me explain. I am not grateful as in I think it should be this way. I am grateful in the sense that I *made meaning* of this injustice. While I don't think that higher education should be inaccessible (as I felt the doctoral program was), I know that it helped me to clarify the kind of academic I wanted to be. This was like when I was twelve years old and experiencing this language oppression, and fueled me to master academic speak and then learn to make choices about when and whether to use it. Through these challenges, I learned that I was indeed a person who belonged in academia. I learned that, indeed, I was the smart girl who mastered English once before. I learned that academic language was just another language to study and master. I learned that academia was a place of unexamined classism, sexism, and racism and that the institution was not designed as a vehicle of social justice. Sadly, I learned that doctoral programs replicate erroneous notions of "intelligence" and deficit thinking about the idea that some people are more intelligent and intellectual than others.

All of this, in turn, helped me to clarify the social justice and language liberation work that must be carried out in higher education. These experiences helped to identify the type of research and writing I would produce: work that was important and always accessible to young people, the general public, teachers, school counselors, and academics alike. The infuriating understanding of language oppression and its intent to further marginalize and alienate people who have been historically marginalized propelled me to challenge these inequities in my everyday work of teaching, scholarship, and service in the academy. Today, I am committed to creating accessible classroom spaces when I teach. I am committed to supporting my students—all of them. I am committed to communicating in a way that does not create distance and hierarchies of intelligence. I have learned that I belong in a place where I can produce knowledge—that I have always belonged. And, I am committed to supporting all of those young people who may question whether or not they belong to be successful scholars.

CHAPTER 12

THE DOCTORAL EXPERIENCE: ONE SINGLE WOMAN'S RESPONSE TO THE (MIS)PERCEPTIONS OF ACADEMIC PEERS AND FAMILY[1]

MAUREEN E. SQUIRES, EdD

State University of New York at Plattsburgh, Plattsburgh, NY, USA

E-mail: msqui001@plattsburgh.edu

12.1 INTRODUCTION

Research on doctoral degree completion reveals surprising data. Of the students enrolled in US doctoral degree programs, 50% will not complete their degree, and many of those will drop out in their first year of study (Jairam & Kahl, Jr., 2012). This attrition rate is well documented in the literature (Ali & Kohun, 2007; Esping, 2010; Lovitts & Nelson, 2000). Though several internal and external contributing factors have been identified, two major factors are stress and the feelings of social isolation (Ali & Kohun, 2007; Jairam & Kahl, Jr., 2012). Not surprisingly, "social support" has been found to mitigate the effects of stress and social isolation. This can be the support provided by academic peers, family, friends, and/or faculty and assume numerous types, including emotional, professional, and practical (Jairam & Kahl, 2012).

I commenced doctoral studies in August 2006 and graduated with my EdD in May 2011. This was an intense five years, filled with heartache and happiness. Completing my doctoral degree was not easy. As a single full-time first-generation woman doctoral student, I wasn't sure what to expect in my doctoral program. Though I relied on some support from academic friends and family, I also had to confront their (mis)conceptions of how lucky I was

---

[1]Dr. Squires' essays address two stages: first year of the program and second year through candidacy.

or their questioning my pursuit of a terminal degree. In the following essay, I describe several assumptions that I challenged and situate my experience in current literature. I conclude with recommendations for doctoral students in similar situations as my own.

12.2   YOU'RE SO LUCKY!

"You're so lucky to be a single full-time doctoral student." Childless was implied. I heard this countless times from peers in my doctoral program. I didn't know it when I matriculated, but I was entering a program where I was the nontraditional student. Most students in the EdD program were nearing retirement as public school teachers and pursuing lifelong goals to obtain a doctorate. For them, this goal had been postponed due to marriage and parenting demands and was suspended over nearly ten years, due to their part-time status in the program. Conversely, I was at the beginning of my career. Having just completed my fifth year as a high school teacher, I was a novice. Moreover, I was enrolled full-time and had none of the perceived distractions of doctoral students who were also wives/husbands and/or mothers/fathers.

When my academic peers remarked that I was lucky, they were referring to the *time* I could devote to my doctoral studies. They perceived themselves as having less time than I to spend on coursework. Though I was free from the responsibilities of being a spouse and parent, I was not completely free from responsibilities. I performed two roles: that of a doctoral student and that of a professional. While in the program, I taught undergraduate courses in human development and eventually graduate courses in special education. As an instructor of record of large and new-to-me courses, I spent a great deal of time preparing for each class, teaching, grading, and holding office hours. This was all time that detracted from doctoral study. Further, I was taking three doctoral courses each semester compared to part-time students who were taking one per semester (or year). The time I had for coursework had to be divided among three courses. Ironically, I remember thinking I wish I could slow down my program, take one course at a time so that I could read deeper and contemplate longer.

In addition to taking classes and teaching at the university, I also had to address daily living tasks on my own. Dishes needed to be washed, laundry needed to be cleaned, groceries needed to be purchased, the apartment needed to be tidied, and so forth. These typical duties of adulthood, which I could not share with or transfer to a spouse, also stole my time. I am not claiming to have less time than my part-time and married academic peers;

I am trying to illustrate how time was allocated to me, a full-time single doctoral student. Tending to all of my responsibilities left no downtime. Although my status had some advantages, it was not a "luxury" as many of my peers remarked.

As the sole financial provider, I had to rely on myself to cover my expenses. Working is not easy as a full-time doctoral student. I was fortunate to be fully funded, and I earned a modest stipend for teaching in the School of Education. Yet the stipend didn't cover basic living expenses. This meant that I had to be frugal, and I had to take out student loans. It also meant that for five years, the duration of my doctoral experience, I was not contributing to savings accounts or retirement plans. Financially, this was a triple burden. First, I took a substantial pay cut by leaving public school teaching to enter the doctoral program. Second, I temporarily accrued debt. Third, I was not saving for my future financial security.

Being a single full-time doctoral student and juggling multiple roles was not easy. I couldn't afford (both financially and career-wise) to slow down or proverbially drop a plate. I was jealous of my academic peers who had spouses to support them financially, emotionally, and practically. I felt isolated, stressed, and exhausted.

Numerous studies have found marital status affects the doctoral experience in positive and negative ways. As a spouse and parent, women doctoral students feel torn between their two roles (Onwuegbuzie, Rosli, & Ingram, 2010). This can add to the married doctoral student's level of stress. A similar phenomenon occurs for single women doctoral students who feel stressed by balancing their roles as students and professionals. Yet spousal support can be a positive factor in the lives of women doctoral students. "Encouragement from husbands had a significant impact on women's academic success" (Onwuegbuzie et al., 2010, p. 2). Spouses can also contribute practical support, such as financial stability and help with chores, housework, and errands (Jairam & Kahl, 2012). For married women doctoral students, practical or tangible support "has been shown to act as a buffer against depression and negative morale" (Schaefer, Coyne, & Lazarus, as cited in Jairam & Kahl, Jr., 2012, p. 319). These benefits are not available to single women doctoral students.

12.3   WHAT DO YOU DO WITH ALL OF YOUR TIME?

"Since you're not teaching, what do you do with all of your time?" I was asked this question often by family members. My family, specifically my parents and sisters, were as supportive of my decision to pursue a doctorate as they could be. They helped me locate housing, pack my belongings, and relocate (multiple times). When I was working on my dissertation, my parents let me live with them for minimal rent. My family surprised me with a party once I graduated. But not having lived the doctoral experience, they couldn't empathize or offer advice about surviving the program. Nor did they understand the intellectual, emotional, or financial stress I endured. They often questioned why I was so stressed, why I spent so much time on coursework, and why I was so removed from the family. This was especially the case during the dissertation stage.

Daily routines during the dissertation stage were mundane but necessary to stay on schedule. When I was writing the first three chapters of my dissertation, I spent my days and evenings on the computer searching for relevant sources, reading articles, or writing. None of these seemed like "real" work to my family. My typical day for six months of data collection was as follows: arrive at school (research site) at 7:00 am; research as a participant observer all day; leave school between 5:00 and 6:00 pm (sometimes later, depending on evening activities); return home to type fieldnotes, transcribe interviews, write memos, and prepare for next day in the field; go to bed, and repeat. When I started analyzing and writing the remainder of my dissertation, I was glued to the computer, surrounded by digital recordings, stacks of transcripts, highlighters, books, notebooks, and coffee. I sat in the basement of my parents' house curled up in blankets typing for what seemed like an eternity.

To outsiders, my time may have appeared to be unstructured or the activities I was immersed in may not have seemed like real work. I wasn't on campus teaching. I didn't have fixed deadlines to meet other than the ones I set for myself. I knew the best practice was to transcribe interviews directly after they ended and write memos or clarify fieldnotes immediately after an observation. These became daily practices. Perhaps my family thought I was listening to music through the headphones (really, it was an interview recording) or reading for pleasure (really, it was a book about theory) because they regularly interrupted me. My parents were the most frequent offenders. When my mom came to the basement to do laundry, she would ask about my day and want to talk about hers. My dad would come to the basement to watch TV and invite me to join him. My parents would prepare dinner and get aggravated when I remained in the basement working rather than eating with them.

I grew increasingly frustrated. I wanted to be a like a ghost in my parents' house: inhabit the basement but not be seen. It was not fair or reasonable of me to expect this. Part of me felt like I was using them. I needed a cheap place to live for a few months. Part of me felt guilty for being annoyed by their intrusions. After all, their intentions were good; they were trying to include me as a family member. But my parents did not understand that I couldn't simply stop transcribing or writing a memo to have a conversation. Stopping midway would cloud my thoughts; I would lose my momentum.

Admittedly, I was distant. Being hyper-focused on my dissertation, I often disregarded family members' requests to spend time together. I was present for big events: Christmas, my sisters' baby and bridal showers, one sister's wedding, the births of several nieces and nephews, and my grandmother's death. But I was not present daily. I grappled with this family absence. As a single woman, I didn't have my "own" nuclear family; I had my parents, sisters and their families, and a large extended family. I missed being with family, yet I perceived them as a distraction. The university also made it clear that I was on a fast track to degree completion. Time was of the essence. Eventually, I had conversations with my family and we established norms. When the "Work in progress. Please do not disturb." sign was hung on the closed basement door, family members agreed not to interrupt me. I agreed to participate in more family events.

As mentioned previously, family support significantly contributes to the doctoral experience. It can be a form of encouragement and discouragement for women doctoral students. Not having a spouse, I relied on my parents and siblings for support. In line with the research, I experienced familial emotional and practical support. "Familial emotional support dealt more with overall encouragement, esteem building, and love" (Jairam & Kahl, 2012, p. 319). Tangible support existed when my parents allowed me to live in their house for minimal rent. While I appreciated this family support, it was also a hindrance. My family's *lack of understanding* was a constant source of frustration. This is a common concern, as doctoral students often report that family members do not understand their rationale for pursuing a doctoral degree or the work involved in obtaining a doctoral degree (Jairam & Kahl, 2012; Onwuegbuzie et al., 2010). In some cases, lack of under-standing from family even discouraged and demotivated doctoral students from completing doctoral programs (Onwuegbuzie et al., 2010).

12.4   REVISING (MIS)CONCEPTIONS

The doctoral experience is an intense period of study where individuals are challenged to process vast amounts of information, make novel contributions in their fields, navigate a complex and unfamiliar culture, and prove themselves as scholars. As such, the doctoral experience can be accompanied by feelings of stress and social isolation. Academic friends and family serve as two social supports that can positively and negatively affect the doctoral journey.

In reflecting on my experience, I realize that I could have better utilized my supports. In regard to academic peers, *time* was a point of contest. Academic peers believed I was "lucky" to pursue doctoral study full-time and as a single woman. Yet, like them, I felt the stress of balancing three roles and limited time. I recommend the following for doctoral students in a similar situation:

- Regarding the scheduling of courses: Ask your advisor and more advanced doctoral students for suggestions. They can recommend the best way to sequence courses or alert you to particularly time-consuming courses and/or semesters. You can then be prepared to make adjustments in your schedule and support network.
- Regarding funding: Ask if scholarships, grants, stipends, and/or fellowships can be used in summer and winter sessions and if these monies can be disbursed over an extended period. This could allow you to spread out coursework, thereby giving you more time to focus on each course and attend to daily responsibilities.
- Regarding finances: One should plan ahead. Prior to entering a doctoral program, pay off or pay down debt. For example, pay the balance on car loans or credit cards. Additionally, put as much money into savings and retirement accounts as possible. Taking these steps will mean you have less debt starting a doctoral program and less need to work during this period, thereby giving you more time to devote to doctoral studies and your personal life.
- Regarding outlook: Simplify your life and let things go. The fewer material things you have to manage, the less time will be devoted to maintaining them. Additionally, be okay with letting the daily responsibilities go, at least a little. The laundry might pile up; the dishes might sit in the sink; the apartment might be messy. It's more important to devote time to your intellectual, professional, and personal life than daily tasks. Remember, the doctoral experience is temporary.

In regard to family, *lack of understanding* was the greatest obstacle. My family members didn't understand the intellectual and emotional demands of the doctoral experience. Additionally, I didn't communicate my needs or expectations well. For doctoral students in a similar situation, I recommend the following:

- Talk with family. Explain the requirements of your doctoral program, the time commitment, and the type of work to be completed. Describe the dissertation process to them. Discuss how your role in the family will change and how family members can shift their roles to best support you. When challenges emerge, address them immediately.
- Establish healthy routines. Set guidelines and deadlines for yourself regarding coursework, family engagements, and personal health. Although you are balancing multiple roles, try not to let one role consume the others.
- Create a "work zone." Carve out a place that is designated as your work space. Explain to family members that when you are in this space, you are working. Ask family members to respect your work zone by not disturbing you, unless there's an emergency. Tell your family members the conditions that are ideal for your productivity.
- Ask for help. If you are overwhelmed by daily tasks, ask for assistance. Family members might do a load of laundry, cook a meal, or clean the house. These tangible supports can relieve some stress and provide more time for your intellectual, professional, and social-emotional well-being.

My grandfather regularly served as a sounding board during my doctoral experience. After listening to me vent about frustrations, he would say, "Nothing worth obtaining comes easily. You must work hard. If you want it, go for it." His words carried great weight. I went for it, and I got it! Unfortunately, this has not been the experience of nearly half of the students who enter doctoral programs. Though it can be stressful and isolating, the doctoral experience does not have to be so daunting. Utilizing social supports effectively can mitigate these factors and make the doctoral journey more favorable and feasible, particularly for a single full-time woman doctoral student.

REFERENCES

Ali, A.; Kohun, F. (2007). Dealing with social isolation to minimize doctoral attrition—a four stage framework. *International Journal of Doctoral Studies, 2,* 33–49. Retrieved from: http://www.informingscience.org/Journals/IJDS/Articles?Volume=2–2007&Search.

Esping, A. (2010). Motivation in doctoral programs: A logotherapeutic perspective. *The International Forum of Logotherapy, 33*, 72–78.

Jairam, D., & Kahl, D. H., Jr. (2012). Navigating the doctoral experience: The role of social support in successful degree completion. *International Journal of Doctoral Studies, 7*, 311–329.

Lovitts, B. E., & Nelson, C. (2000). The hidden crisis in graduate education: Attrition from PhD programs. *Academe, 86*(6), 44–50.

Onwuegbuzie, A. J., Rosli, R., Ingram, J. M., & Frels, R. K. (2014). A critical dialectical pluralistic examination of the lived experiences of select women doctoral students. *The Qualitative Report, 19*(5), 1–35. Retrieved from: http://www.nova.edu/ssss/QR/QR19/onwuegbuzie5.pdf.

CHAPTER 13

MY FIRST YEAR: IS WORK–LIFE BALANCE ACHIEVABLE?

CHERIE L. KING, ScD

Central Connecticut State University, New Britain, CT, USA

E-mail: kingche@ccsu.edu

I started my program at Boston University in the fall of 2002 as my twins started kindergarten and my daughter started fourth grade. Leading up to my first day of school, I spent weeks organizing the house, coordinating with my husband, arranging schedules, hiring babysitters, stocking up on groceries and toilet paper, and finishing the laundry. I was exhausted before the start of classes.

The morning of my first day of school was a combination of excitement and disappointment. My husband and I had an upsetting argument. I was anxious and needed to know he had everything covered. He was difficult and dismissive, and I felt unsupported and disheartened. I left for the campus in tears and angry. I was so angry that I packed a bag and decided to stay with friends for a couple nights near campus. After calling him in the late afternoon to tell him I wasn't coming home, I walked into my first doctoral class. I did not go home for four days. He knew I was serious. In retrospect, I would not have changed my response to our fight. I still stand firm on my decision to make my point with my actions. I was serious about getting my doctorate, and he needed to get on board. We had always been a two-career couple with kids. We never had the traditional "Mom stays home and Dad goes to work" kind of family. My husband's mother worked full-time with four kids as he grew up so it was not a foreign concept to him. But my question throughout my program was: Why was my pursuit of an advanced degree such an inconvenience to him?

In starting my program, I carried 18 credits per semester, and this included weekly supervision with my mentor. I traveled to the campus in

Boston from Connecticut (90 miles one way) twice a week for supervision and classes. These were long days where I would leave the house at 10 am and get home around 11:30 pm and then get up the next morning to get the kids out the door for school. After a lot of discussion and compromise, my husband's attitude improved and he became a more cooperative team player. We shared the workload but it was a big change in our weekly routine. I was even more aware of working mom's guilt. But I was determined. The days I was not on campus were spent reading, reading, and more reading. I wrote endless papers and finished homework. As someone who never perceived herself as a good student, I proved to myself that I had what it takes. I had a lot of professional experience that complemented my studies. I felt my experience added depth to assignments and participation in classes. My nemesis, Statistics, was a tough course. But every week, I went to my professor's office hours to make sure I understood what I was doing and applying it correctly. I also kept working part time in my practice. I took on a few cases a month so I could retain income. I also continued my leadership responsibilities in my professional associations. These professional activities were hard to give up, and I found ways to integrate them into my doctoral studies. For example, I organized a professional development day on campus for members and master's students from rehabilitation counseling programs in New England. It was a great way to connect academia to the professionals in the field as well as connect master's students to private rehabilitation practitioners.

Since I was the only student accepted into the program that year, my courses were combination doctoral-level courses, such as statistics with doctoral students from other programs at the university. I had been out of school for a while so I was advised to re-familiarize myself with research methods by taking a master's-level course. This is when I became acutely aware that I was a "nontraditional" student. In the research course, we were learning the use of surveys by collecting data from the class through a random life activity questionnaire. My professor then demonstrated data analysis using SPSS. One survey question was "How many loads of laundry do you do a week?" My answer was 15, and the mean of my classmates' responses was 1.5 loads per week. I had "outed" myself and learned an important concept in data analysis—outliers.

I also discovered my "practitioner bias" related to research findings and application to the real world. After working in the field for close to 20 years, I had become accustomed to utilizing what worked with clients. Rehabilitation counseling services were results-oriented, and although the practice was informed by research, it was not a driver in my practice. I knew what worked to help individuals with disabilities respond to acquired disabilities and get back to work. I used counseling as a motivator to move cases along to a positive result. Many times, the result was not necessarily driven by the client. It was an expectation of the payer of services. Mine was a very different world from conducting research to improve practice and service delivery. Although I never saw myself as a researcher, I became more open to the mindset and felt stronger in developing a research agenda and skills to study my interests and utilize in my practice.

Luckily, I had peers who were working professionals, most with kids. They knew what I was up against since they had experienced it too. This was extremely comforting and motivating to me. I developed strong connections with several of these peers and fostered these relationships. My doctoral mentor was the quintessential university professor: white hair, beard with a mustache, and an inquisitive gaze. I was petrified in our weekly supervision meetings. He was a kind man with a good sense of humor but he was a classic counselor who loved the silence to ponder my answers and ramblings. Yes, I rambled. Most of the time, I felt like an idiot and I was sure he thought he had made a big mistake taking me on as his student. Luckily, I had a fellow doctorate student who helped me through the anxiety of supervision. She said that our mentor was just contemplating how great I was. What? Was that possible? I went with it and it worked. I became more relaxed and confident in our supervision sessions. This proved to be entirely true throughout my doctoral experience with this fantastic man. I knew my experience was quite different than many of my peers in other doctoral programs who felt judged or ignored by their advisors. I was fortunate that my program had created an environment in which I was understood as a doctoral student, experienced professional, and mother. I exposed and integrated my kids into my school life by occasionally bringing them to campus to meet my professors and peers, have lunch in the cafeteria, and to sit quietly and color during a doctoral seminar class. In retrospect, I think this was an attempt to balance the pull I felt in both directions, that is, home and school. By occasionally combining my family with school, I could be who I was and allow the faculty to see my life and get to know my family.

Although I was invigorated with my new life in academia, I started showing the effects of stress in the first year. I was doing too much and trying to do everything perfectly. Coursework, reading, marriage, kids, work, and home were a constant juggling act, with balls dropping everywhere. The biggest ball drop was my health. Either I wasn't sleeping well or sleeping too much. I ate fast food in the car. I did not have time for exercise. I was drinking to decompress. I gained weight. I was impatient with my husband

and kids. Body aches, pains, and headaches were more common than not. My blood sugar was high, and my skin was a mess. Time became my enemy and there was never enough for me. Hormones out of whack, 50 pounds heavier, dysfunctional adrenals, and feeling awful were not enough to make me stop and look at myself. I marched on, determined to push through and ignore my body.

Completion of a doctoral degree is an enormous feat, especially for nontraditional students including women and mothers. Women in doctoral programs "struggle with competing demands for their time and attention" (Trepal, Stinchfield, & Haiyasos, 2013, p. 30). Offstein, Larson, McNeill, & Mwale (2004) suggest that stress is at the core of the doctoral experience. Health problems, including mental health issues, are an additional stressor that impacts completion of a doctoral degree (Maher, Ford, & Thompson, 2004). The well-being of a doctoral student is not addressed readily in the literature. However, a few authors have assessed doctoral student experiences related to work–life balance and have included the issues of health, stress, and managing time and priorities as contributing factors impacting balance (Brus, 2006; Haynes, Bulosan, Citty, Grant-Harris, Hudson, & Koro-Ljungsberg 2012; Martinez, Ordu, Della Sala, & McFarlane, 2013). I describe it as a slow and steady marathon just to sustain the pace to keep the ball moving forward. However, it is very common for doctoral students, whether single with no children or with families, to struggle with managing time and attention to both personal and academic demands. In my experience, it was all consuming to "stay on top" of my life priorities and make it look easy. As mentioned, my health was one thing in my life that was not a priority. I did not use any coping mechanisms, which is common for doctoral students. My health was just one more stressful "thing" I had to attend to and then pushed aside. At the time, I felt taking time to exercise or to prepare healthy meals would create more pressure on me and get in the way of finishing a paper or preparing to teach a class or spending time with my family.

I feel the residual physical and emotional health effects of being in a doctoral program, working, and family was the price I paid for my degree. Luckily, my story ends well. It took me eight years after completion of my degree to get healthy. I am now 50 pounds lighter, exercise regularly, and off medications. This is not to discourage any woman from pursuing an advanced degree, but it is important to be aware of the effects that no one talks about. I learned an important but hard lesson that I pass on to my graduate students frequently. Nothing is more important than self-care.

REFERENCES

Brus, C. P. (2006). Seeking balance in graduate school: A realistic expectation or dangerous dilemma. *New Directions for Student Services, 115*, 31–45.

Haynes, C., Bulosan, M., Citty, J., Grant-Harris, M., Hudson, J., & Koro-Ljungberg, M. (2012). My world is not my doctoral program ... or is it? Female students' perceptions of well-being. *International Journal of Doctoral Studies, 7*, 1–16. Retrieved from: http://www.informingscience.com/ijds/Volume7/IJDSv7p001–017Haynes329.pdf.

Martinez, E., Ordu, C., Della Sala, M. R., & McFarlane, A. (2013). Striving to obtain school-work–life balance: The fulltime doctoral student. *International Journal of Doctoral Studies, 8*, 39–57.

Offstein, E. H., Larson, M. B., McNeill, A. L., & Mwale, H. M. (2004). Are we doing enough for today's graduate students? *International Journal of Educational Management, 18*(7), 396–407.

Trepal, H., Stichfield, T., & Haiyasoso, M. (2014). Great expectations: Doctoral student mothers in counselor education. *Adultspan Journal, 13*(1), 30–45. DOI: 10.1002/j.2161.2014.00024.x.

CHAPTER 14

AHEAD OF THE CURVE

DEBORAH J. SMITH, EdD

Empire State College, Saratoga Springs, NY, USA

E-mail: Deborah.Smith@esc.edu

In 1994, my dad had a stroke that left him paralyzed in the vocal chords and unable to swallow. Fitted with a tracheostomy and a polyethylene glycol gastric tube, he spent the next five years until his death being fed liquid nourishment, watching the Food Channel on TV, attempting to eat food that he wanted but shouldn't eat, and coughing up what small bits of food slid into his lungs. He also spent his remaining days on the "swinging door" cycle of our local hospital emergency room (ER). We never knew when he'd go in: if he inhaled something, if the tube or the trach became blocked, if he spiked a fever, or maybe fell down, unable to get up.

My mother was his full-time caregiver, but she couldn't drive a car. In an emergency, she'd call the ambulance and then she'd call me, her daughter— the nurse and the doctoral student. I worked full-time as a nursing instructor while I pursued my doctorate cross-country at Pepperdine University while also trying to take care of my immediate family.

As a nurse, my experience of the ER from both sides of the curtain confirms it's a setting where adrenalin junkies thrive. You're either triaging patients right and left or waiting for them to arrive when the heralding ambulance call comes in. Family members sit and worry next to a loved one's gurney or in the waiting room, trying to pass the time with notoriously crappy magazines all around them.

The ER isn't the best setting for doctoral students with a dozen books to read in a single course, even if you're an advanced-practice psychiatric nurse like me. But nursing, a rigorous intellectual pursuit, teaches theory and skills. In reality, it's up to you to take those procedural instructions and safely fit them to the situation and your patients: whether that's maintaining sterility, keeping a therapeutic relationship going, or getting that pesky IV to run at the specified drops per minute. You have a plan, maybe two or three. Often you have payoff waiting too, for following the plan, because you really do deserve it.

It's an understatement, but pursuing any advanced academic degree requires a huge amount of reading. Right here, I was a woman with a plan. Every time I drove my parents to the ER or the offices of assorted physicians for my father, I also dropped a textbook into my handbag. Once everyone was settled in for the inevitable lengthy wait, I opened the book and started reading. Books for class in my car, or in my bag, were a constant.

Credit goes to my fellow classmates at Pepperdine University as well. As a cohort, we'd make a point of getting the reading list *first* from the various professors. The reading list was emailed to everyone, titles available on Amazon linked within the email. Just click and order.

My friend Barb, a technology teacher, showed me how to cut through the more boring business books on the list quickly: read the introduction and the first and last sentence of every paragraph in the chapter. If there's a summary of each chapter, read that too. Without having to plow through every daunting word, with this technique I got a grip on the topics for each class discussion. In our Pepperdine residency classes or in the online environment, I knew enough of the material to follow the class and tackle the issues intelligently. Which is what professors hope doctoral students will do, right?

I spent the endless hours with my father and my mother in the ER or in medical offices reading about chaos theory, leadership with soul, technology and the future, scaffolding learning, learning communities, change theories, and on and on. The end result each term was getting through a pile of work at a steady rate. It also left time (when I wasn't at work or in virtual classes online) to keep up with writing papers and eventually my dissertation. If I left all that "wait time" vacant, I'd have to use my writing time for reading, further crowding up my life and my pursuit of a doctorate. My family—my professor-husband and my small son—would have seen far less of me than they already did on any given night.

Here's the thing: by nature and by nurture I am a voracious reader. Reading is one of my favorite things to do in life, so I keep right on doing it. My parents always encouraged me to bring a book everywhere with me. My mom got me a library card at an early age; I've had one ever since everywhere I lived. This was practical for mom, especially when my sisters came along. If the adults wanted to talk and I was bored, I could read. If the car ride was long, I could read. On rainy vacation days in our camper, I read.

Flash forward to my doctoral program in the pre-Kindle era. I read printed books on the plane trips to and from the California campus. I read in the hotel where I stayed and at my friend's homes when I crashed with them for our residencies in Culver City. I toted the books with a heavy laptop from coast to coast. Now, I borrow digitally from our local library or buy the e-book, downloading and reading as I go, on several portable devices. And I can do this as I fly across the globe. Isn't technology great?

In the end, the space you make in reading ahead of the curve allows you to do things you enjoy, knowing the required stuff is out of the way. That's the payoff to the plan, and it works as marvelously as any reinforcement of behavior tends to do.

Sometimes though, the plan can unexpectedly go awry. Once I arrived at Los Angeles Airport with my course books packed in my checked baggage, but a novel tucked under my arm. Smugly thrilled with myself in the shuttle van to my hotel, I didn't notice Robert, another doctoral student from my cohort, until he asked to sit with me. Sliding into the seat, Robert glanced down at my book and quickly looked up into my face. Our eyes locked.

> *"What book is that?" he exclaimed, dumbfounded I was reading for pleasure.*
> *"A novel I was reading ...," I said quietly, flipping the front cover away from him.*
> *"What about the books for Dr. Canning's class? And McManus' class? All those things? I've barely gotten through the half of them."*
> *"Ummm ..., I've read them all."*
> *"You are kidding, right?"*

The look of disbelief on Robert's face was palpable. Sure, some of our courses required us to read novels about technology, like *Blade Runner* or *A Hitchhiker's Guide to the Galaxy*. The novel now on my lap was by Andrew M. Greeley, a locked-door mystery clearly unrelated to technology. While I felt caught out, I almost felt victorious too. In class that evening, the cohort started discussing our workload and the amount of reading. I was doodling away on paper when I heard a disembodied voice speak:

> *"And then there's her!" It was Robert, still in shock, as 18 sets of eyes shot my way.*
> *"I can't believe it ... She has all the books read already. I met her on the shuttle to the hotel today and she's reading a novel—and not one for class either!"*

So maybe that's the point: *read everywhere you can*. Get ahead of the curve and get the required stuff done. You may not do this in an emergency room like I did, but there are plenty of places in any given day where idled time can push you ahead of the pack and increase your understanding of the course material. Use the wait in line, the Starbucks break, the commute on the subway to read material required for your doctoral courses. Maybe someday you'll unwittingly shock your classmates; maybe you never will.

But if you follow the plan, I guarantee there's a novel waiting that will keep you glued to the pages once you crack it open when the required reading is done. And someday beyond the novels, there'll be the real payoff—a completed dissertation by you, Doctor.

Yes, you. And as they like to say at Harvard, that's the *Veritas*.

CHAPTER 15

"YOU CAN'T MAKE A SILK PURSE OUT OF A SOW'S EAR," MY MOTHER SAID

SIGNE M. KASTBERG, PhD

St. John Fisher College, Rochester, NY, USA

E-mail: signe.jag@gmail.com

Using the Ali & Kohun (2007) four stages of doctoral study as a guide, I discuss my experience in Stage 2. This consists of the first year of academic coursework and the process of acclimating to the culture of the program, including student identity and interactions with fellow students and faculty members. I write from both feminist- and social-class-informed perspectives. I will refer to the "factory model of education" as well as to historical lived-experience analysis that informs the filter through which I reflect upon my experience as a doctoral student. These frameworks will be introduced first.

15.1 FACTORY MODEL OF EDUCATION

Formal education in the 1900s and beyond focused on the "industrial model" in which the educator's role was to prepare students for eventual occupations on the factory floor (Callahan, 1962; Horn & Evans, 2013; Kastberg, 2007; Leland & Kasten, 2002; Tolley, 2015). In such a model, students are trained to conform to expected codes of behavior, to memorize and regurgitate information accurately, and to perform repetitive tasks. The industrial era required a focus on increasing worker productivity, so nonconformity and unique perspectives were not welcome. Thus, educators at the kindergarten through high school levels would teach all students as if they were all the same. Individuality was problematic. A number of assumptions exist to make the industrial system of education work. Among these are the following:

- All entering students have equal preparation.
- All students require the same education while enrolled.
- All students will have the same kind of jobs in the future.
- Disempowerment of the individual is required to engender respect for authority.
- Teachers should stimulate competition among students for grades/recognition.
- Cooperation or teamwork is counter to individual accountability and will be penalized.
- Struggling learners are allowed to fail (a la social Darwinism), and the failing learner is blamed rather than the system.

One size fits all, particularly in blue-collar and non-White communities. The encouragement of critical thinking skills is reserved for the elite student from a privileged background in upper-class environments, such as private schools, where networking for future career takes place (Cookson & Persell, 1985).

In the postindustrial era, where preparation for assembly-line work would be nearly obsolete, one would think that education delivery systems would change dramatically. In the university, however, order and efficiency are more prized than ever; the student is a product to be processed and conformity is still expected. Tokarczyk & Fay (1993) have written a book subtitled *Laborers in the Knowledge Factory* that concludes as much, and the laborers are, of course, faculty. In the current university model, getting grants is prized, publications in top tier journals are necessary to maintain employment, service on multiple committees is required, and students come last. To maintain such a model, faculty originality in the classroom and attention to the actual learning enterprise must be voiced as an aspirational value, but in practice minimized.

These were my experiences, as will be narrated below. But first, a bit more about the training of individuals.

15.2   THE DISEMPOWERMENT PROJECT

In the 1600s, a vicar named Ralph Josselin chronicled not only the financial accounts of his farm and agricultural products but also his relationships with his wife and rearing of his children (Macfarlane, 1977). In essence, Ralph Josselin shared a psychological and emotional chronicle of how to break the will of a child.

Most models of human development would agree that children have predictable energy toward independent decision-making that first emerges in the two-year-old's incessant "no" with which most parents are familiar. Ralph Josselin, like his 17th century peers, needed a smooth-running household and farm, so his children were molded to meet the will of their father. Children were to be silent, obedient, and to follow directives accurately and immediately. The running of a farm in that century and the next changed very little; and arguably conformity to expectations of children as farm laborers was a necessity of the era.

I will argue that my experience as a 37-year-old doctoral student was not unlike being a child of Ralph Josselin, as follows.

15.3   THE FIRST YEAR OF SIGNE M. KASTBERG

There was some fanfare at my arrival in the PhD program in Human Development at the University of Rochester. I had been awarded a full-tuition scholarship as a sort of "most likely to succeed" anointment. This was due to my prior master's from Harvard University, a Fulbright scholarship for independent research in Denmark, significant accomplishments professionally as a Director of Continuing Education for over ten years, and active leadership roles in national organizations. I had already published one book chapter on social class issues and two articles, in addition to a number of conference presentations.

Upon arrival at the university, I was assigned a graduate assistantship under the tutelage of my advisor, a recognized expert on moral development. My advisor was also my employer in that sense. She refused to support my request to have credits from my master's degree count toward my doctorate, and thus, I had to take four full years of courses, including courses that could have been waived. This was disappointing, as I was not independently wealthy and one year of lost wages was significant to my family. I was mainstreamed with students who came straight from completion of their baccalaureate degree and individuals with significant professional experience. But at this university, one size fits all.

While at Harvard, I had the good fortune to take classes with renowned experts on moral psychology, Lawrence Kohlberg and Carol Gilligan. When I and the other graduate assistants were sent out to collect data for my advisor's research, we were coached to "shape" the responses of the children we were interviewing in order to get "codable responses." In many cases, the children's responses did not fit the narrow set of codes assigned to this project, codes designed to replicate the findings of previous studies, and I voiced my objection to the tacit manipulation we were expected to perform. I was taken off the project and reassigned. Students should be silent, obedient, and follow directives.

In my next assignment as a "research assistant," I spent roughly 15 hours per week standing in front of a photocopier, making copies for a faculty member's tenure file. I filed and photocopied. Then, I photocopied and filed. At first, I enjoyed the dark humor, observing myself doing work that normally I wouldn't even have given to my secretaries in my prior jobs. As a work-study student nearly 20 years prior, I had done this work. What a good lesson in humility, but coming from a blue-collar background I was already humble and had a long history of humbling. It got old. Another faculty member approached me at the photocopier one day and indicated that some faculty members were talking about how inappropriate this was, some commiserated with me, but the hazing continued. The student's will must be broken.

To my surprise, I became pregnant early in the spring semester. I approached my advisor and requested that I take off the fall semester when my second child was due, and then return part-time in the following semester. I was told by her, "You can come back full time or not at all." The student must respect authority figures; empowerment is denied.

One of my courses in that first year was taught by a professor of philosophy. The students of color were frequently offended by indirect racist comments made by this self-indulgent professor, who routinely gave these students poor grades. On a particularly memorable occasion, the professor spent over two hours in the class discussing the structure of one paragraph of our assigned reading. When we students became restless entering third hour on that same few sentences, the professor told us that we were "not sophisticated thinkers." The disempowerment of students was real, as was the disrespect.

The faculty members were concerned that the students were becoming rebellious as we had many complaints about the program and our significant lack of authority over our learning experience in a very lockstep program. Students were invited to a "focus group" where we could air our dissatisfactions. Apparently, the faculty was not well versed in what a "focus group" is, or how it is conducted, as a good number of faculty members were present in the room, and debated students' concerns, great and small, as one would crush ants at a picnic. For example, a student mentioned as a side note something about the shape of the path from classrooms to the library, and this was soundly rejected by a vocal faculty member who insisted on her interpretation of the shape of the path. In short, students were reminded of our place in the hierarchy, and our views and concerns rejected.

Doctoral students referred to the faculty members' offices as "the culture of closed doors" because faculty members were too busy to answer students' questions other than during the obligatory two hours per week. Faculty members might be in those offices, but they signaled their unavailability with a closed door because their research and grant-seeking took precedence. One faculty member dared to reject the dominant paradigm and spent significant time with students and on student projects and papers. His collaborative inquiry approach and originality in classroom instruction were widely respected and appreciated by students. He did not get tenure, and was gone. Students come last.

Our first-year exams materialized from under a cloud of secrecy. That is, the processes, procedures, and policies regarding the exam were strictly by word of mouth from student to student; there were no official written notifications or explanations. It was important to be mentored by a doctoral student with more time under his/her belt so you could learn what kind of preparation was needed, and what, at least anecdotally, was considered acceptable. Interestingly, rewrites were often required by faculty, whether the questions were answered correctly or not; it was just part of the initiation ritual. Some students were subjected to multiple rewrites with no explanation given, just "rewrite." Sadly, many very bright and capable students dropped out of the doctoral program after so many disempowering experiences. Students must listen and obey.

15.4 STRATEGIES FOR COMPLETING YEAR ONE

The reader of this essay may be wondering how a mature feminist could have succeeded in completing this harrowing first year of doctoral study. It required multiple adjustments on my part, and keeping an active sense of humor.

One of my tactics, established prior to entering the program, was due to my focus on balance; as a mother and wife I wanted to keep my studies in perspective as my family was of utmost importance to me. So, I decided up front that my goal would be to get "B" grades; if I got "As" that would mean I was working too hard. Establishing priorities congruent with my values and ethical grounding was essential to my survival in the program.

Upon encountering the reality of my advisor's agenda to break my will, I had to balance my native assertiveness with an abundance of humility and flexibility. This was difficult but made easier when I reminded myself of my goal: to complete the doctorate. The lockstep program was discouraging, but I made sure that any opportunity to individualize and personalize assignments in line with my interests was capitalized upon. Thus, I explored many areas of interest.

I was respectful with faculty while also advocating for myself as a mature learner who truly wanted a positive learning experience. Within myself, I had to grieve and let go of my hope that the doctoral experience would be just as rewarding as my master's degree experience had been. As my mother used to say, "You can't make a silk purse out of a sow's ear."

15.5 CONCLUSION

In the factory model of doctoral education, homogeneity is assumed across race, class, gender, socioeconomic status, parenting status, age, and all other markers of diversity. Learners are recipients of knowledge, not co-creators of knowledge, as replication is privileged and originality discouraged. Disempowerment of students requires their conformity and obedience, just as in Ralph Josselin's family. Students are not assessed for appropriate placement; they are placed in lockstep sequences that suit the needs of the teacher/institution and ignore the lived experiences and skills of a diverse student body. Thus, a uniform, standardized course of instruction can efficiently be delivered to the passive learner. And finally, the doctoral student, who completes a program run according to these models, is prepared to replicate the social order in their future role as a faculty member in the knowledge factory (Bourdieu & Passeron, 1990). The rules for such social reproduction are: one size fits all, students come last, research and publication come first, research must be completed with expedience while ethics are given lip service, grading is subjective at best, conformity and obedience are required, homogeneity is assumed, and struggling learners will be allowed to fail.

As an epilogue, I must note that after a career in higher education spanning over 35 years, I recently left the professoriate bruised and embattled as I repeatedly tried, unsuccessfully, to challenge the factory disempowerment model of education.

REFERENCES

Ali, A.; Kohun, F. (2007). Dealing with social isolation to minimize doctoral attrition—a four stage framework. *International Journal of Doctoral Studies, 2*, 33–49. Retrieved from: http://www.informingscience.org/Journals/IJDS/Articles?Volume=2–2007&Search.

Bourdieu, P., & Passeron, J. C. (1990). *Reproduction in education, society, and culture.* London, UK: Sage.

Callahan, R. E. (1962). *Education and the cult of efficiency.* Chicago, IL: University of Chicago.

Cookson, P. W., Jr., & Persell, C. H. (1985). *Preparing for power: America's elite boarding schools.* New York, NY: Basic Books.

Horn, M. B., & Evans, M. (2013). A factory model for schools no longer works. *Milwaukee-Wisconsin Journal Sentinel,* June 29, 2013.

Kastberg, S. (2007). Servants in the house of the masters: A social class primer for educators, helping professionals, and others who want to change the world. New York, NY: iUniverse.

Leland, C. H., & Kasten, W. C. (2002). Literacy education for the 21st century: It's time to close the factory. *Reading and Writing Quarterly.* Abingdon, UK: Taylor & Francis.

Macfarlane, A. (1977). *The family life of Ralph Josselin.* New York, NY: Norton.

Tokarczyk, M., & Fay, E., Eds. (1993). *Working-class women in the academy: Laborers in the knowledge factory.* Amherst, MA: University of Massachusetts.

Tolley, W. (2015). Why the factory model of schools persists, and how we can change it. *Education Week: Teacher,* Nov 3, 2015.

CHAPTER 16

WIDENING THE CIRCLE

KIM R. HARRIS PhD, with additional stories by LUCILLE W. IJOY EdD

Loyola Marymount University, Los Angeles, CA, USA

It took so long to find his office. This uncertainty only served to extend and deepen my fears. The very idea of challenging the actions of the professor on the first night of my first class in graduate school pounded in my brain and churned in my stomach. He politely invited me inside. My eyes quickly scanned the room. Pictures of Black people hung on the office walls of this White Catholic priest. I internally noted surprise. Textiles and carvings from Central and South America lay on the chairs and sat on flat surfaces. Most White people I knew did not have images of Black and brown people on their walls, especially pictures of African Americans. The artwork in his office extended hospitality to me more quickly than any words could accomplish. Through my viewing of these images of the People of Color, could I imagine the possibility of an honest dialogue about race with the professor, despite the difference in our race and in power, given our academic positions? Would his responses to my challenge live up to the promise of his choices for the office environment?

I'd expected no racial hospitality or obvious allies among those gathered for the first night of class. Coming into the graduate program for ministry in the diocese, I instinctively knew I'd be the only African American. Unlike several dioceses in New York state, my adopted home diocese of Albany featured exactly one predominantly Black parish, located too far from my home for me to attend conveniently. By choice or because of distance, other Black Catholics, relatively few in number, worshipped in scattered parishes throughout the diocese, as did I.

In general, I felt accepted, though culturally unknown in my small-town parish and at diocesan functions. As a new Black student in the White graduate theological academic community, however, I anticipated an awkward beginning. Preemptively, I brought a "shield" to class. The book was actually more of a divining rod and deflector. Holding it high, I introduced myself and the book as we went from person to person around the room. "I'm Kim Harris from Schoharie County. My new favorite book is this one, *When Women Were Priests: Women's Leadership in the Early Church and the Scandal of Their Subordination in the Rise of Christianity* by Karen J. Torjesen." The course I attended was about ministry as a means of community building. If this room was filled with like-minded classmates, seeking to build a more forward-thinking Catholic community, we'd find each other after my "show and tell." Additionally, the interjection of the book provided a subject for conversation apart from my lonely social location as the new Black student among White classmates.

So far, so good. No one offered contrary remarks after I showed the book. A few in the room, including the professor, seemed to discern and appreciate my progressive leanings. At the very least, I'd found a few allies in the struggle for women's ordained leadership in the Roman Catholic Church we shared. The students in the class from other Christian denominations also included women on the "ordination track." This class could to be "interesting" indeed!

After the round of introductions and a look through the syllabus, the class discussed and practiced the format for the upcoming assignment: Critical Incident Reports. I was new to this process, though not surprised about its use in a class on pastoral ministry. Each person planned to recount a difficult incident involving their ministry experiences. As a class, we would analyze the situation and imagine different choices for their actions and responses.

To help us better understand the assignment and experience the format, the professor recounted a ministry incident of his own for the class to analyze. I appreciated his lack of embarrassment, as well as his humility as a teacher willing to offer his own story for our evaluation. He told us of a night during which he heard a fight escalating outside of the rectory door. By choice, he lived and ministered in a predominantly African-American, working-class and working-poor neighborhood. Hoping to be a moderating influence, he opened the rectory door. Did his presence and purpose help or hinder a peaceful solution in that situation? What range of actions might be appropriate for him to take? How might his social location as a White, male clergyperson, interacting with a group Black men, affect possible outcomes?

My first thought was that I, as a woman, in ministry or not, would never choose to open the door as a group of men, of any race or culture, moved toward an altercation. In a split second my initial appreciation for the critical incident process turned to dread when I also realized that this incident had racial implications. Would people in the class be listening intently for my reaction given the racial component of the interaction? The professor interrupted my thoughts with a direct question. "Kim, what do you think?"

Truthfully, I cannot recall his exact words or question. I began to disassociate from my body, sensing the danger of a conversation about race within a group of potential classmates and colleagues, all White people I'd just met. One hour of the class did not offer me sufficient opportunity to assess the group for racial experience, knowledge, and attitudes nor time to decide what "part" I would play in the mix. The deflection of the progressive position I staked out with the "show and tell" book provided me no cover for a discussion of race.

I certainly faced no physical danger in that classroom. Intellectual, emotional, social, and professional danger, however, was imminent. Even among long-standing White friends, a discussion of the race could easily become a relationship-ending encounter. On this first night of class, who would I show myself to be? Scholarly? Friendly? Militant? Conciliatory? Joking? Cooperative? Challenging? The list goes on, overlaid, of course, with the element of my social location as an African-American woman.

My feigned calm and experience with microaggressions and ongoing racial neurosis provided a few seconds for me to don a quick "mask" while I answered the professor's question. I have no real memory of my answer. I imagine, however, that I chose the role of the "friendly, scholarly, Black person."

Racial neurosis is often described as the daily, hourly, and minute-by-minute mental gymnastics performed by Black people during encounters with White people. The observations and adjustments, common to any social encounter, are overlaid with questions concerning race with emotionally, intellectually, and physically exhausting regularity. Is he saying that because I'm Black? Does she really mean what I just heard her say? Do they possibly know or understand how that sounds to me? If I am in emotional or intellectual danger, will there be an understanding, knowledgeable, and experienced ally in this room? Am I expected to remain constantly on guard? Is it my responsibility to always be in a teaching position among White people? Why am I always under a magnifying glass? Stress!

Mercifully, the class break came quickly after the critical incident discussion, and I fled to the restroom while attempting to breathe. Given the chance or finding an "appropriate" excuse, I planned to leave the class early, ditching the idea of graduate school right then and drive home. As an auditor, I had nothing to lose. As a potential Black graduate theological student and a member of the diocese, my scholarly, social, and ecclesial losses could quickly outnumber the possible gains of ministry. As a potential scholar for the relatively small national Black Catholic community, any loss of personnel is heartbreaking and unacceptable.

Damn it! I should have taken my coat and bag with me to the restroom! I had to go back into that classroom to retrieve them after the break. I entered after class began again, trying to be "invisible" for a moment before bolting. Not sure why I sat still and stayed until the end. The rest of the class proceeded without incident that I recall. The remaining class time felt interminable and the stress, oppressive. My "friendly scholar" persona forced me to answer a question or two on another subject in a jovial manner. I drove home distracted and spent that sleepless night in bed with the covers up over my head.

In the morning, I contacted various friends in academia, both Black and White. They suggested meeting privately with the professor before making my final decision about continuing with the course. One friend suggested that I offer my first night's experience for the critical incident assignment the following week. Friends held split opinions on the question of alerting the professor about my plan in advance. I chose to nervously offer him fair warning. In his office, the professor shared that he'd expected my call and mentioned looking forward to our conversation. He apologized after listening closely to my experience of the classroom interaction and made no attempt to smooth things over. Together, we planned for the next class. I would return to the school at least one more time, a few nights later.

My anticipation and anxiety grew as the week progressed. Anger and appreciation came and went along with resentment that my student responsibilities included educating a class about racial sensitivities while simultaneously grappling with the choices surrounding my entrance into academia. On the night of the next class, I volunteered to share my assignment toward the end of the evening. Yes, I was scared, but grew steadily concerned as the night progressed that I might run out of time. After the break, I invited the group to gather their chairs into a circle and spoke. Classmates listened with close attention. They also, after all, witnessed and had their own memory and perception of the interaction. The responses covered the usual range for a conversation about race with a group of White people. A few understood the difficulty of the situation. Two women reported that they planned to go looking for me if I did not return to class after the break. Other student responses showed a general, not unusual, lack of racial understanding, yet revealed the genuine kindness I often experienced in diocesan gatherings.

As in our private conversation, the professor did not attempt to control or derail the conversation nor downplay the racially cued aspects of the situation. He displayed the same honesty, contrition, and openness to expanding his knowledge. We both discussed the choice to display art and physical objects from a diversity of cultural traditions as an unspoken gesture of hospitality in a pastoral setting. His support and assistance in setting an example for the tone of the classroom conversation influenced my choice to return to class for the third week. I eventually registered for the class, matriculated in the program, and remained the only person of color in the school and one of two the following year.

New, lasting friendships came into being that second night in class. Two female classmates and I eventually formed a group, a circle of women, which continues to meet periodically in support of each other's ministry and life journeys. I returned to meet with the professor later in the semester and marveled at how much easier my entrance into his office felt the second time. Together we imagined my future in theological studies, agreeing that I needed to find a school with more diversity among the students and the professors. He encouraged and supported my eventual transfer to Union Theological Seminary in the City of New York for the completion of my Master of Divinity (and PhD).

Recalling my beginning in graduate school, I reflect that during the chill of those first difficult moments, my family's academic memories and stories did not immediately rise to my consciousness to wrap me in the warmth and strength of their successful outcomes. I am the second generation in my family to attend graduate school. When I called to commiserate with my mother after the first class, she reminded me of her experiences on the road to receiving her doctorate. Like me, she began her higher education with one "trial" course in a class filled with White people. Unlike me, her road was also paved with dirty diapers and the backdrop of the modern Civil Rights Movement.

My mother loved high school and attended the school to which I would eventually go, The Philadelphia High School for Girls in Pennsylvania. As a first-generation college aspirant, she knew little of the mechanics of the college application process. In 1950, a White high school guidance counselor curtly advised that there was "nothing for her." All of the college information was "gone." Mom graduated with honors, went to work, and married not long after high-school. When my older sister was four years old, my mother taught her and a few playmates to read on the front steps of our house. Our Baptist church would not take her on as a religious educator, preferring instead Sunday School teachers with college degrees. The idea of continuing her education and a bit of anger with the "church folk" finally moved mom to action.

Each credit hour cost $11 at St. Joseph's College (Philadelphia) in 1957. With difficulty, mom saved $33 dollars for her "trial" course, Spanish. Most students in her evening division class were 18-year-old White young men. She was 27, Negro, and married with two small children in 1957.

A high-school girl in the neighborhood watched my sister and me while Mom attended class. I was three months old. As Mom says, she could go to school and still be home by the time I had "one bottle, one burp, two diapers, three boops, a nap, and a throw-up." The divide of race, class, gender, and her need to multitask combined to severely limit her interaction with other students and professors. A few St. Joe's administrators and Jesuit priests kindly guided Mom toward scholarship funds and the best course choices toward her degree in education.

By 1963, our family was well used to mom's school routine. Dad, then working for the US Postal Service in Philadelphia, also began attending Civil Rights Movement planning meetings and nonviolent resistance training sessions. On August 28, 1963, Mom stayed home to study and to care for my sister and me as my father traveled south for the March on Washington. At home, we gathered around the black and white console TV to watch the proceedings. My sister moved in very close to the small screen, poking it with her finger. Could she somehow find our daddy in the crowd?

My parents carefully guided our education, making sometimes difficult choices to further our best interests. They chose to permit me to integrate a White elementary school, in close proximity, though outside of my immediate Philadelphia neighborhood, despite the "politely" hostile parents and teachers who looked down on the few entering Black students. The White parents cried in parent–teacher association meetings, being upset and thinking that the admission of Black children would lower the status of the school. My mother did not tell me of their overt feelings. My experience at the school was generally positive. All the while, Mom successfully continued her studies at night and completed her degree in seven years. She was genuinely surprised to receive three awards during her St. Joseph's College graduation in 1964. The headline in the *Philadelphia Inquirer* read "Negro Mom Graduates First in Her Class."

As my mother continued her education with graduate studies at Temple University in Philadelphia, she added working full-time as an elementary school teacher to her growing list of tasks. The graduate student body in education at Temple contained a representative amount of African Americans. While preparing to enter the doctoral program in education, however, Mom experienced a searing experience with a college administrator. She needed one last signature. My mother waited respectfully outside of the open door. Eventually, a voice gruffly called her inside. "Why do you want to get this doctorate? It's very hard work and you won't get any more money." Mom heard what sounded like anger and aggression pushing the question toward her. She felt overwhelmed by racial stress and general student fears.

What was behind the questions and statements of the White administrator? There was truth to the fact about little potential change in salary, especially for women with doctorates in education. Was the roughness of the administrator's response due to her own experience with sexism or was it racial aggression meant to discourage a Black woman's advancement? Even with the little potential for an increase in pay, an increase in respect and positions in higher education required the doctorate. Mom does not clearly remember her response to the administrator's questions. She does remember her abject fear. If this woman refused a signature, Mom's chance to enter the program might be lost. The administrator finally signed the form and Mom quickly left the room. After closing the door behind her, my mother literally fell against the wall in exhaustion and relief. One more obstacle surmounted; one more step toward becoming Dr. Lucille W. Ijoy.

This would not be the only time that a White administrator attempted to thwart my mother's progress. Luckily, Black and White allies filled in "missing" information and opened "locked" doors. Such information included computer work over a weekend at the home of a Jewish administrator. Her husband assisted my mother with the statistical analysis required for chapter two of her dissertation. His 1970s home computer was large enough to fill the entire basement.

My mother received her doctorate in education from Temple University in 1972. By the time I began my undergraduate studies at Temple in 1974, she was an administrator of the Career Opportunity Program, along with the same administrator who guided her to skilled help with statistics. Mom's work included helping older women navigate the academic path to become teachers. As her daughter, I received the advantage of her employee benefits and attended the university free of charge. When I finally began my graduate school career in 1992, thanks to my mother's academic journey, I was blessedly free of student debt.

I often wonder how African-American students, professors, and scholars in the past survived the abuse of overt and covert racism, many with few economic resources or allies and oppressive laws against them during their tenure in academia. I also know and have experienced that "missing" information and those "locked" doors, along with the stress of having to deal with daily macro- and microaggressions that continues in the present-day academic lives of Black students, staff, administrators and scholars.

As I remembered these stories in ongoing conversation with Mom, I find myself being grateful that though my situation was difficult and could have thwarted my academic career, I did not have to play "guessing games" during my first night of graduate school. I knew immediately that the classroom conversation was about race. I never doubted the professor's good intentions, just his timing and method. To his credit, he now uses the story of that night in his classes. He illustrates the critical incident process, offers ideas about creating a safer climate and a wider circle of hospitality for students of underrepresented groups, and opens a conversation about race in each class he teaches. We remain esteemed colleagues and friends to this day.

Now, several years into my own teaching career in liturgy and religious studies, I offer courses on Negro spirituals and Civil Rights Movement freedom songs, African-American religious experience, and surveys of major religious traditions. When I set up my newest office space, I continued to follow my first professor's lead with a local "twist." On the first day of my visiting position at Loyola Marymount University in Los Angeles, I observed a practice among the professors in almost every department. Office doors are festooned with pictures, slogans, banners, and notices of events. I quickly made my own contributions to the tradition: African-American art, photos, poetry, and notices of events from the Office of Black Student Services. I am also particular about including notices of events that welcome and lift the concerns of students, staff, and faculty of underrepresented and oppressed groups on campus.

Students of color entering my office can experience the hospitality of environment both on the doors and windows, as well as inside. In choosing door notices, I do, however, feel the racial stress of expecting African-American notices on the outside of my door to be defaced, especially during this current climate of overt, active racial, religious, sexual, cultural, and identity aggression in a sharply divided nation.

During my first semester at Loyola Marymount, a majority of the Theological Studies faculty members added the same sign to various notices on our office doors: "DON'T DEPORT MY STUDENTS! No human being is illegal." One morning we came into the Theological Village to find all of the signs ripped down. We quickly replaced them. My single defaced sign multiplied eightfold. All of them now face outward, taped on the inside of the glass windows of my office, out of reach, but not out of sight.

We do not know who committed the vandalism. With the exception of a few professor-advisors, we also do not know which students are undocumented. I choose, however, to draw the circle of hospitality wider to include not only students of color but also refugees, "dreamers," and the undocumented among my students. This circle must now widen to include them, also, as well as the at-risk international faculty, scholars, and members of oppressed and excluded religious traditions. My story, as well as my mother's, continues to be my guide for the shape of my interactions.

Within this mix of diversity, I, like my first graduate school professor, make missteps, at times. It is my hope, however, that my students will challenge me toward growth and later take their places as scholars, professors, and administrators who will offer hospitality in an ever-widening circle within the academic world.

CHAPTER 17

"MY KEEPERS": THE POWER OF MENTORSHIP DURING THE FIRST-YEAR DOCTORAL EXPERIENCE

MARKESHA MILLER, PhD

South University, Savannah, GA, USA

E-mail: markmiller@southuniversity.edu, drmiller@thecebc.com

If someone had told me during my early childhood years that I would enter a doctoral program at a traditionally white institution (TWI) and success-fully obtain my PhD, I would have dismissed it. As a child, I knew that my beam traveled far, tracking the level of success that I could imagine for myself. However, I had not fully taken an understanding of how a young, Black girl from a small, southern town would manifest that success. I grew up in a family where education was respected, and it was expected that I would move further than my parents. My mother, now a retired educator, taught school for over 40 years. My father, never completing high school, was disabled and worked as a farmer. In my family, the idea of "holding on to each other" was planted as the foundation that moved us through. In other words, "We were each other's keepers."

My brother chose to join the military, and I chose the road that was expected of me, college. I knew that I wanted to attend the University of South Carolina at an early age. My mother always made sure that I knew that my road would be tough. During high school, I completed college prep courses and was challenged by my mother to always keep my bar high. I can recall being in many of my high school courses and not seeing people who resembled me, being accepted into talented and gifted programs and being the only Black. My mother assured me at an early age that this was okay. The lessons that she taught me, from what could deem to be uncomfortable for some, was that the path to success may at times be lonely. However, my mother made sure that I understood that I was there because I deserved to be there: I earned it! With this seed of motivation sowed into my mind, I always made sure that I was recognized for what I brought to the table with my academics. For I knew that I deserved to have a seat at the table!

After pursuing my undergraduate degree at the University of South Carolina and my EdS in Marriage and Family Therapy, I went through a variety of identity phases. As I often tell my students, I had to take a little time to find myself. For so long, I thought that I would be a neurologist, then an attorney; however, my purpose was grounded in that I knew I wanted to be a change agent. I wanted to help people be better, help families be better, and help the community and society be better. I worked various jobs after completing my graduate degree in the psychology field. The experiences that I obtained were invaluable. For so long, I was very comfortable with working and growing in the career. However, I began to recognize facets in the field that were alarming to me. I recognized that minorities were not very well informed about mental health needs and, often times, are very uneducated about the process. In addition, I recognized that mental health issues ranked very high among African-American women (i.e., depression); however, many times our psychological well-being was neither valued nor understood. It was at this time that I knew that in order to change the game, I had to get into the game. I decided to pursue my PhD at the University of South Carolina so that I could ultimately highlight these issues and have an opportunity to enhance the field not only in practice but also through research and teaching.

During my first year of doctoral studies, I struggled. I did not struggle academically. I struggled with the culture of the program. I struggled with others looking at me and assumed that they were asking the question to themselves, "Why is she here?" As an African-American female who matriculated through the program with a cohort of White females, there were times when I even posed the question to myself. Then I would always remember what my mother had instilled in me: "I am here because I deserve to be here." It is almost like the old jubilee spiritual that my grandparents sang, "The World Didn't Give It and the World Can't Take It Away." I felt that I had earned my place at this time, and no one was going to deprive me of it.

However, during the first year, I developed a fear. Not a physical fear, but a mental and emotional fear. For the first time in my life, I feared failure. I recognized that I had taken on new heights into unfamiliar territory. This was a time in my life that I felt alone in the process. My parents continued to give me their best! They prayed with me and for me. They validated me throughout the course of my matriculation. However, there were aspects of my fear that my parents could not soothe. As I stated, I was the first in my family to pursue an advanced degree. My mother graduated from a histori-cally Black college and therefore could relate to the collegiate experience, but not necessarily the environment. Although I attended the University of South Carolina throughout my bachelor's degree and my educational specialist degree, there was a different feeling about being there for my doctoral program. Maybe it was because the environment was more intimate as a doctoral student, and therefore, it was easier to feel the isolation. I real-ized that during my doctoral program, I had to embrace the social changes and begin to understand my environment and how I would rise above and beyond it.

I discovered this through mentorship! I would encourage any candidate interested in a doctoral program to seek mentorship and nourish the rela-tionship. I was fortunate to find three women who literally changed my life and with whom I developed everlasting relationships. Two of these women were Black professors in the program, and one was a White second-year student. The beautiful thing about mentorship in a doctoral program is that it provides guidance on what can be deemed as a dark and gloomy territory. The uniqueness of the mentorship experience for me was that I had two distinct viewpoints, a professor and student. The professors were able to help me understand three specific roles in my life: "A Black woman pursuing a doctoral program at a TWI." There were various microaggressions that I needed to have validated for me … they were able to do that. I specifi-cally recall a White professor telling me that my participation was needed "because they had to have a Black." I was bothered by this statement and questioned whether it was my skin being noticed or my ability and depth of knowledge. I think this traces back to my mother always making sure that I understood that the reason that I had a seat at the table was because I deserved a seat because of my intellect and my abilities, not to serve as a token. I felt for a professor to insinuate to me otherwise was not acceptable. My mentors were able to advocate for me on various occasions when I felt oppressed. By the end of my doctoral program, these women had taken the voice that my mother and grandmother gave me years ago and amplified that voice. They had guaranteed me that I needed to be at the "head" of the table.

I also strongly encourage peer mentorship. I developed a relationship with a second-year doctoral student that has grown into an everlasting relationship. She is more than my friend and my colleague; she is my sister. There were many levels to the program that I did not understand and, at times, may not have been made aware of. She took me under her wing and guided me from a student's perspective. I took on a leadership role my first year in our honor society because she nominated me for it and encouraged me to do it. We often went to lunch together to talk about the daily trials of being a student and how to navigate through those successfully. We presented together at various conferences and still do! Now as professionals in the field, we continue to make time to check in on each other; though we live in different states, we arrange lunches or dinners according to availability.

Through mentorship, you are able to get not only the guidance and support you need but also to build relationships that you will need throughout your professional journey. The experiences that I had through mentorship definitely helped to sustain me throughout my doctoral program. Is the first year the toughest? Absolutely! It is during this time that you have to make the adjustment and figure out your needs and how to meet them. I knew I needed guidance and support. I am not speaking of the guidance and support that I receive undeservingly, at times, from my parents. I am speaking of the guidance and support that is rendered because someone sees a vision inside of you that is bigger than what you can see. In a sense, they take a chance on you. I recall near the end of my program when I had a deep conversation with one of my professor mentors. I was sincerely thankful for EVERYTHING that she had done. She gave me the opportunities that I probably would not have had and helped me to grow professionally and personally. During our discussion, she was very clear to explain to me that I would never be able to pay her back—but I was obligated to pay it forward. I now understand that this is the process of mentoring. We all rise by lifting each other.

Currently, as a scholar, I have the opportunity to teach, practice, and research. I also am fortunate to have the ability to share my voice across different platforms on issues that affect individuals, our communities, and society. I have always had a voice because my mother and grandmother instilled that in me. I always knew that I had a purpose that was bigger than my understanding. However, I am fortunate that even in the midst of my doubt during my doctoral program I had strong women to remind me of myself. Let's just say the roots of my family values traveled with me to my doctoral studies, and I found women who would serve as my "keepers." They kept me grounded, focused, motivated, and encouraged.

CHAPTER 18

MAKING THE PhD HAPPEN: STAGE 2—FIRST YEAR OF THE PROGRAM

ANNE TOOLAN ROWLEY, PhD

The College of Saint Rose, Albany, NY, USA

After successfully ending the investigative process, I selected the best program of study that would be beneficial for my career. I reflected on the changes to my family dynamics and successfully achieved admission to the desired major. I began to adjust to the expectations that I anticipated and to immerse myself into the actual coursework of the program. I had taken on a new identity as a student while maintaining my work and family obligations. In retrospect, I can identify this stage as "consciously incompetent" (Beeler, 1991, p. 166) with regard to the academic requirements and challenges that were arrayed before me. In this chapter, I will describe and discuss advisement, enrollment, and rationale for pursuing the degree from both a personal perspective and from peer discussions.

The advisement process should begin before the actual courses commence. This should take place with an advisor who is seasoned with the process and can review master's-level courses with an eye to the student's background and possible transfer of credits toward the doctoral degree. My initial advisor had just been hired, did not have a complete understanding of the doctoral program or the avenue of study that I wanted to pursue, and often commented, "You are my first advisee." The advisor did offer to seek the information that I requested, but it took some time and I often felt that I was pestering for the answers. Although some courses from my related master's degree were accepted, it took a while for the actual documentation to be recorded. Now, I began to realize that the advisement process on a doctoral scale was very different from the kinds of support that I had received in the past at the undergraduate and graduate academic levels, particularly related to course selections.

The process of choosing courses needed for degree completion was a daunting task, as much is left to the student's choice with a basic number of required courses and credits set forth. Discussions with peers revealed different advisement situations that were better or worse than my experiences. Later issues arose when the advisor scheduled a sabbatical, and it was suggested by the department chair to find my own new advisor. This was an intimidating task to find another person interested in my goals and enrollment needs without having any introduction to the full-time faculty.

When talking with other students, I learned that their enrollment schedules varied based on their personal lives and when they were accepted. Many individuals pursued the advanced degree as full-time or part-time students or in the capacity as full-time research assistants. Many of the full-time students were continuing on directly from a master's degree and were able to dedicate three years toward doctoral degree completion. They were devoting all their time to studies without an outside work commitment. However, some of the full-time students were tied into research assistant scholarships and were required to work ten to twenty hours weekly on a faculty project destined for publication. The pressure of the work varied depending on the faculty member's needs. This type of student balanced the postsecondary courses and the scholarship demands while feeling overwhelmed and possibly "incompetent" during the first year.

The part-time student, such as me, usually maintained full-time employment and had limited time to juggle courses and complete the required work per course due to family issues and needs. The family issues may be related to child care and children's academic needs, family or personal health, and household demands. In these cases, the ages of the doctoral students in the first year varied and became a challenging factor when bonding with each other professionally and socially. For me, the social isolation came in the form of age differences. Coming back to school after a successful career as a college professor put me in an older age bracket compared with the individuals who were in their late twenties and early thirties. When I did meet older classmates, they usually had the same limited time available to socialize that I had. The age difference became apparent to me on the first night of my classes. I was looking for my classroom in a building which was unfamiliar to me. Two young women ahead of me in the hall mentioned the room number. I asked them where the room was located. They responded with the location and asked me if I was the professor. When I responded that I was a new student, their faces registered an amazed look. I really was not that old!

Looking back on my choice of courses, I recalled that although some students were helpful when discussing the track of courses to take, the role taken by my advisor was less supportive. One's advisor should be aware of the student's life situation. Selection of coursework could be considered based on the student's timeline. This would require the advisor to offer suggestions related to the difficulty of some courses, the demands of courses, and how to plan a schedule as needed. The advisor should be aware of the availability of courses in the doctoral schedule. For example, some programs work on a rotating schedule where a course may be taught only once every two years.

This information would have been helpful for me as a part-time student. After reviewing the suggested courses required and those to be considered as electives, I found that a prerequisite for another course would not be offered until two semesters later. This resulted in the need for me to take an additional course to maintain my part-time status. This was also voiced by full-time peers. However, these students were often tracked more closely by their advisors and had more flexibility in their schedules. Personally, I came from an academic profession, and as a college advisor, I had provided undergraduate and graduate advisement to many students. In these situations, I made every effort to help a part-time or full-time student complete the program in two to four years as required. Moreover, projected changes in degree requirements should be voiced in the planning of courses.

A challenge to my plans was the one-year residency requirement for all doctoral students. Since I worked full-time and did not have the option of taking nine to ten months off, I designed a plan on my own and submitted it for the advisor and departmental approval. After much discussion, I was permitted to complete a ten-credit fall semester, a six-credit spring semester, and a nine-credit summer enrollment. Although this was a challenging compromise with my full-time work, I was able to complete the three semesters as planned. However, as I began the summer challenge, the department announced that it was dropping the full-time residency year requirement effective the fall semester of that year for newly enrolled and current students in the doctoral program! Although the change would have helped me, I completed the proposed course track and justified for myself the need to finish course work early before comprehensive exams.

I do understand that a doctoral program schedule needs to be flexible for a small group or cohort of students on an annual basis. However, I think that advisors need training during faculty meetings or time should be set aside for the updating of changes on course planning from the department's purview. In this way, the faculty member would be better prepared for the different needs of each student. This type of support within the first year could make a difference in one's frustration and feelings of "incompetence" related to the student's expectations and rationale for undertaking the long journey ahead.

Again an advisor's role should be one that discusses and supports the student's rationale for the path of study. Students often continue in a major that requires advanced study for professional credentials. The professions of law, medicine, psychology, and business come to mind. The path of study has often been predetermined, and areas of specialty within the profession need more guidance. Others return to pursue an advanced degree after working in a field that requires credentials for employment or promotion. After several years of employment, an individual may feel the need for a change in one's field or a new career opportunity, prompting the desire for a doctoral degree.

My rationale for pursuing the degree came from two perspectives, namely, promotion as a college professor and the desire to acquire knowledge in a related subject area. Although these ideas were conveyed to my advisor, the one that seemed to be most meaningful was related to the college promotion aspect. Initially, he did not grasp my desire to bridge the connection between language and literacy. As I began to take courses, I had Beeler's (1991) "consciously incompetent" feeling (p. 166) through the first year of part-time enrollment. However, the instructors in the courses were more helpful when I discussed my goals and topics for exploration. In time, my competence in the career choice was bolstered.

As I reflect on the first year and subsequent years prior to the dissertation process, I thought of how the feeling of social isolation might have been addressed. First, I thought that incoming students could have been offered group advisement and then individual meetings with an advisor who was savvy with the "ins and outs" of the degree requirements. The group opportunity would let students meet each other as a cohort and provide an opportunity to chat about their goals. Initial connections could be made prior to meeting in classes. An early social event for all the students in the program could afford the time to hear how others have progressed toward the degree completion and give firsthand suggestions and "need to know" aspects of the program. While age and life experiences were factors, I did not find these to be glaring issues as I developed acquaintances with fellow students who also struggled with course selection and advisement support.

Although not required, advisors should periodically touch base with their advisees for just a "how are you doing?" contact. This may actually occur, but it didn't in my experience. As mentioned above, in my fourth semester, I found my second advisor on my own through a process of "selling" my goals and aspirations to an interested faculty member. This person was more available for discussion and guidance when I requested a meeting. I should note that by subsequent semesters, I began to feel more confident in my career choice, though "unconsciously competent" (Beeler, p. 166) in the coursework.

A positive first-year experience may be a deciding factor in shrinking the attrition numbers. Advisement support for enrollment, course selection, and interest in the student's motivation and commitment expectations would have been helpful to me. Moreover, opportunities for peer (full-time and part-time) social events and/or program updates and forums throughout the years would have been supportive from the beginning of the journey.

REFERENCES

Ali, A., & Kohun, F. (2006). Dealing with isolation feelings in IS doctoral programs. *International Journal of Doctoral Studies, 1*, 21–22. Retrieved from: http://www.informingscience.org/Journals/IJDS/Articles?Volume=1–2006&Search.

Beeler, K. D. (1991) Graduate student adjustment to academic life: A four-stage framework. *NASPA Journal, 28*(2), 163–171.

CHAPTER 19

THIS WAS NOT THE ORIGINAL PLAN

JAMIE S. SWITZER, EdD

Colorado State University, Fort Collins, CO, USA

I'll start at the beginning.

Growing up in football-mad Texas, in the shadow of the old Texas Stadium where the Dallas Cowboys used to play (NOT the billion-dollar monstrosity where they play now, but I digress), I was going to be a sports reporter and an editor for NFL Films. I love most all sports, ever since I was little and my father taught me what a "down" was in football. I was a soccer referee for many years; that's how I made my spending money in high school and college. I was also a soccer coach. So yeah, sports were my thing. I was a news junkie too; I was probably the only kid reading *Time* magazine in junior high.

I went to Texas Christian University and majored in Radio/TV/Film, while at the same time interning in the sports department of the local National Broadcasting Company affiliate. Sports reporter, here I come. Alas, it was not to be, for several reasons. The biggest obstacle was the fact that I was female, and there were *very* few females working in sports at a national level, and almost none at local levels in 1983. I tried again and again, waiting on tables in the meantime.

I was very discouraged, so I moved to Colorado, where my mother and brother had moved several years prior. I continued to wait tables while sending out an endless number of demo reels. I finally landed a part-time job at the local school district's cable outlet channel. It wasn't exactly perfect (televising school board meetings is not quite the same as a football game!), but it was a start. And I was still sending out those demo reels.

Fast forward a few years. The College of Business at Colorado State University (CSU) called, looking for someone with television experience. They were going to launch a partnership with a cable company to broadcast their MBA programs, so students around the country could earn a master's degree on their own schedule. It was also a part-time job, so I took it.

I immediately fell in love with the university environment. I loved every-thing about it—the vibe, the students, the faculty—academia in general. (I also fell in love with a business law professor; we married three years later, but again I digress.) I stopped sending out demo reels. Soon that job became full time, and with that came additional employee benefits. Six credits a year for free, so I decided to get my master's in the Journalism department. It took a while, taking only one class a semester and working full time, but I did it.

Once I graduated, the department asked me to teach a class for them as an adjunct. My boss at the College of Business said it was Okay, so I started teaching Broadcast Newswriting. And that's when it hit me—this is what I want to do for the rest of my life. But to get to that point, I needed a doctorate.

And that's where the rest of this story begins.

I started researching programs. I could have gone to CSU and used my employee benefits, but the Journalism department did not have a PhD program at the time (we do now) and no other doctoral program was suit-able. I looked at other universities in and around Denver. There were a few programs that would have worked, but they were offered at night, and I didn't want to drive on the interstate in the dark during the winter when it can be very snowy. Since I was working in distance education at the time I knew a lot about it, so I decided to search for a program I could do at a distance. Long story short, I found a doctoral program in Educational Tech-nology at Pepperdine. The program of study was perfect for me, Pepperdine is a world-renown university with a stellar reputation, but best of all I could do the program online with some trips to campus in California. Not the Malibu campus unfortunately, but in a building in an industrial area about ten minutes from LAX.

Our first meeting face to face as a cohort was for one week in the summer before classes began. I vividly remember walking into the classroom for the first time and seeing a bunch of adults nervously sitting in chairs. My first thought was "What have I gotten myself into—can I really do this?" We all smiled apprehensively at one another. Then, the orientation session began. We did the usual teambuilding exercises, and we all slowly began to relax and start to get to know one another. "Maybe I *can* do this," I thought to myself.

My classmates came from all over the country. Many were from Cali-fornia but still had to fly to get to campus. Some came all the way from the East Coast. Pepperdine had an arrangement with a nearby hotel so we could stay there at a discount during the times we were on-site, which was one week every quarter plus a few three-day weekends per quarter. The rest of the time we "met" online.

It was at the hotel, our home for the next two years, that we all really became close. We'd go out to dinner together, sit in the lobby and have a drink; we talked about everything under the sun. I loved the camaraderie we had. We relied upon each other since we were all in the same situation: trying to earn a doctorate and write a dissertation while still working full time and raising families.

It was not easy. Paying for tuition and flying back and forth to California was a financial burden. It was difficult to get back into "school" mode since it had been a long time since most of us had been in a classroom as a student. Some relationships unraveled. I gained weight, then lost a lot of weight. There were a lot of tears, a lot of frustrations, and a lot of nights getting little sleep.

I remember one night in class, about halfway through our first year, when our professor realized we all were at a breaking point. She brought out a felt board, the kind you see in kindergarten, and pieces of felt and scissors. She asked us to demonstrate how we were feeling using the felt board. We all just needed to vent, to unload, because we were all so overwhelmed. I cut out a pink oblong oval and put it on the board. "Oh yeah—Paxil!" the class shouted.

Don't be afraid to ask for help. Sure, the meds may help take a bit of the edge off, but help came in other forms too. My family, classmates, wonderful professors, awesome committee members (who are so important to any doctoral student), and my little black toy poodle, Roxy, all got me through the process. That first year was particularly stressful, but I did it. And two years later, overlooking the blue waters of the Pacific Ocean (graduation *was* on the Malibu campus), walking across the stage in flip-flops with my family, friends, classmates, and professors present, I felt really strong and empowered. I could do *anything*.

I was incredibly lucky. I had a husband who could take over everything: cooking, cleaning, laundry, grocery shopping, etc. I know many of my classmates did not have that luxury. My husband, as a professor, was able to travel with me, so we had a lot of fun exploring everything Southern California had to offer when I wasn't in class. I was incredibly fortunate. Yet even in my situation, it was still a tremendously stressful three years. But they were also very rewarding years, and I hold dear the relationships I made with my classmates and professors. I wouldn't change a thing; it was all worth it.

It took three tries—the first job opening I was still all but dissertation (ABD), the second search was cancelled—but here I am today a tenured associate professor in the Department of Journalism and Media Communication at CSU.

But that wasn't the original plan.

CHAPTER 20

WHO WOULD HAVE THOUGHT?

JELANE A. KENNEDY, EdD

Central Connecticut State University, New Britain, CT, USA

Having worked in higher education for a number of years before I went back to school for my doctorate, I was aware of the importance of doing some exploration about whether the culture of the program was a good fit. As a first-generation college student, I always have felt a bit behind and found that developing good research skills to learn how things are done has served me well, and this was not an exception to the case.

The admissions process for the doctoral program had a unique two-step system; the first step was to be accepted into the Educational Specialist program with the intent to go on to the doctorate. Once you had completed some classes toward the degree, you then prepared for and took a written doctoral entrance exam. If you succeeded, then you would be asked to meet with the full faculty to discuss your research agenda. After that conversation, you then could be invited on to complete the doctoral degree. Once in the doctoral program, besides completing classes, there were written and oral comprehensive exams and the required original research for the dissertation. If you were not invited into the doctoral program, you would stop after completing the Educational Specialist degree.

I actually took a couple classes as a nonmatriculated student. I had wanted to be sure I had found a good fit as I had several options in the nearby area and had taken classes at another university when I was employed there but did not like the program. When I chose The College of William and Mary, I was happy to see that a number of dissertations had been done around diversity issues. I also liked the couple of classes I took. The program was very practice-oriented, and I liked the connections that were made to practice. There was not a lot of emphasis on going on into the professoriate.

By the time I reached my second matriculated semester, I had settled into classes and my graduate assistantship working for two professors, my advisor, and another professor in the program. During my first semester, I had been part time and did not have a graduate assistantship. Just before the start of the spring semester, an opening occurred, and I was asked if I'd like to move to full-time study and a graduate assistantship position. I thought all I needed to worry about was classes and what my research topic would be. I did not think that I would need to worry about potential microaggressions in the classroom. I felt like I had done my homework. Besides, most of the time southern hospitality included more subtle undercurrents that I had learned to negotiate over the years.

Since I was still early in my studies, I was just starting to develop relation-ships with my fellow doctoral students and my advisor. During that second semester, I took a class in psychometrics, and each night when we met we discussed assessment, how to develop assessments, and how to critically examine the assessments we might want to use with clients and for research. The class was interesting and seemed pretty straightforward.

One night, we discussed how people might informally pick up on hunches and consider developing assessments to test their hunches. Our instructor began to share with us that he had a stepson who identified as gay and told us that his stepson had a "sense" that was pretty accurate in that he could pick out when he met someone that they also were gay. He told us that this was called "gaydar." At this point, I grew a bit apprehensive at where this was going but thought he would soon make his point and move on.

Moments later, the instructor looked out into the class and said, "So, Bill, Greg, and Jelane, could you please explain this phenomenon more to us?"

I was stunned for three reasons: one, I had not told my instructor or anyone in my program that I identified as a lesbian; two, he had broken a cardinal rule in the gay community that one does not "out" someone without their permission; and three, it felt really inappropriate to be discussing this in a doctoral-level class. I don't remember much more about the class that night or how the three of us responded other than to move the focus along as quickly as possible. I think we all were stunned and just wanted to move on to new material, pretending that this calling us out had not just happened. The instructor was a well-known person in the field and had just been made a Professor Emeritus of the program. I had actually had this professor for the two classes I had taken as a nonmatriculated student. But that evening as I drove home, I was furious. I wondered how what had happened in class would impact my relationship with my fellow doctoral students who were primarily southern men whom I had yet to know well, and, as an emerging diversity educator, what was my responsibility to step up and talk to my instructor about the mistake he had made?

The next day after a restless night of sleep I decided I needed to reach out to the two men in class who had been "outed" to see how they wanted to handle it. Their response was to ignore what happened and just forget about it. Not satisfied and feeling the need to do more, I decided to approach my advisor. She was an African-American woman, and even though I knew this could be risky because of the tension within the African-American community around LGBT issues, I decided to take the risk. She was the only African-American person in the department and in the whole school of education. She also was the only full-time woman faculty person in the department.

Since I knew I would see her that day, as she was both my advisor and the person I worked for as a graduate assistant, I decided I would approach her and discuss my options. I was nervous about having this conversation; I had never approached my professors in the past to discuss what I was experiencing as a student. Luckily, she was very supportive and understood my concerns. She also supported me in going back to my instructor and discussing the situation.

I, then, went individually to each of my classmates from the Psychometrics class with whom I shared my graduate assistantship office to talk about what had happened in class that week. My classmates seemed to not see it as a big deal and didn't question the professor's discussion of "gaydar." Although I felt that one student colleague, who was also an older pastor, was a little more standoffish during the rest of my time in the program, my other graduate assistant colleague seemed to take it well, and we shared more personally from then on. It was a lot of emotional and logistical work that week to do what I felt was important.

The following week after class, I spoke with my instructor about how I had felt in class and the mistake he had made that night related to "outing" people. This was not something that I thought I would be doing in my doctoral program. I had never before in my life talked with a professor in this way; I had never challenged a professor about their behavior or thought it was important. In the past, during my master's program, if I was not happy about something, I kept my mouth shut; who was I to confront a professor? I think he was surprised that I had actually pulled him aside. I'm not sure he really got it. Sometimes folks who identify as allies don't understand why this code of ethics is important; they are accepting and don't/can't see why others are not. They don't always understand the complex ramifications of being "out" or "outing" and why this code of ethics is important to the gay community. "Not understanding" is part of heterosexual privilege. But he heard me out and seemed to ponder my response. I had hoped for more of a dialogue, more curiosity from him, but I think he may have felt that because he had a stepson (this was very clear—"stepson"), that he was in the know. I, though, felt at peace that I had done what I thought was right, and maybe in the future he would hesitate before he made that kind of a leap again.

Ultimately, I believe that I did the right thing; my relationship with my advisor was strengthened, and near the end of the semester my instructor approached me for consultation about a client he was working with in his private practice. I had moved from being just a student to being seen as a budding colleague. I also felt that I had honored my integrity. This was not the last time I would feel the cold hand of a microaggression. Months later, while working on a project with classmates one evening, I would head off to the ladies room and find myself as I left the restroom confronted by the cold stare of a janitor with her arms folded over her waist, thinking I was a man with my short hair, jeans, and bulky sweater. I wanted to do something rash, but this time I just smiled and gave a little wave. I actually got a bit of a kick out of my ability to be a gender bender, and that day I didn't let it bother me—keep them guessing. I now actually use this story in classes to talk about misperceptions and gender.

CHAPTER 21

AGAINST ALL ODDS: PERSEVERING WHILE PURSUING THE PhD

NADJA C. JOHNSON, PhD

Clark University, Worcester, MA, USA

E-mail: nadjajohnson@yahoo.com

I was reading a novel, sitting on the couch when the email arrived; I had been admitted into the PhD program in Comparative Studies at Florida Atlantic University with a full tuition waiver and a stipend of $12,000 a year. I remember that day very well because this was the first time I cried due to overwhelming joy. After seeing the email, I went straight to the beach; I ran in the sand and splashed in the water. I was genuinely happy, and I just could not believe that I was afforded this opportunity. I thought to myself, finally, I would have my chance at achieving something that at one point seemed virtually impossible. I was so grateful and utterly surprised. I never believed or imagined that I would have had the opportunity to be the first in my family to get a PhD.

Still, as an international student with very limited resources, I was nervous because I lacked many basic resources that others had. I was admitted to a PhD program, but I did not have a computer of my own. I started my PhD program without a computer! That is unheard of these days. Still, I was confident that I would somehow find a way to make it work, which is just what I always did. I also had very limited money and was unable to find accommodation because I would only be able to afford rent after getting my first stipend check at the end of August. I had no money saved and was not sure how I would be able to fund this new journey. As the start day for classes approached, we began to receive emails regarding classes and reading lists. While I was excited, the first thought that came to my mind was that I would not have been able to afford to buy any books on the reading list, definitely not before receiving my first check from the graduate assistantship. Something in me said, well, if I can make it to the class for the first day of school, I was sure I would be able to figure it all out.

That summer before the start of my PhD program, I returned to Jamaica to spend some time with my family. Unfortunately, right before it was time to return to the United States and start my PhD, a hurricane hit Jamaica. Luckily, the damage was minimal, and my family remained safe. However, the hurricane meant that all flights out of the country were cancelled and there was chaos trying to get a flight out. I arrived to Florida the first day of classes and literally went from the airport to the classroom. This is how my PhD program began, in a whirlwind of chaos, uncertainty, and tragedy.

21.1   SURVIVAL

It was difficult at first, but I persevered. I have always been someone who found it difficult to complain or ask for help. So I started by strategizing and seeing what problems I could solve on my own. I did all my work and research in the library and computer labs. I checked email and responded to professors and classmates at school before going home. I also found an apartment to rent very near to the campus. So I walked to school and could walk home easily. Still, the most helpful asset I had was my family. I include my friends in that category. They helped me get through what would have otherwise been an extremely difficult situation. They provided the love, care, and support I needed to get through the initial transition.

Oftentimes, women of color try to do it all, alone. This can be dangerous as we feel the need to appear competent, show people how brilliant we truly are, and that we can manage on our own. This is rooted in societal complexes that force women of color to constantly prove that they belong. I did not want to be the one woman of color in my cohort complaining or sharing my story of challenges. I felt a need to show everyone that I deserved to be there as much as they did. While this mindset kept me motivated and persevering, I was not taking care of myself. I felt overwhelmed very quickly in those first few days of school.

I openly share with people that one resource I found extremely helpful was counseling services. As someone trained in counseling and therapeutic services, I always knew the value and benefit of counseling. However, it was not until I began my doctoral degree that I enrolled in counseling at my institution. This was one of the best decisions I ever made on the graduate school journey. I used the time with my therapist well to address the concerns, issues, and challenges to adjustment that I was facing. The hour per week was well worth it. I know that in many communities, especially in under-served and marginalized communities, going to a therapist is often viewed as a sign of weakness or worse, a betrayal by airing dirty laundry in public. However, in my case, I surmised that the benefits of therapy far outweighed the disadvantages. I can recall all the "aha" and "lightbulb" moments that I had during those sessions. It was helpful to have an objective person in the room as I navigated the concerns I was facing.

So I made it through those first months relying heavily on my support systems. Here are some other strategies that were helpful in making it through the entire degree:

1. It takes a village to read all those books: Find colleagues you trust and to whom you feel connected. Form a study group and split up the readings. In your meetings, you will then "teach each other." This was an extremely helpful strategy as we were able to provide each other with the summaries and main points for all the readings and spend time discussing them to gain a more in-depth understanding.

2. Designing your committee: Once you have identified your chair or main advisor, work with that person to help you select the other members of your committee. While it is nice and cool to have people on your committee whom you relate well with and whose work you admire, I found that having a committee who can function together is possibly more important. So be sure all members of your committee feel comfortable working together or have already established some form of successful working relationship. Any unharmonious rela-tionship could adversely affect your work!

3. Chapter 1 starts now: As soon as you have thought about what you want to write about, start the background research and groundwork immediately! Whatever your topic, find a way to bring it into every final paper for every course. That way, when you sit down to start writing, you already have started the literature review and have some work you can build on.

4. Explore the world outside your department: Intentionally go to intellectual and educational events on campus. Think about joining a student organization or volunteering for another department in student affairs. I found it extremely valuable to form relationships and connections outside the classroom. We often think of our road to the "D" as just between us and our committee. In reality, you will have to work with staff in the degree completion department, the registrar's office, the library, the graduate school, etc. All these

departments can make a huge impact on your experience. Make friends there and you will be surprised how much easier the process can be!

5. Use the resources that you pay for: Some of the best support I received on my journey happened outside the classroom setting. If it is helpful, connect with staff in the counseling center and career services. Although I was doing a PhD, I knew I did not want to limit myself, after graduation, to faculty positions in higher education. A staff member in career services met with me and helped me reorganize my resume and cover letter as well as provided me with interview tips to showcase skills that were transferrable to nonfaculty roles. This is some of the best help I received to launch my career in student affairs.

6. Your professors expect you to "pop the question": I found it very difficult to ask professors to be on my committee. I did not want to feel like I was burdening them or giving them more work to do. However, I had to constantly remind myself that they signed up for this job when they chose to teach graduate students. They knew that students would be looking for advisors and committee members, and they must have figured that the chances were high that we would one day ask them. It sounds very straightforward, but for those of us who already have the burden of not feeling like we belong ("imposter syndrome"), this can be a difficult task. I openly tell my friends and colleagues that the first time I asked a professor to be my advisor, I had a mild panic attack just before entering the professor's office. I was shaking and having difficulty breathing and was clearly not looking good. The professor was kind enough to realize what was going on, offered me a seat, and told me to take all the time I needed to breathe and feel better. It was hard, but I got through it, I asked, and the answer was yes.

7. Put the PhD in perspective: There were many times when I felt like my entire life was consumed by this PhD I woke up thinking about my dissertation, I went to bed thinking about it, I went on vacation stressing about it. That is a common feeling, and many of us experience this throughout the process. Still, it was always helpful for me to remember—and say out loud all the other things in my life that were important to me: my family, my partner, dancing, food, my favorite TV shows. It was helpful to remember that even though the doctorate seemed like the only important thing in my life that mattered, it definitely was not. I constantly reminded myself of this.

8. You bring knowledge to the table: One of the most memorable moments in my doctoral career happened in a classroom after an introduction of all classmates. I listened as everyone around the table spoke eloquently of all their accomplishments, research, list of favorite authors, and just generally how much they had contributed to the world. At the time I was doing my doctorate, I did not feel confident enough to share anything. In fact, I thought the only thing I had accomplished was the luck of being accepted into the program. One day, a professor asked me how I was adjusting to the program. I told her the truth: that I felt extremely underprepared and not as knowledgeable as my classmates. She shook her head immediately and said, "Nadja, there is so much you bring to the table. There is so much information you know that no one else here knows." At first I thought, okay, this must be a lie and wondered why she would say that. It took a while, but eventually I got what she was saying. For this reason, I started to validate my lived experience. Even though it was different from my classmates, it was real and very much something I could bring to the table that they could not.

9. Give back early and often: One of the most helpful strategies was finding ways to connect with new incoming students facing similar challenges. Fortunately for me, I was employed in an office where I had the opportunity to work with new graduate students from the first day they arrived on campus and experienced orientation. Just knowing that I had an opportunity to help create a positive transitional experience helped me value my contribution to the program as well as reaffirmed my own resilience and achievement. Whenever possible, try to find either formal or informal ways to work with other students who are new to navigating the program. Another thing I was able to do was serve on the student council of the program, using my voice to advocate for my colleagues. That was such a rewarding and fulfilling experience!

10. Have fun! There is nothing in life worth doing if, at the end of it all, you do not feel a sense of satisfaction and fulfillment. If you hear your favorite song in the middle of writing your literature review, sing along (loudly). It is a PhD, but it does not have to be a bore! You have the option to experience this program exactly the way you want to. Laugh at yourself often, even laugh at the readings if they amuse you. Just do not take it too seriously and surround yourself with others who do not.

CHAPTER 22

MENTORING: A REAL RELATIONSHIP

ALLISON M. HROVAT, MEd[1] and MELISSA LUKE, PhD[2]

[1]*Holyoke Community College, Holyoke, MA, USA,*
E-mail: ahrovat@hcc.edu

[2]*Syracuse University, Syracuse, NY, USA, E-mail: mmluke@syr.edu*

Allison Hrovat: In the first year of my doctoral program, I was filled with a lot of questions about the professional shift that I was undertaking. I had, of course, thought long and hard about my decision to pursue a doctoral degree, but I had thought about the endeavor more in terms of wanting to learn more about my discipline of counseling than potentially undertaking a professional identity shift from practitioner to scholar. It was, somehow, surprising to me that within the doctoral program, there seemed to be a great deal of emphasis placed on the development of scholarly identity and comparatively less placed on teaching and clinical practice.

As my path unfolded in the doctoral program, I came to see that the choices that I made would determine the direction of my professional life and that there was support to be found for any avenue I wanted to pursue. Early on, though, these were questions I really struggled with, in part because I wanted to be a "good student" and I knew that, within my department, academic scholarship was certainly valued over teaching and clinical practice.

I was fortunate enough to be paired with a wonderful advisor and mentor, Dr. Melissa Luke, who has always been encouraging, candid, and loving in helping me to navigate these questions. During a summer course on narrative inquiry, I asked her to join me in a research design that would involve the two of us writing back and forth via e-mail about the topic of professional identity. Our communication occurred over a span of five days, during which Dr. Luke was at a professional conference and I was immersed in the work of summer courses. I am presenting here parts of our dialogue—my contributions appear in italics *(AH)* and hers appear in bold text (ML).

AH: I'm writing to you to ask for some of your time to engage in a different type of research experience with me .... I think you know by now that I see you as a mentor and as someone who consistently supports me through challenges and wonderings as I move forward in my profes- sional development. It's, therefore, likely not a surprise to you that I struggle to think about my developing identity as a counselor educator and researcher and how that will or will not alter the professional identity that I love, that of a counselor. I know that the pressures and responsibilities that come with becoming an academic and a full-time faculty member push people toward focusing on research and academic pursuits and, as a necessity of time, leaving behind much or all of their clinical work. Thus, I've been wondering recently about the personal side of this research-practice gap: is it just about problems with effec- tive information dissemination or is there something about the impact of identity shift as well?

ML: Let's begin! I can write while I am at the supervision conference and then we can meet the week after.

AH: I thought I'd begin by sending you the following excerpt. This was written in class in response to a prompt for us to write a vignette that we might use as part of our research project. This vignette is about a client whom I worked with—let's call him Alec—who was an African-American male who had spent years incarcerated for jewel theft, and who expressed that his painful experiences of racial oppression were what motivated so many of his lifestyle choices. So that day I asked him: What is it like to come here and work with a White woman like me? And we talked about it. For weeks. For months. When I'd process his case with colleagues, some would say but how is this helping him with his depression? He is just avoiding the issue. But something inside told me differently. Something told me that this WAS the issue, at least it was our issue. My supervisor and teachers encouraged me to trust this path, to trust what I knew and what I sensed he needed. I felt that for that time, it was our work to do and it needed to be done. With me. I needed for me to try to see me as he saw me and figure out what that meant, and I needed to push past simply the counseling persona I thought was so important to being a professional to being, to just being present."

ML: The intrapersonal exists within the interpersonal and the larger group system. So, again to bring this back to your professional development, I suggest there might be several layers taking place simultaneously and that these likely even interact with one another. It gets even more existentially complicated as

I consider this is also the case for me and everyone else in your "system." So there is a whole lot going on all at once, huh, no wonder things can get squishy.

AH: It got me thinking about whether that is often a part of career choice and professional identity—looking to create a corrective experience?

ML: However, before I do this, I want to note that I am acutely aware that I am amidst the development that defines the process. While my identity as a counselor educator has evolved greatly since I entered doctoral study, I strongly suspect that it is still unfolding.

AH: "Counselor" is the only professional identifier I've used for myself in the noun form. I "taught Spanish," I "wrote press releases and did design work," but I can never remember calling myself a teacher or a journalist. Same with other activities—I "run races" but I did not call myself a "runner," I "make jewelry and love photography," but am not an artist, etc. etc. It's a weird realization that I think is born from insecurity, but I also think there is some connection to other constructs of identity, too.

Allison: As a new doctoral student, it was refreshing and validating to learn that my advisor had asked herself similar questions along her professional identity path. Our email dialogue continued through the sharing of our own personal stories of professional identity seeking and finding. Here, we are presenting excerpts from those longer dialogues as a way of demonstrating the various experiences and accompanying emotions that marked each of our journeys.

ML: Messy is the first descriptor that comes to mind related to my experience. I found that the "edges" were and remain irregular and ill-defined. Moreover, I can see when looking back, that there were points wherein I was actively resistant, contributing to "tugs" and tears so to speak. I'm pretty sure that there were other interpersonal pieces that contributed to the stops and starts, shifting the pieces and contributing factors in haphazard ways. For me, my initial entry into teaching was born out of practicality, not passion. As a first in the family to attend college, my family's working-class values strongly influenced the professional decisions I made.

AH: I think I am a counselor because my parents died. That's weird to think, but my life wasn't so clearly on that path until they died. I don't know that I'd be here without that experience.

ML: I don't know what constellation of factors attributes it to, but there was a marked shift for me a couple years ago. Like I say to students, I realized

professional identity for me was not either–or. Ironically, though I did not set out to, consciously, so much of my work as a counselor educator actually touches on professional identity development. Perhaps my own growth was influenced through, by, and because of my work exploring others' experiences of such.

AH: I remember when I interviewed, you asked me how I expected my doctoral experience to be different than other prior academic work. I answered that while I didn't have so many specific expectations of how the program would differ, I did have expectations of myself and how I would be different in that I hoped to be more invested in the process, less grade- and outcome-focused, and more present for what I was experiencing, learning, and doing.

ML: Though I really liked the work, I never wanted to be a teacher and, truthfully, didn't like many aspects of the work, namely classroom management and the politics that preferenced academics over social/emotional learning. Because I am who I am, I was always drawn to work with the kids no one else wanted to be around, and understandably, these students always found me anyway.

AH: I don't see a time in my near future where I would want to abandon clinical work completely, but maybe there is a part of me ready for a different challenge. I can say that I've been surprised that I have liked teaching, especially the clinical courses, and while not surprising I have also loved supervising. Research, though, has been a total shock. As a researcher, I've learned so much about myself, different than what I've learned as a counselor. It really pushes me to think. It unexpectedly draws from the skills I learned as a journalist that I thought I'd never use.

ML: After about 10 years of teaching on and off, I took a class in group counseling as a means to better facilitate the daily group that I was running in a high school. I loved being back in school, as there was minimal sustained intellectual stimulation for me as a teacher. I found myself feeling more and more validated (through experience but also the literature) in my identity as a counselor. I wasn't sure what I would do with a PhD, and at several points, I wondered if I would even finish. I felt "different" than my classmates on many levels, and there is much truth to that experience but part of the difference was that I did not want to give up my practitioner self. My professional identity development within the PhD program comprised myself wanting access and credibility in one respect, while also desperately wanting to hang on to myself, if that makes any sense. I sometimes wondered if I needed to chop off pieces and parts that I had so carefully grown. I might have even told you that at the end of my first semester, I felt like I was a Venus deMilo statue. Over time, I developed a sense of efficacy as a scholar, but even with a growing CV, I was sure that my research capabilities were inferior to my other skills. Because I am an over-functioner, despite many years of therapy, I worked doing both.

AH: I remember this time in third grade when we had to take the presidential fitness tests in gym class. I was always quite good at these tests but sucked at the balance beam. So I obsessed over this balance beam test, wanting to master it. My parents told me that I could do it and, however, it turned out they'd know I'd done my best and that really in life the balance beam is not what matters. Those platitudes and lessons on the meaning of life meant nothing to me, I needed PROOF that I was good enough, and proof would come in the form of a flawless balance beam routine. My dad, sweet and spontaneous as he was, and while challenging of my motives also supportive of my fragile little ego, spent a long evening after work building me a balance beam in the garage; he did the hard work, I helped out with the smaller tasks that wouldn't compromise the eventual design and product. The finished beam placed in the backyard, I practiced and practiced and practiced. To be honest, I don't even remember how I did on the test. But I remember well the sawing and the measuring, the building and the practicing. That's how my parents were—we came up with an idea, they'd encourage us and give us the tools to make it happen. But they also wanted to show us that life had to be more than a series of As and Bs and passes and fails, that we had to figure out what really mattered to us and what we wanted to spend our time doing.

I think they wanted us to be able to think bigger and explore more broadly than they ever had, while my natural inclination was to simply kill myself in order to succeed at the task before me, no matter how meaningless it seemed. I remember that, and stand in awe of how different that thought process is to how I "evaluate" my work as a counselor. In a way (and this awareness is only coming to me now as I write this), I suppose what I wanted for myself was what my parents wanted for me all along.

Some of the only horrible arguments I can remember between me and my parents were me, up at two in the morning, freaking out about a test or a grade and screaming at my parents that they'd given birth to a failure and why don't they care? My mom told me later in life that not only were these arguments tiresome and difficult but also heartbreaking for her. She told me how hard it was to give birth to and raise a child that she just knew was full of goodness and possibility, only to send her into a world that made her think there was nothing about her that was good enough.

ML: I am not sure I feel worthy in the scholarly sense, yikes! Hard to put in writing, but true. I have read about the "imposter" syndrome, and it

doesn't professionally resonate with me. I don't feel like I am playing a part, fearing that I will be discovered. That said, I recognize a mismatch between my self-perceptions and those of others in my local professional world, and more largely. I struggle with "owning" certain things, but that isn't new. Paralleled in lots of places in my life.

> *AH: What you said about the imposter syndrome is also resonant for me. The mismatch you're describing between what you see and what others see feels big to me personally too.*

ML: I gained a resonance that I am me at my core, and I can retain my values and the main elements of the work that I do across identities of teacher, counselor, and scholar. I have found, probably better to say am finding, ways to integrate these and sequence them so that they uniquely meet different needs that I have. I want to stress the sequencing piece because this is also a theme in my personal/family life.

> *AH: I know that you are a really driven person, but I think there is a great divide between achievement for the sake of achievement and achievement for a greater meaning and value.*

ML: I do not believe "having it all" means having it all at once. Thus, I'm good with sequencing, I see value in it. So, this is part of my professional identity now; I can't be all three of those things at once, but because being a teacher/advisor is very meaningful work to me, I hold this very dear and invest in doing it well. I also value being a counselor/supervisor. In many ways, academia values these interpersonal roles least, though the interpersonal holds the most potential to change people, I think. I also really love the process of doing research and the products that I produce through my writing (the process of writing isn't uniformly fun for me). I like the creative aspects, but I can feel the pressure that gets in my way.

I am sure your goal in this project was not to facilitate my self-awareness, but I must say that I just had an epiphany. My above-expressed ambivalence and struggle are about loss. Letting go of my uncertainty about myself, which is much deeper than humility, would likely bring many positive things, but it is also a loss of who I have been. I know this process well, as it is part of much of my personal growth over my life. Hmm, this gives me something to ponder more.

I am a person who wishes to kindly and gently move through the world being true to myself and others. I hope to be part of others' growth, academically, psychologically, and professionally, as well as make the world's suffering a bit easier to bear. I can do these from all of my professional roles, but only through combining them can I do so comprehensively. I don't want to give up

any of the parts really. Somehow, it would be as false as saying that I am not a mother, even though my daughter's needs have drastically shifted and she doesn't need to be fed, clothed, or bathed by me.

Allison: As our dialogue continued over the course of several days, the conversation shifted slightly away from the professional identity questions and toward the role of relationships in the journey of professional development. We wrestled with questions of where the personal stopped and the professional began, and whether those neat boundaries could really be drawn in a process so complex and inherently personal. Reading this dialogue now, years later and after significant personal and professional challenges, I am struck by the nearly impossible dilemma that is created by the illusion of being able to contain the personal as separate from the professional. Of all of the things that I have learned in my work with Dr. Melissa Luke, by far the most significant has been this concept of a "real relationship." Our "real relationship" has required risk, vulnerability, compassion, and mutuality, and has not been without its challenges and ruptures, but it has, in so many ways, mirrored what the journey through academia *really* requires.

ML: One perhaps unexpected outcome of your project is my recognition that in addition to our professional relationship as advisor–advisee, there is what Gelso refers to as a "real relationship" too. In therapy, the concept refers to the interpersonal relationship that is outside of but impacting the working alliance. Ironically, Ed Watkins presented on this related to supervision at the conference. There, at his roundtable, I publically owned to him that I am giving myself permission in this regard. Incidentally, all supported this!

AH: I know that on the advisee side of things, I have juggled the same question. We have talked about this somewhat before—the boundaries surrounding these relationships are fuzzy, at best anyway, and the added experience of feeling like we are both on stage in a sense, watched by our colleagues and peers, makes it all feel more complicated than it likely ought to be.

ML: I enjoyed reading your material for several reasons. This more personal narrative displays your creativity in a different way than I had access to before. It makes sense to me from other things that I have observed (e.g., creative arts counseling work, jewelry making). It was also nice for me to be able to "know" you in a deeper way. We have talked before about our relationship, in all its complexity, but in addition to our advisor–advisee professor–student

relationship, I do really value you as a person. As such, I appreciated you sharing yourself openly in this way.

> *AH: For me, though, you have been the utmost example of what it means to try to find a way to be a congruent self, and how important that is to personal and, yes, also professional identity development. What you shared about your experience of finding your way to this career path underscored all of that. I had no idea that you were not born wanting to be a teacher, and yet when you described the journey, it all made a lot of sense. The fact that through a series of experiences, you found yourself in the teacher role and managed to find a way to make incredible meaning of that role is very you.*

ML: I really appreciated the stories you offered and I found them so beautiful to illustrate the valuable gifts you received from your parents. The rich detail helped me not only to visualize and have a tactile sense that put me sensually into the memory (something about the sawing in the garage to make the balance beam) but also have a fuller recognition of who you are and how you came to be. That feels like a treasured and treasurable gift. Is this resonant to what you have learned about narrative? I wonder.

> *AH: I wanted to add here just a piece because it's about you and it feels really relevant to say here. And I mean it sincerely. The paper is called "Relinquishing Definition". And now my advisor and mentor, who strives to navigate her place in academia with a kind of bravery, honesty, and authenticity that could turn institutions of higher education on their heads into something more progressive, more empowering, more sincere, more accepting and less oppressive—if only all would be as courageous and genuine as she. She brings herself to the work that she does in such a way that her compassion becomes a foundation upon which any challenges are seen navigable; any interaction seems meaningful and important. I sometimes imagine these women to be gifts from my mom—that if she couldn't be here with me, she wanted to find the best companions to share my journey.*

ML: I need to share that for a long time I have felt that there was a larger purpose or meaning to our meeting. The thought that your mother steered our overlapping path in any fashion fits for me too. I can only hope to do right by that. What I can say is that I am certain if your mom could/can see/ know you over the past two years in the way that I have been fortunate to have, she is undoubtedly beaming with satisfaction and pride. You are truly something. (I am aware that I am prematurely ending this strand of writing b/c I am tearing up—not something to do in a conference session, no matter how uninteresting.)

> *AH: I can absolutely say I wouldn't have that perspective if not for you and our work together. And I really agree with you—the perspective came from experiences, yes, but also from my connection to you.*

ML: This has been an unusually emotionally evocative email exchange, and it makes me even more intrigued about narrative as a method. Without a better understanding of the methodology, your course, and the specific project you have developed, I cannot tell to what I attribute the emotion. Regardless, I have found myself teary with each reading/writing, and a few times more than that! My initial attribution was that the sentiment reflected more about our relationship, but I suspect there may be numerous contributing factors.

> *AH: My parents and I unfortunately never got to have those "I am about to die and here is what I want you to know" conversations, because we were perpetually denying the reality before us, but I think what they'd probably say is that they would want me to live my best life to do what I love and love what I do; to choose the people I love and love the people I choose; to be who I am and somehow know that is enough.*

ML: I also feel like I need to be very honest about something. I was greatly impacted by your sharing how your family's denial of the possibility of each of your parent's deaths, and knowing you, perhaps even the unlabeled over-functioning that went on as part of coping, prevented you all from having some conversations that it sounds like you would now value. Probably the biggest part of my reaction was in empathy for your losses that are associated with this, but I also felt like there was a "woo woo" message in there too. I'm not classically religious at all, but I felt like there was something that I needed to learn, largely about what I might need to more explicitly communicate to those I deeply love, even if I am not facing an about-to-die moment.

> *AH: Something I realized in this class—in writing an essay from the perspectives of all of my family members during the initial days of my mom's illness—is that considering I am basically a professional empathizer, I don't take as much time as I want to practice empathy on my own time for the people I love. And so I am thinking a lot about you, about all the balls you keep in the air in your life, and the people that surround you and love you so much.*

ML: This is certainly not regular teacher–student boundary material, but one of those "real relationship" moments that I want to bravely embrace.

AH: It's hard to shift from a daily life of being driven by one thing to a life of being more in the moment. I think of it like when they are resurfacing the highway and there are huge ridges between the lanes. It feels like in order to change lanes, I might end up being bumped off course by the ridges, and so sometimes I stay in the wrong lane longer than I should because of the anxiety of switching. My wish for you is that you can change lanes to be present for what you want for yourself in this moment.

ML: That is a danger everywhere I guess, as a person in any profession can live with their proverbial eyes closed, but for me, it is very pronounced in academia. We have talked about it as balance and self-care, but neither completely captures it for me. There is something about the "job" that can suck the self, and I know that part of my "task" at my current stage of professional identity development involves figuring out how to be fully present, and not lose myself, in the job.

AH: I really valued what you said about the stress in academia being about more than just balance and boundaries. I think that must be true, and I think it is what turns me off/scares me. As I am writing this, I am thinking that the product in academia is YOU. Sure the parts that make that are publications, presentations, teaching, research, grants, etc. but the ultimate commodity that is bought by universities and sold by you is you. But the struggle of deciding the personal parts that become part of the product sold in academia seems big. How does one package themselves? And in doing so, what gets lost and left behind?

ML: I think I am suggesting that there are false dichotomies all over; perhaps professional identity is one place. You are Allison Hrovat and perhaps I am naive and/or overly simplistic, but you may not have to choose beyond that. I am nonetheless confident that you will engage in doing good in the world, bringing comfort and healing to others, and facilitating their becoming. I am so grateful to be a witness to and part of the process with you.

Melissa Luke: And so, it has gone over the succeeding many years. The ongoing unfolding of both an advisor–advisee professional collaboration and a miraculous and messy real relationship, in tandem. Somehow though, without much more meta-processing, what ensued became a weaving of the two, instead of separate, parallel ways of relating. Just as I was assuring Allison that she could/would integrate her personal and professional identities, so also did our formal and real relationships synthesize into something larger, something more whole.

It has been many years since we exchanged email for Allison's class project. By looking back, I can recognize that those years have contained triumphs and challenges, great successes and deep despair. Both of us have continued to evolve as women, as counselors, and as counselor educators. Within our relationship, we have also experienced moments of interpersonal angst and times of great resonance. Through it all, we have continued to better know ourselves and each other. There is a bit of irony in that in Allison's search for professional identity and in my quest to be a good advisor in the process, we each found more of our personal selves. This is the raw stuff that is both real and surreal all at once.

PART III:
Stage 3: Second Year Through Candidacy

This is the period after completion of the first year of study until attainment of candidacy, signified by successful completion of the comprehensive or qualifying exams. During this time, the student continues with coursework, completes the comprehensive or qualifying exam, identifies a dissertation topic, selects a dissertation advisor and committee, and prepares and defends a dissertation proposal (Ali & Kohun, 2007).

COMPLETING COURSEWORK

You have a full year of coursework under your belt! This is both an exciting time and a time when you will be required to have some grit because you are enjoying your coursework but you are also getting tired. The work is piling on a bit more as you prepare for your comps. You are experiencing the stress and excitement of the academic experience, connecting with colleagues, and deepening your professional identity. You're in the groove, doing your thing, and starting to feel both a sense of "I've got this!" as well as a sense of being in a place of limbo—no longer a novice, yet not quite done; in fact, you are nowhere near done. You take a deep breath and recommit to keep on keeping on.

COMPREHENSIVE OR QUALIFYING EXAMINATIONS

Comprehensive/qualifying exams can be written, oral, or both; they generally come upon the completion of coursework and before developing the dissertation proposal. Every program is unique in how these are completed, but the exams generally cover the breadth and depth of material you are expected to know as a scholar in your discipline. Study groups are highly recommended. If the exams include an oral component, generally the written component comes first with a follow-up in which faculty members can ask questions or for clarifications of anything you have written (or not written).

These exams determine whether you can go on; if you pass, you become a doctoral candidate.

DISSERTATION PREPARATION

Once you are a doctoral candidate, you will need to identify your dissertation topic, your dissertation chair/advisor, and your dissertation committee, and create your dissertation proposal/prospectus. Your dissertation chair/ advisor will be a university faculty member, generally within your academic department, who has agreed to serve as an advisor/mentor to guide your process of completion of the dissertation. Sometimes this person is assigned, but most often the chair is chosen by you after careful consideration of your needs and interests and the needs and interests of potential advisors. This person may be the same or distinct from the academic advisor who helps you select courses and typically possesses content expertise related to your research topic.

Your dissertation committee will be a group of two or more university faculty members who, like the dissertation advisor, have agreed to provide you guidance in completion of your dissertation. The dissertation advisor is the chair of the dissertation committee and is the member of the committee with whom you will work most closely. The committee consists of a total of three or four members, two of whom must be in your field of study. Dissertation committee members may also be referred to as "readers." It is wise to work with your dissertation chair to carefully select your committee members.

The following are some tips and strategies for successfully preparing for the execution of your dissertation research:

1. ***Do not take on too large of a dissertation topic:*** Sometimes students want to make a big splash, thinking that their dissertation will be a seminal piece of work. They create an enormous project that could realistically be broken down into several studies. Students can become so committed to the project they get lost in the research. There must be a balance, enough commitment, and discipline to keep going but not so much that you cannot get out of your own way when feedback is provided.
2. ***Keep track of and meet deadlines:*** The dissertation is an independent project, as all of the steps are leading up to collecting and analyzing one's data. It is easy to get distracted with life and get lost without the college timetable for framing due dates. Things happen, babies

are born, marriages and divorces take place, parents need assistance, someone important may pass away, a job might end, someone gets sick, and so forth. It is important to develop a timeline with tangible goals and markers. You may need to talk with family/friends and others about how they can support you, what works and what does not. When you are sidetracked, do not get discouraged and stop; instead create a new timeline and recommit to finishing. No self-judgment—only observe, notice, and get back on track.

3. ***Give yourself permission to find your own rhythm to write***: Students sometimes feel like they need to write all day. They forget to figure out what feeds their writing and how to keep things in balance. There needs to be time to read, contemplate, reflect, write, and edit. It is a process. Some people write five days a week and play/rest for two days; some people write every morning and then take the afternoon off to do other things. There must be a balance of eating, exercise, rest, and family/friends to feed the writing. Not everything you read must be about your dissertation. Be sure to read some fun things to break it up a bit. It is important to make a schedule, have designated workspace to write, and time. Find the rhythm that makes sense for *you*, not your best friend.

4. ***See Part IV for more tips***!

STAGE 3 NARRATIVES

In describing their experiences in this stage of the doctoral process, our authors address the stress and challenges of getting through the comprehensive (or qualifying) exams, which must be successfully completed in order to become a doctoral candidate, that is, someone who completed all but the dissertation in order to attain the doctoral degree. When all coursework is completed, the exams will assess the student's cumulative knowledge within the academic discipline she is studying.

Successful completion of the dissertation begins in this stage with narrowing one's interests sufficiently to identify a viable research topic, finding a faculty member who will serve as a supportive and available dissertation advisor (and committee chair), and constructing a dissertation committee that will provide the well-rounded guidance needed to complete the project successfully. The final tasks of this stage are development of the dissertation proposal and presentation of the proposal to the committee for approval to go forward with the study.

Our authors caution readers that unless a doctoral student makes the effort to continue engagement with the members of her support group, preparing for the comprehensive exams and the work on the dissertation becomes more solitary and the student can begin to feel more isolated and stressed, with an accompanying feeling that time is slowing down. Study groups, writing groups, and social connections with doctoral peers are noted as essential for staying on track. Balancing family and other non doctoral responsibilities becomes more challenging as the doctoral journey moves away from the scheduled and shared environment of classes to the more isolated and unstructured process of studying for the exams and then work on the dissertation.

REFERENCE

Ali, A.; & Kohun, F. (2007). Dealing with social isolation to minimize doctoral attrition—a four stage framework. *International Journal of Doctoral Studies, 2*, 33–49. Retrieved from: http://www.informingscience.org/Journals/IJDS/Articles?Volume=2–2007&Search.

CHAPTER 23

"LIFT AS WE CLIMB": COMMUNITY IN DOCTORAL EDUCATION

LIZA A. TALUSAN, PhD

Educational Consultant and Speaker, Brockton, MA, USA

I was so relieved to see a multicolored rug in the room where my dissertation defense was going to take place. I knew, at some point during the defense, that my son's bag of M&Ms would explode all over the floor, despite his best efforts to be quiet. At least the multicolored industrial rug would absorb the sound of M&Ms hitting the floor and be only minimally distracting.

Going into my defense, I had prepared a bag of goodies for my three children. Evan, age 6, got the small, brown pouch of candy that I had frantically grabbed at the last minute in line at the grocery store. Jada, age 8, brought a pack of colored pencils and a new drawing pad. Joli, age 12, was allowed to bring her electronic device, as long as she promised to take a few photos of me in action.

For the past five years, my children had been passengers on my journey toward completing my doctoral coursework and dissertation. And today, at my big defense, they would be physically present. But I did not have high hopes that they would follow along with my 22 slides of statistics and narrative. After all, what could I possibly expect from three young children who have just realized they are missing recess and pizza day at school. Coming to my dissertation defense felt like punishment. "Join the club," I thought, as my nerves got the best of me.

For nearly a decade, I had wanted to pursue my doctorate. For five consecutive years prior to my actual start, I had printed up the application and written the essays, but I always failed to send in the packet. I kept telling myself, "My children are too young" or "I'm just not ready" or "I don't have time to breathe. How would I have time for doctoral work?" or "There is too much to do at work." I wish I could say there was a distinct moment in time when I decided to actually send in the application. Truth is, I was just tired of putting it off.

Within the first week of my graduate school semester, I knew life was going to change. Habits, routines, expectations, and everyday activities now had to include scholarly reading, writing, and the all elusive "head space." Instead of being an active audience member at my daughter's dance class, I was highlighting journal articles and digesting problem statements. When my other daughter was doing homework, I sat next to her frantically typing away to make a course deadline. And, while my son was busy throwing macaroni and cheese from the high chair onto the linoleum floor, I was attempting to read an SPSS assignment that was due the next day. On and off, my "mommy guilt" played out in my head. I questioned whether I was being a good-enough doctoral student or a good-enough graduate assistant or a good-enough mom or a good-enough student affairs director. Layered on top of those roles, I wondered if I was being a good-enough wife, a good-enough daughter, and a good-enough friend to people who noticed the abrupt absence of my text messages and invitations to have dinner or coffee. I kept asking myself why: "Why didn't I know it would be this hard?"

Around this time in my doctoral studies, I was beginning to learn about socialization, the process by which an individual is influenced by the professional expectations of the field, discipline, or role (Clark & Corcoran, 1986; Van Maanen & Schein, 1979). I began to reflect on the professional expectations of my field, particularly around what it meant to be a doctoral student and what I was expected to produce and begin publishing. I began to explore literature on the socialization of doctoral students and the ways in which doctoral students can impact a bidirectional process—one in which the organization socializes the student and the student can, in turn, influence the organization (Tierney & Rhoads, 1993). I began reading more about the experiences of doctoral student mothers (e.g., Evans & Grant, 2008) and the challenges of being a practitioner-scholar (e.g., Barnett & Muth, 2008).

While I found support through these identities in the socialization process, there was one aspect of my socialization process in which I felt marginalized and invisible: my identity as an Asian American. I distinctly remember a moment in my History of Higher Education class where we were wrapping up the semester. We had been assigned one of the foundational texts in higher education—a textbook that weighed more than each of my individual children at birth—which was filled with the contributions, struggles, and issues related to different racial, ethnic, immigrant, and political groups. One of our final assignments was to read pages 792–800: "Asian Americans in Higher Education." While I should have been overjoyed that the evening's reading was only eight pages, I found myself angry, frustrated, upset, and confused. Did my reading assignment on Asian Americans really only take up eight pages? But, there it was: eight pages of "Asian Americans in Higher Education."

My people took up only eight pages.

I began to think about why I had felt so out of place in my field. Though I had read a dozen articles and almost a hundred pages on socialization, I never felt like those pages were talking about me or my journey. I began to think about why socialization models and student development theories and the experiences of adult learners seemed to miss the mark of my own life.

Then, the truth hit me right in that moment. For, in that moment, I had realized that for nearly 32 years of formal education, I was invisible to the very system that promised to educate me.

While I entered into my doctoral program set on exploring how general issues of diversity and inclusion informed structural policies, these happenstance eight pages from my history book and the swirl of invisibility that was leading up to this moment soon became the foundation of my research. I dove quickly into statistics about the number of Asian Americans and Pacific Islanders in higher education programs and the representation of Asian Americans and Pacific Islanders in my field at large. I thought about the anticipatory aspects of doctoral student socialization that extended beyond the time when individuals applied to schools; instead, I looked at the anticipation and the messages we received from a very early age about *who* goes to graduate school, *why* people go to graduate school, and *what kind of people* go to graduate school.

The existing models of socialization and development did not speak to me because they were missing a major component of what makes *me*: my cultural background, my race, and my racialized identities. Over the course of a year, my research began to fine-tune itself as I developed an insatiable appetite for learning about my own people. I began to explore that anticipatory time—the period during which one explores doctoral studies—from a cultural perspective, asking participants about how family identity, responsibility, language, gender, ethnicity, and experiences in school informed their decisions to pursue graduate degrees. I listened to stories of my peers—Asian-American and Pacific-Islander doctoral students—share similar stories of feeling invisible in their curriculum. I heard the pause and disappointment in their voices when they told me about how all their teachers were White and how their only understanding of Asian-American history was Pearl Harbor and the Vietnam War. I recognized the shake in their voices when, just like me, they were called "ching-chong" and came face-to-face with that one kid on the playground who pulled at the corners of his eyes, and how we hung on for dear life to the metal bars with the chipped paint out of fear we would fall off the monkey bars and cry. I talked to people all over the country, at different stages of their doctoral studies, from different ethnic backgrounds, and from different schooling structures. Our stories, surprisingly, were the same. And, despite our different pathways to doctoral studies, we were experiencing similar socialization and development in our graduate programs, processes that ignored our racialized identities.

I realized that existing models of socialization and development failed to address the experiences of doctoral students who, on a daily basis, faced microaggressions and macroaggressions from peers and professors. They did not address what it takes to keep showing up to a place that does not treat you like you belong, thereby leaving you out of the history books and not including you in aggregated data about students of color. They did not address the fear a student feels when she is tired of being called by the wrong name, and being confused with the other Asian woman in the class, yet still shows up to class each day and grinds out paper after paper. They did not address the persistence it takes to constantly say, "So, what would that data on Asian Americans look like if it was disaggregated by ethnic identities?" and have everyone in the class—classmates who will become researchers and leaders in higher education—roll their eyes. They did not address what it means to get rejection letters from conferences with feedback like "this isn't a scholarly area" or "not sure anyone cares about this issue" when you have submitted critical scholarship about marginalized identities.

Existing literature addressed socialization and development as two separate processes; yet, for me, they were interdependent. I was unable to experience positive socialization without acknowledging that my development—my ability to navigate self-growth—was dependent upon opportunities to learn about my field, to be exposed to professional experiences, to have mentors and role models and advocates who understood my Asian-American experience, and to engage in critical discourse with my professors and peers. Anticipatory socialization, in education at least, began with who our own teachers were, what we were taught, and whether or not we saw ourselves reflected in our curriculum. Anticipatory socialization was impacted by our ability to believe we were a part of the system, a part of the narrative, and a part of the change.

So, how did I navigate this territory that treated me as a visitor? I had to find where my people were. I had to find my support network, my *barkada*, my scholar sisters, my lovelies, and my Ride-or-die people. I went to conferences and immersed myself in the presence of Asian-American and Pacific-Islander scholars and practitioners. I filled my emotional and psychological tank with scholarship and people who affirmed my identity and helped me feel like I wasn't going crazy (e.g., Gildersleeve, Croom, & Vasquez, 2011). And, though I ran into many scholars who continued to perpetuate my worst fears—that my scholarship was not "worthy" enough—I had my crew I could turn to who reminded me that it was. I threw myself into studying the impact of White supremacy on our educational systems, and I began to understand why the undercurrent of delegitimizing the study of race was pervasive. I shifted from taking these slights of rejection personally to examining how a system of oppression created conditions that allowed others to dismiss my work and my interests. I joined social media support and dialogue groups. I saved articles that I could pull up at the ready. I organized my own "Committee of Love" (people who give me feedback, critique, and support). I connected with senior scholars who had also faced similar battles in their journey. I worked in solidarity with communities who are also pushed to the margins. And, I made sure I found my group of "Scholar Mamas" who understood what it meant to have parts of your dissertation deleted because your three-year-old got hold of your computer or who struggled with the tensions of taking care of everyone but yourself. I connected with faculty members who also approached their work from a liberatory framework and who are committed to "lifting as we climb."

I end this piece as a scholar, as an Asian-American educator, and as a mother who is committed to identity-conscious education. I found that pathway while in my doctoral program. In the first days of my doctoral journey back in 2011, I did not anticipate the transformation that I would go through while writing my dissertation, hearing the stories of others, and experiencing socialization and development in higher education. There are still days when I feel like that student waving the 800–page, maroon-colored textbook in the air, demanding to know why my people were missing from the history of higher education. There are days when I am impatient about the lack of research or the misuse of data or the marginalization of my people. There are days when I wonder if we have made any changes in how we understand Asian Americans and Pacific Islanders—when I eagerly await scholarship or a new publication or book that helps us to understand the needs of our community. There are days when I wait for that change, and there are moments when I realize, that I am a part of that transformation. My contribution to the field, to the lives of other doctoral students, to the transformation of our shared approaches to graduate study, and to the educational experiences of my children are deeply rooted in the "lift as we climb" approach to community building.

My children still do not understand what my research is or why it was important. They still remember that day when "Evan spilled his M&Ms all over the carpet" and not the day that "Mommy defended her dissertation." And, that is fine with me. Because, my hope is that my contributions will not be as relevant to them and their education as we make changes. My hope is that they go through school knowing their community and their people and their worth. My hope is that they read books about the history of this country where their people are given more than eight pages in the back.

Currently, my dissertation sits on the coffee table in my living room. While it may never be opened by my children, the presence of my dissertation in our shared space serves as a reminder of what I achieved. It serves as a reminder of the work that still needs to get done. And, it serves as a reminder of what I sacrificed to cross the finish line. My first line of the dissertation was dedicated to my children, and they deserved this success as much as I did. "Joli Irene, Jada Grace, and Evan Eduardo—I began this journey toward my doctorate while you were learning how to read, write, talk, and even walk. There were many nights during which my work seemed to have been more important than your chapter books, juice boxes, and after-school activities. For four years, you may have felt as if you were not as important, and I assure you, you were. In fact, you were the reasons why I saw this journey to the end. I wanted you to see that learning about our community and our people is important. I wanted you to understand that we can achieve beyond our own imagination." Let us climb together.

REFERENCES

Barnett, B. G., & Muth, R. (2008). Using action-research strategies and cohort structures to ensure research competence for practitioner-scholar leaders. *Journal of Research on Leadership Education, 3*(1), 1–42.

Clark, S. M., & Corcoran, M. (1986). Perspectives on the professional socialization of women faculty: A case of accumulative disadvantage?. *The Journal of Higher Education, 57*(1), 20–43.

Evans, E., & Grant, C. (2008). *Mama, Ph.D: Women write about motherhood and academic life.* New Brunswick, NJ: Rutgers University Press.

Gildersleeve, R., Croom, N., & Vazquez, P. (2011). "Am I going crazy?!": A critical race analysis of doctoral education. *Equity & Excellence in Education, 44(1),* 93–114.

Tierney, W. G., & Rhoads, R. A. (1993). *Enhancing promotion, tenure and beyond: Faculty socialization as a cultural process. ASHE-ERIC Higher Education Report No. 6.* ASHE-ERIC Higher Education Reports, The George Washington University, One Dupont Circle, Suite 630, Washington, DC, 1993; 20036–1183.

Van Maanen, J., & Schein, E. (1979). Towards a theory of organizational socialization. In B. M. Staw (Ed.). *Research in Organizational Behavior, Vol. 1,* (pp 209–264). Greenwich, CT: JAI Press.

CHAPTER 24

AND THIS TOO SHALL PASS

NANCY L. ELWESS, PhD

The State University of New York at Plattsburgh, Plattsburgh, NY, USA

Here it was, the beginning of my second year of my doctoral journey, but was I ready? I was already knee deep into my research and approved dissertation topic, when my next challenge was slowly rearing its ugly head on the horizon, those dreaded comprehensive exams. It seemed just when I had put out one fire, surviving my first year, another blaze was taking root. Even though these exams were nine months away, I had to put a plan of readiness in place if I were to endure the inferno that was yet to come. After all, my mother always told me that "preparation brings success." My research and doctoral program was in the area of molecular biology; this determined how my comprehensive exams were to be administered. And, of course, my selected doctoral program proved to have the most challenging approach for these exams. "Why did I choose this program? Ugh!"

You see, the doctoral program in which one was enrolled would dictate the form of the comprehensive exams at the end of the second year. This just didn't seem fair. For example, if one was using a cellular approach to research, the "comprehensive exams" were a series of monthly quizzes started during the first month of the first year. If one passed the quiz, two points were awarded toward the total 14 points needed. Once the magic number of 14 was obtained, then one had passed one's comprehensive exams. Had one taken a biochemical approach to research, their comprehensive exams were to write a practice National Science Foundation grant based on their determined dissertation topic. This type of "exam" would have been so helpful to all graduate students in any concentration of science. I believe this approach was the best because it allowed each student to immerse themselves into the literature, which was needed not only for the grant but also for the dissertation, and it provided a great exercise in preparing graduate students for writing grants, something that was inevitable in our future. So, for me, this approach would have been the most beneficial. By far, the easiest form of the exams was for those taking an environmental approach to research. Much to their relief, they had a take-home exam that they were given a week to complete. That was it!

But, my exams, the exams for those taking a molecular approach to research, were the most taxing out of the bunch. They were composed of four different exams covering four distinctive subject areas. My four exams were in biochemistry, cell biology, genetics, and molecular biology. When I asked what areas in each of these subjects I should focus on, I was told any and all were fair game. My exams were four three-hour exams, to be taken over the course of two consecutive days. "What? What had I gotten myself into?" I had to find Martha, the smartest graduate student in the program; she had survived these exams and was still standing. I knew I had to seek her out and ask what I needed in my survival kit for getting through these gut-wrenching exams that ultimately would determine my future. Her answer was simple—discipline.

I only had nine months to prepare for my exams; this did not seem to be nearly enough time. Much like how a marathon runner trains to go the distance, I too needed to discipline myself so I could finish the race set before me. This was a case where I truly needed to be the tortoise and not the hare.

My typical day as a graduate student had me either in class, in the lab with research, or teaching a class, since my PhD was being funded by a teaching fellowship. There was no time in my day for preparing for my upcoming exams. This was done strictly at night. I typically got home at 7 pm, ate dinner from 7:00 to 7:30 pm, then studied from 7:30 until 11:30 pm, and then in bed by midnight. Discipline! Monday night was biochemistry night, studying chapters from a textbook for two hours, followed by reviewing journal articles for another two hours. Tuesday night was cell biology night, Wednesday was genetics, and Thursday molecular biology. Discipline! Friday, Saturday, and Sunday were reserved for studying for my classes, preparing my lectures, and grading papers. More discipline. When I reflect back, I am thankful that I just kept thinking "and this too shall pass," reminding myself that even though it felt like it, nine months was not an eternity.

However, it seemed like the months were flying by, and I was not nearly covering or remembering all the material I needed for these exams. I recall getting so frustrated by and jealous of the second-year graduate students in the environmental program; they shared how they would go out at night or skiing over a given weekend. They actually had a life, which I was lacking. "And this too shall pass." They were all just waiting for the time when they were to bury themselves in the library for a week, working on their take-home comprehensive exams.

Ultimately, the time had come to set the date for my exams. They were the Thursday and Friday before Memorial Day weekend. Thursday's exams were biochemistry (9 am–noon) and cell biology (1–4 pm), followed by Friday's exams of genetics and molecular biology. My exam questions were written by members of my dissertation committee. For the final two months of preparation, I changed my approach and included studying the areas of research in which my committee members were engaged. This proved to be extremely helpful, by possibly providing the motivation of their questions in each of the four disciplines. I first had laid the foundation in my initial studies, and then later incorporated what I felt was the focus.

With a week to go before my exams, I had the same nightmare over and over. It was that my exam questions were on the Russian Revolution and my answers had to be written in Russian. "And this too shall pass." I needed to get these exams over as quickly as possible for my own sanity. At long last, Thursday, day one of my exam had arrived. First up was biochemistry. Question one, "Who was awarded the Nobel Prize in Chemistry in 1980, and explain the experiment that this prize was based upon." Question two, "What successful research has been done in this area since then?" Question three, "What experiments would you design if you were to continue this research?" I remember thinking, "Are you kidding me? This is why I studied for nine months?" After I calmed down (and stopped hyperventilating), I thought about which Nobel Laureate's research might have laid the groundwork for the current research being done by one of my committee members. This approach paid off, even though at the time I thought it was a "shot in the dark." This one exam brought together a chapter from a biochemistry textbook with some of the journal articles I had read, together with the research I had done on my committee members' own research. Discipline was paying off.

By 4 pm on Friday, I had written well over 40 pages and was done with my exams. And yes, I was still standing; now the waiting game began. I was told it would take up to two weeks to get my results. In the meantime, however, friends wanted to take me out that Friday night; I just wanted to head home. My mind had been tested, I felt I had no more to give, it was completely purged of any and all thoughts. My dinner was cereal, after which I flopped across the futon in my apartment. I don't remember moving much from that spot for the next three days, challenging my mind only with watching infomercials. That was when I actually learned what an infomercial was.

Finally, the news of my comprehensive exams was given to me, the exams in which approximately 50% of all graduate students in the molecular biology program historically fail. Thankfully, I had passed, and all of this finally came to pass. Now on to face year three of my program. "And this too shall pass."

CHAPTER 25

FROM ABD, TO EdD/PhD

YETTIEVE A. MARQUEZ-SANTANA, EdD

New York University, New York City, NY, USA,

E-mail: yettieve.marquez@gmail.com

To say that I was the unlikeliest of persons to earn my doctorate degree is an understatement. However, as each year passed and my determination to ascend to a senior-level position within higher education increased, I realized I had no alternative but to earn my terminal degree. This resolution would lead me on a four-year life-changing journey marked by struggle, sacrifice, and resilience. With each accomplishment, I would overcome a hurdle and find myself doubting my resolve to reach my goal, but I drew inspiration from a simple phrase echoing in my mind: "Doctor before thirty!" This became my guidepost spurring me forward, inspiring me to press on until the moment I walked across the stage and earned my terminal degree.

Throughout my life, I have often been the "only" and became accustomed to this experience. I came to acknowledge that as a first-generation, physically disabled Latina from the South Bronx, I would be hard-pressed to find someone who fully understood my journey or experience. In many ways, the cards were stacked against me, and I had every reason not to pursue my doctoral studies, yet in the fall of 2010 I found myself enrolled in my first EdD course. According to the National Center for Education Statistics (2014), of the 10,920 educational doctorates conferred in 2013–2014, only 7.5% were earned by Latinas. That's only 819 degrees, nationally. Then if you were to further cross-tab those numbers with women, first-generation students, or doctoral students with disabilities—such as me, you would probably find few, if any, aside from me. I was the definition of an anomaly.

Regardless of your social identities, whether dominant or marginalized, many doctoral students face challenges once they reach the dissertation phase. Completing coursework is undoubtedly a huge accomplishment, but it does not complete the doctoral journey. It is disheartening to watch many women and/or people of color get stuck in the dissertation phase and never graduate. It is my hope that the five practical tips shared and lessons learned can assist you in successfully completing your dissertation and moving from all but dissertation (ABD) to EdD/PhD

Tip #1: Choose a Topic That You Love

You may have heard the statement "The best dissertation is a done dissertation." While this is definitely the end goal, the process of getting it done will be more bearable and fulfilling if you choose a topic you love. Often people choose what may be the most assessable or what is seen as a topic that can lead to faster completion. This can be a double-edged sword. I suggest avoiding situations in which you are so disinterested in your topic that you then dread working on it. Keep in mind that by the end of your dissertation journey, you will be coined as the expert on your specific topic. Therefore, choosing a topic that sparks passion and inspires writing momentum is key to completion. You will be living, breathing, sleeping, and, at times, dreaming about this working document for at least a year. Personally, it was the first thing I thought about when I woke up and the last thing I thought about before going to bed. So the topic should provoke excitement and ignite an ongoing fervor to completion. As I reflect on my life post-dissertation, I have been able to share my research at regional and national conferences in various formats and recently published two of my salient findings in a chapter within a book focused on women. It is empowering to take ownership of your work as the researcher and share this knowledge with others.

Tip #2: Select a Committee That Works for You

I feel incredibly fortunate to have selected and worked with what I considered to be the perfect dissertation committee. I was led to believe that your committee should be comprised of those who are experts in your topic or have conducted research that relates to your topic. This was not the case with my committee, and I never felt at a disadvantage. In fact, they all played unique yet essential roles throughout my process. My dissertation mentor was excellent at qualitative research and very knowledgeable of my chosen methodology, my internal reader was also very knowledgeable on qualitative research and my theoretical framework, and my external reader is a talented writer and had recently graduated from an EdD program. She was able to assist as an editor and also had American Psychological Association (APA) formatting rules fresh in her mind. She was also familiar with my topic and understood the student affairs jargon. All three were very responsive and never delayed me throughout the different phases of the dissertation. Most importantly, I felt a personal connection with them and believed they were all rooting for my success to completion. Overall, you should look forward to hear back from your committee throughout the stages of the dissertation and feel confident incorporating their many ongoing edits and suggestions. In the end, if you pick the right committee, they will guide you to the finish line.

Tip # 3: Committing the Time to Write

Recognizing my privilege and where I was positioned both professionally and personally, I had the ability to treat my dissertation as a part-time job. This was made possible because I was not married at the time, I was not a parent, and I worked as a Residence Hall Director in which I worked and lived in the same building, eliminating any commute. I adhered to a very strict and disciplined schedule. After work hours, I dedicated Monday through Thursday from 6:30 pm to 12:30 am as dissertation work time. This may seem unrealistic and a schedule leading to exhaustion and burnout, but for me it was highly effective. Although I was indeed exhausted, I worked to ensure I arranged personal time in my schedule while still maintaining a momentum of productivity. I was able to integrate my work and life by not relinquishing my weekends. This provided a separation from my academic and personal commitments. During the weekends, I wanted to be present and spend quality time with my partner, friends, and family. This also permitted time for household chores and personal errands so that I still felt like a person. Moreover, during the week, I did not compromise my lunch hour, allowing me to step away from the office and spend time with my colleagues. Lastly, I would be remiss if I did not share the importance of having a strong cohort that served as my support system every step of the way, especially beyond the classroom. I hosted "Dissertation Tuesdays," which was incredibly helpful for all who attended. Weekly my cohort would write in silence and ask pertinent questions that did not hinder anyone's productivity. We supported one another and we persevered together. Overall, this process, and its completion, is your own responsibility so you have to motivate yourself to push forward and get it done.

Tip # 4: Utilizing Helpful Resources

The unspoken reality is that research courses, dissertation seminars, your dissertation handbook, and the latest APA manual will only take you so far. To be entirely candid, I felt clueless on how to structure my dissertation and what each chapter should entail. I soon learned that the best guide is other completed dissertations. You will have access to your school's database that has every completed dissertation from that institution, and outside disserta-tions can be easily found online. I recommend saving three dissertations for your frequent reference: one that has been overseen by your dissertation mentor, allowing you to gauge their style and expectations; a dissertation that used a similar methodology and/or theoretical framework; and another that is related to your topic, which will help with finding extensive sources for your literature review and framing your survey and/or interview questions.

Notably, it is a very common practice to use at least one external service to assist with the dissertation, such as a transcriber for qualitative studies, a statistician for quantitative studies, and an editor regardless of your meth-odology. While these services are highly beneficial, they are also costly. For example, transcribing services can average around $100 per hour-long interview. Keep in mind that some dissertation mentors will require their doctoral students to transcribe their own data, so verify this before pursuing this service. If you are taking the quantitative route, a statistician can average around $800–$1000 depending on how many tables you are requesting. An editor, which can range from $45 to $75 an hour, is very beneficial before submitting your defended dissertation to your school's format review for the final approval. The editor will not only correct your writing but will also ensure you are following APA guidelines and your school's dissertation format requirements. This is an added expense but one I highly recommend as I have heard of several cases in which students successfully defended their dissertations but did not pass the external review guidelines, thus delaying their graduation. Remember, utilizing these resources does not make you less of a doctor but instead will progressively help you get to a place in which you've completed your dissertation.

Tip #5: Having Self-Confidence

It may sound cliché, but you have to have self-confidence and believe you can accomplish any task no matter the odds, difficulty, or adversity. This confidence will help take you to the finish line, and that's becoming a doctor! Throughout my doctoral journey, the greatest lesson I learned was to stop comparing myself with others. Each person's path, success, expe-rience, trials, and tribulations look different. As a first-generation college student who grew up attending failing public schools, I would compare my speaking and writing abilities to those of members of my cohort. I would always admire how eloquently and articulately they spoke and how they could write a 10-page paper in a couple of hours and, without fail, earn an A. In my case, I have physical limitations as I type with one hand, resulting in one page of text taking up to two hours to compose. Therefore, the completion of a 10-page paper generally took me approximately 20 hours. I would still receive an A, but the process of getting there looked different due to my disability. It wasn't until recently that I consider my writing one of my strongest competencies. It takes practice and patience, but it is a skill that can be mastered with time. When my dissertation mentor saw that I was in low spirits, she gave me the best advice, "Yetty, stop comparing yourself with your cohort. Once you remove this self-imposed barrier, you will be on your way to doctor." I took her advice and was able to overcome my feelings of "imposter syndrome." I accepted my personal strengths and challenges and was on my way to achieve my goal. I share this story in full vulnerability and humility in hopes that you too can overcome the feelings of not belonging and being inferiority, but will instead recognize your worth and ability to earn a doctorate regardless of the intersections of your marginalized identities.

25.1 LESSONS LEARNED

Having a strong support system is nonnegotiable. It is important to ask yourself, "How will this journey impact my responsibilities? Will my loved ones be understanding of the time commitment required?" My doctorate would not have been possible without the unwavering support of my family, friends, and cohort. I am a firm believer in the importance of writing down your goals, reviewing them, visualizing them, but also having your personal "board of trustees" hold you accountable. My partner was often selfless and never made me feel guilty when I couldn't spend quality time with him once I entered the dissertation phase. My cohort operated in a "we are in this together" mindset. My supervisor provided the most important aspect of support, which was flexibility at my workplace. This unwavering support, accompanied with having the confidence to persevere against all obstacles, was necessary. These mechanisms kept my eyes on the goal—"Doctor before 30"—until I successfully achieved it. Ultimately, relationships matter, and this process can't be done alone, so having a support system is necessary.

Earning a doctorate can be academically, personally, mentally, emotionally, physically, and financially taxing. Learn from my mistakes by not comparing yourself with others and remember that your doctoral journey is your own. It is a path that is filled with personal sacrifices that may make you question if this taxing lifestyle is worth it. Completing the dissertation is a long and arduous process, but I have no regrets, and graduating was by far the happiest day of my life. Realistically speaking, when unexpected life challenges occur, you may feel stuck in the ABD phase. Should you have to push back graduation, it is completely acceptable to do so as long as you are determined to get back on track and make it to the finish line. Ultimately, anything is possible if you have the persistence to persevere until the end goal and that's—Doctor!

REFERENCE

National Center for Education Statistics. Table 324.25. 2015. Retrieved from: https://nces. ed.gov/programs/digest/d15/tables/dt15_324.25.asp?current=yes.

CHAPTER 26

MAKING THE PhD HAPPEN: STAGE 3

ANNE TOOLAN ROWLEY, PhD

The College of Saint Rose, Albany, NY, USA

From the second year of the program to the candidacy stage, much happens with regard to completion of required courses, the passing of comprehensive exams, the selection of a research topic, and the preparation and defense of a doctoral proposal. Ali & Kohun (2006) point out that during these few years, periods of social isolation may occur.

26.1 STAGE III: SECOND YEAR THROUGH CANDIDACY

The next few years of part-time study seemed to go on forever. However, after seeking and securing a new faculty advisor, the advice that I needed for course selections improved. My new advisor seemed to show interest in my plans and recognized my goal to bridge my language development background with literacy achievement. Selection of courses was still a problem at times as my part-time status required a six-credit enrollment each semester, and a needed prerequisite course for the program might not have been available for additional one or two semesters. As mentioned earlier, this is a common scheduling pattern for doctoral programs based on small classes. Course scheduling is determined with full-time enrollment in mind. As a result, this required me to take an extra course at times to maintain my status. By the second and third year, I was able to acquire suggestions from some of the full-time students as to which courses in other departments would complement this major. Advisement sessions were more productive when I was prepared with these suggestions that needed department approval. These courses were designed to review literacy topics and to prepare students for the comprehensive exam.

At my institution, two comprehensive exam options were available. The first choice was an in-person written exam for several hours. Questions were generated by the faculty and presented to the examinee on a specified date.

The second option, which I selected, was to prepare major papers in three domains related to literacy. In some of the required courses, the topics could be explored in written projects. However, limited information was given on what was expected, and I sought advice from full-time students who had already completed the second option. During some semesters, I took extra credits to complete an independent study with a professor whose specialty was in the area of one of the domains. The end result was the submission of three 50-page papers with extensive bibliographies. For doctoral students, this can be a turning point. Some of my peers opted to postpone the comprehensive exam or added course time as a result of struggling with the papers needed for the second option. As I breathed a sigh of relief when my papers were accepted, the next layer of stress began. During this time, social isolation comes into play again. The few acquaintances that I had made during the various courses began to slip away because we were at different junctions in the program. As mentioned, some opted to extend another semester to complete the comprehensive exams while others had moved into the dissertation stage ahead of me.

Even at the beginning of the program, the idea of a dissertation looms before the student. It is a topic frequently discussed among the full- and part-time students depending on their year and semester. Throughout the time for courses and preparation for doctoral candidacy, students are focusing on topics of interest that may become the idea for a dissertation. The process requires selecting the topics for research, narrowing the focus, and working with their advisor to prepare a proposal for presentation to the full faculty. Here the advisor should be interested in the topic, have expertise in the area, and be supportive of the endeavor. In preparation for a proposal, the literature review is done, the research questions are established, and the plan for the research is designed. Although the proposal is only an overview of the research that is ahead, it needs to be well developed and easily understood by the full faculty who will vote to accept or reject the plan.

I was fortunate that my academic advisor was knowledgeable of my area of interest and eventually willing to become the chair of my dissertation committee. However, there was no preparation for what could be accepted as a proposal. The advisor can offer suggestions related to shaping research questions, recruiting participants, and determining the statistical approach to the problem. The format for the defense of the proposal might vary. Although defenses do not occur frequently, depending on the size of the department, the dates and times are generally posted so that students may observe. I was not so fortunate to have an opportunity to observe in advance. My advisor stated that I would be allowed 20 minutes to present the proposal and then respond to questions from the faculty. If I went over the 20 minutes, I would be signaled to stop even if I had not reached the end. Moreover, my advisor instructed that her students should practice the prepared PowerPoint™ presentation with her before a date would be scheduled for the defense.

The day finally arrived, and two of us were scheduled, each with different advisors. I was introduced first. As I was about to begin, a fire alarm was activated, and we needed to evacuate the premises. It was not just a drill, and we were instructed to remain outside until an "all clear" was given. Twenty-five minutes later, we rushed up three flights of stairs to the conference room, and I was told that I might have less time to present. I managed to stick to the time and fielded several faculty questions. The decision on the acceptance of the proposal comes later, after the faculty discusses the student's readiness for candidacy.

I was expected to remain in the conference room as the next student defended her proposal. I had assumed that the guidelines for the proposal presentation were specified by the department, so I was greatly surprised when the student was allowed to speak for 45 minutes without any signal to stop after 20 minutes. Since we each had a different advisor, this was my first experience with the fact that expectations might be different from now on. Discussions with others confirmed that the next part of the process could be a unique experience. Within a few days, I was notified that my proposal was accepted, and the ideas suggested by the faculty during the defense should be pursued.

Doctoral credits are accrued when working on the dissertation and submitting scheduled chapters to the committee chair and the members. Now I was considered a doctoral candidate, ready to invite faculty to guide me through the last major stage of the process. This is a challenging moment as students are not offered any guidance on this process. My experience was to review faculty backgrounds and areas of expertise. While taking courses, a student will not encounter every faculty member as an instructor. I relied on fellow candidates who were further along in the process for advice. Also, through the "grapevine," one learns about faculty members' personalities, engagement skills with students, and promptness with returning classwork in a timely fashion.

Selecting a collegial and collaborative committee is important. When inviting a faculty member to be on a committee, it is essential to explain the intended research and seek someone with genuine interest in the topic. I needed to select members who had experience on dissertation committees and were willing to provide me with that support. As I selected my committee, I informed the committee chair of the other potential committee members and inquired if they had worked together in the past. Fellow doctoral candidates often suggest whether certain faculty members respond with chapter feedback in a timely fashion. It was important for me to discuss with the chair what her expectations would be for the other committee members. When an outside committee member is selected, it is important to describe her/his qualifications that make the person an important asset to the committee. Since my extra member was in another state, I introduced her to the committee via phone and email contacts. Initially, this was a positive move. However, although she requested that she be included in all committee meetings via conference calls, this did not always happen or it was assumed that I would make the arrangement. The committee met her in person when she traveled east to be present at my dissertation defense.

Knowing the steps and requirements for the completion of the dissertation are also learned on one's own. There was no orientation to the process for me and, in my time, no detailed online source to review. I was fortunate that my academic advisor was interested in my topic and agreed to be my dissertation committee chair. The department required a committee composed of a minimum of two additional department faculty members with the option to invite another professional outside the department. I invited two faculty members with whom I had taken courses and had developed a good rapport. Being able to invite an additional member outside of the department was a bonus for me as I invited a colleague from my profession who later was instrumental in explaining aspects of my work that were new to my committee members.

As I invited the additional faculty members, I considered if they were planning a sabbatical or possible retirement during the next two years. Any break in their availability would mean a postponement in my plan for completion. My committee consisted of three faculty women who were renowned in their fields and with whom I had completed coursework. My additional member was an outstanding professional whose work was highly regarded. Although I was proud to have made it this far, I was fearful of the continued journey ahead. As so many before me had come to this juncture, we all feared the possibility of stopping along the way and becoming another candidate designated as "ABD," if we did not finish.

REFERENCE

Ali, S., & Kohun, F. (2006). Dealing with isolation feelings at IS doctoral programs. *International Journal of Doctoral Studies, 1,* 21–33. Available at: http://ijds.org/Volume1/ IJDSv1p021-033Ali13.pdf.

CHAPTER 27

THE BIG PUSH

CHERIE L. KING, ScD

Central Connecticut State University, New Britain, CT, USA

E-mail: kingche@ccsu.edu

In the second year of my program, my responsibilities expanded into a teaching fellowship. I taught one master's-level course each semester at Boston University. I was given excellent supervision from my mentor and other faculty regarding pedagogy, teaching skills, how to handle a class, and designing class activities. I also took on additional adjunct teaching in a counselor education program in my state. It's what I had been waiting to do: to teach live students in a classroom. I was so happy in the classroom but nervous. Did I know what I was talking about? How could I make the dry material interesting? Was I engaging students? Was I helping students to be introspective and grow? These questions whirled in my mind as I drove home from each class. I questioned my competence as a counselor and ability to teach what I knew. Did I know anything? The more I studied and prepared, the less I felt I knew.

I had supervised and trained rehabilitation counselors in my previous employment, but pre-professional teaching and supervision of graduate students was different. Clinical supervision was an art as far as I was concerned. I read as much as I could about different models, tried new techniques with my interns, and sought out feedback from faculty. As I taught more and sought feedback, I gradually became more confident. As I relaxed more and allowed myself to be authentic, I found my way and developed my own style as a teacher and supervisor. This is where the seeds of my dissertation research were planted.

I completed the remaining coursework in my third year, which involved research courses, teaching, and clinical supervision. Prior to starting my doctoral program, I was active in the leadership of my professional association, and I was asked to represent the organization on an accreditation board.

The board, The Council on Rehabilitation Education (CORE), accredited graduate-level rehabilitation counseling programs in the United States. I could integrate my service on this board into my program. I learned accreditation standards, reviewed and evaluated other graduate programs, made recommendations to the programs, and wrote reports. This immersion in the graduate accreditation process was crucial in my development as a counselor educator. I observed and evaluated other programs, which gave me an in-depth understanding of program design, curriculum, and the nuances from program to program. I spent many hours dedicated to this organization and moved into leadership as chair of its Standards and Accreditation Commission. My mentor and program faculty were very supportive. They felt this was an important and unique experience that doctoral students in my field do not necessarily receive as part of the doctoral program. I used my knowledge and experience in accreditation standards to consult with the counselor education program where I was a part-time adjunct instructor. The program had been in existence for 25 years and had not pursued accreditation. I completed a comprehensive program evaluation, made curriculum updates and changes, completed the self-study, and coordinated and led the site visit, which resulted in the program's first national accreditation in rehabilitation counselor education.

In my fourth year, I took on an additional role that I considered part of my education. I accepted a part-time position as a training coordinator under a federal training grant for community rehabilitation programs. This exposed me to the community-based training of entry-level rehabilitation personnel. Unlike graduate training of counselors, the job provided me with a broader perspective of the continuum of education and training needed to provide services to individuals with disabilities. It also required a lot of travel and time away from my family. While this was a great opportunity, it created more stress for my family and me. After four years, the demands of school, work, and family responsibilities were taking its toll on me, the kids, and my marriage. The time I was away from home was difficult, and when I was home, it was tense. I could feel the divide between us. My husband was angry, I was angry, and the kids were stressed.

Although limited research exists on the experiences of female doctoral students, including mothers, a few studies show that they face uniquely complex challenges compared with their male counterparts, including family concerns or relationship conflict (Maher, Ford, & Thompson, 2004; Trepal, Stinchfield, & Haiyasoso, 2014; Willis & Carmichael, 2011). I experienced these challenges firsthand. I could not figure out a way to make everyone happy and fulfill my dream. This was the only time I considered quitting my doctoral program. My husband never asked me to quit or modify my pace. But I could feel myself becoming resentful. It was not pretty and created more strain on our marriage. I was relying on him to hold everything together in my absence, and he was looking for some relief after four years. We had to dig down hard to figure it out and, at times, it did not seem that either of us was satisfied with our compromises or choices. We considered separating until I was done with my degree, but I felt incredible guilty putting my degree ahead of my family. I was in a classic bind—I did not want to quit my program or my marriage. We sought counseling and negotiated our way to the end, which worked for us and the kids. I also quit the training coordinator job.

Fortunately, I completed my academic coursework and teaching experiences soon after, which created more flexibility for me. I walked into the comprehensive exam phase of my program ready. I was given a choice to complete the traditional written examinations or complete a comprehensive review of literature as a springboard into my dissertation. I chose the latter. This was an excellent experience for me to dive into the literature. I was required to have a "comp" committee that comprised my mentor and two other faculty members from the program. All the work I had completed up to this point had been focused on educational standards and clinical supervision for rehabilitation counselors. Most of my professional experience was in the private rehabilitation counseling field, which was a unique area of practice. I wanted to combine my knowledge of this area of practice with my developing research interests.

I choose to explore clinical supervision for rehabilitation counselors in the private sector. There was no existing research on this topic so I knew I was onto an important area for examination. As I dove into the literature, I realized that there were only a few researchers in my field who had examined clinical supervision. I studied the literature and became proficient in the critical analysis of study results. My mentor was instrumental in supporting the direction I was taking with the topic. I also discovered the importance of reaching out to other researchers. There was one researcher who published most of the literature on clinical supervision in rehabilitation counseling. I attended all his presentations at conferences and then emailed him. Fortunately for me, he did not think I was stalking him. He was incredibly nice and generous with his thoughts on my research focus and suggested several ideas when I moved into the dissertation phase. He also became my outside reviewer for my dissertation.

Completing the review of research, writing, and submitting drafts to my committee took several months but served as the basis for my dissertation research topic. Although many doctoral programs have different comprehensive exam processes, I felt this was the most valuable for me to springboard into the dissertation phase. I completed the final review of literature—chapter two for my dissertation. Part of the comprehensive exam process was to present the review of literature to my committee as well as a brief proposal of possible research questions and design of the study. This was a great experience as I had a taste of what the dissertation defense would feel like. I successfully presented for my comprehensive exam and was approved to start the dissertation stage.

After I had completed my comprehensive exam and before starting the dissertation proposal phase, a full-time faculty opportunity at my local university became available. I had been working part time as an adjunct instructor and then as emergency hire for this program for three years and had completed their accreditation. It was a strong program, and I knew I had a lot to offer them as a full-time faculty member. I applied as an ABD and, after the search process, I was hired to start in a full-time tenure-track position in the fall of 2007 with the understanding that I was expected to complete my dissertation and degree by the end of 2008. I was thrilled but did not realize how hard it would be to be on the tenure track and complete a dissertation at the same time. And, one more thing, I still had school-aged kids.

I approached both the new job and the dissertation with the same determination I had over the previous four years. I knew it was not a normal process for any doctoral student to get the job before the degree, but for me the life of a full-time assistant professor was conducive to have more flexibility to manage work, family, data collection, analysis, and writing. I spent one summer break driving to upstate New York and around New England to conduct interviews; my daughter was my research assistant. This was the light at the end of the tunnel, and I could see it.

REFERENCES

Maher, M. A., Ford, M. E., & Thompson, C. M. (2004). Degree progress of women doctoral students: Factors that constrain, facilitate, and differentiate. *The Review of Higher Education, 27*(3), 385–408. https://muse-jhu-edu.ccsu.idm.oclc.org/article/53327.

Trepal, H., Stichfield, T., & Haiyasoso, M. (2014). Great expectations: Doctoral student mothers in counselor education. *Adultspan Journal, 13*(1), 30–45. DOI:10.1002/j.2161.2014.00024.x.

Willis, B., & Carmichael, K. D. (2011). The lived experiences of late-stage doctoral student attrition in counselor education. *The Qualitative Report, 16*(1), 192–207. http://nova.edu/sss/QR/QR16-1/willis.pdf.

CHAPTER 28

ADVANCING THROUGH CANDIDACY: SELECTING A DISSERTATION TOPIC, CHAIR, AND COMMITTEE

MAUREEN E. SQUIRES, EdD

State University of New York at Plattsburgh, Plattsburgh, NY, USA

E-mail: msqui001@plattsburgh.edu

28.1 INTRODUCTION

Ten years ago, I never would have imagined writing this chapter. In 2006, after five years teaching high-school English at a rural public school in New York, I took a leave of absence to pursue doctoral study. Initially, my intent was to gain more knowledge and skills to apply in the secondary classroom. I wanted to better serve my diverse students. (I taught in a school district where one-fourth of the students are Native American and classes are inclusive.) My goal was not to leave the high-school classroom for the halls of academia, but here I am. That professional journey is a story for another time.

I was one of the few doctoral students in my program to matriculate full time. I was also one of the few who successfully completed two programs (an EdD in Educational Theory and Practice and a CAS in Educational Leadership) simultaneously and within five years. I began doctoral study at the age of 27 and defended my dissertation at the age of 32. This was a period of my life marked by, among other things, social isolation. So much of my time and energy was devoted to doctoral work that I sacrificed meaningful connections with friends and family. Even peer support was limited (save two close relationships), as I did not fit the typical profile of doctoral students enrolled in this program nor was there an established culture of systemic peer support in the School of Education. So how did I survive these five years of doctoral work? I drew on personal fortitude and the support of faculty.

In their research on successful doctoral degree completion, Jairam & Kahl (2012) describe the social supports and/or hindrances provided by three groups: academic friends, family, and faculty. Moreover, they cite numerous studies that indicate doctoral student attrition primarily is linked to stress and/or social isolation. Ali & Kohun (2007), in their research on attrition among doctoral students, generated a four-stage framework for analyzing causes and remedies to social isolation. The stages, in order, include preadmission to enrollment, the first year of the program, the second year through candidacy, and the dissertation. In this chapter, I present my experience navigating the stage of candidacy, specifically in selecting a dissertation topic, chair, and committee. Additionally, I describe how faculty support can work as a positive factor during this stage. Finally, I share tips for navigating this process.

28.2 SELECTING A DISSERTATION TOPIC

I wanted my dissertation to be unique, powerful, and contribute something novel and meaningful to the world of education. Building from my recent teaching experience, I was fascinated with anything related to Native American education. I realized that I had a lot to learn in this field and that I wanted to give voice to a historically marginalized group of people. Before starting my first doctoral course, I *knew* Native American education would be the focus of my dissertation. More accurately, I *hoped*, even *expected*, it would be the focus. Three proposals later, it was not.

Starting a doctoral program (at least one with a broad focus such as Educational Theory and Practice) with an idea for your dissertation topic is great. Starting a doctoral program with your mind set on a specific dissertation topic is not great. If you have a general idea of your dissertation topic, you can build this into your coursework. For instance, in the Special Education course, I focused on overrepresentation of Native American students in stigmatized disability categories. In the Discourse Analysis course, I researched language patterns and participation structures of Native American students in elementary and secondary schools. In the Curriculum courses, I explored theories and practices that support culturally relevant pedagogy. In this way, each course contributed to my *anticipated* dissertation. Without realizing it, I was building elements of the literature review, theoretical framework, methodology, and research questions of my prospectus. Moreover, each course was personally and professionally relevant because I brought my passion and curiosity to the course. By making the courses "my own," I motivated myself to engage, find meaning, and not simply view the course as a required element to be completed.

Selecting, and committing to, my *actual* dissertation topic was a laborious, anxiety-provoking, and agonizing journey. Initially, I found inspiration for my dissertation topic from a required reading, *Black Teachers on Teaching* (Foster, 1997). I was interested in the content of the stories told and the method used to share the stories. This would be the perfect model for my future, though never accomplished, dissertation: *Native American Teachers on Teaching*. I began exploring the topic and found limited publications. I discussed my topic with a former colleague who was Native American, and she believed the study had merit. I wrote and defended my first prospectus. After making revisions, I was given approval by my committee to begin my dissertation.

I spent one semester trying to recruit a sufficient number of participants but was unsuccessful. As a White woman pursuing a dissertation with Native American participants, I was an outsider. I needed time to build trust and rapport with participants; I also needed to rely on respondents, via snowball sampling, to locate future participants. This was difficult due to the few participants who fit this category. In the 2011–2012 academic year, Native American teachers comprised 5% of the entire public and private elementary and secondary schools teacher population (USDOE, 2013). Knowing that my graduate funding was limited and that recruiting more participants would take time, I decided to abandon my first dissertation topic. I was disappointed.

Still determined to research in the field of Native American education, I spent one year developing a second prospectus. This time, I intended to explore how Native American culture was represented and experienced by students and teachers in a K–8 school for Native American students. I read widely for the literature review and methodology. I sought advice from Native American scholars and professors. I worked with members of the Nation to gain permissions and entrée. I defended my second prospectus and received approval from my dissertation committee. But at the last minute, school leadership at the research site changed, and I was denied access to the school by a new principal. I was devastated.

It was at this point that a faculty mentor gave me some advice. She told me, "A good dissertation is a defended dissertation." She also convinced me that the two initial dissertation attempts were not failed; they were simply topics meant to be pursued in the future. I needed to complete a dissertation that was quality, not spectacular, and that I found interesting, albeit not my ideal topic. At my university, I was simultaneously enrolled in an EdD program and a CAS program. When I opened myself to the possibility of a dissertation in educational leadership, opportunities emerged. When one door closes, another opens. The third dissertation topic was the charm. (Choose your idiom.) I defended another prospectus, conducted the study, and successfully defended my *actual* dissertation: *Educational Leadership at Lyon Big Picture School, a Non-traditional High School: A Case Study*.

Tips

Tip #1: In the beginning of your doctoral program, consider your dissertation topic globally, and remain open to other options. Do not cleave steadfastly to your initial dissertation topic.

Tip #2: Keep a log of all potential dissertation topics. No matter how rough the idea is, record it. This serves two purposes: (1) retaining a record for you to peruse in the future and (2) transferring ideas from your head to the paper, thereby unclogging your mind and freeing it to ponder other ideas.

Tip #3: To the extent possible, individualize your coursework to your intellectual and professional interests, questions, or concerns. When the opportunity arises, dabble with elements of your *potential* dissertation topic (s) in coursework. Doing so early on provides insight about your true passion (or not) for the topic and can reveal possibilities and pitfalls of pursing the topic later on.

Tip #4: Plan with the end in mind. As educators, we often talk about "backward design." When designing lessons, we identify desired results, then plan instruction to help students reach these goals. Do the same when selecting and designing your dissertation topic. Determine where you want to be professionally after the dissertation: doing research, teaching in higher education, working for a nonprofit organization, returning to your previous position, and so forth. Then align your dissertation topic with your desired career trajectory. The dissertation is the last project you complete before re-entering your career. It's also the project you know the best. Make this the springboard to your next professional step.

Tip #5: Select a doable dissertation topic. Choose a topic where you can readily recruit participants and gain entrée in a timely manner.

Tip #6: Resolve to complete a quality dissertation, not necessarily a perfect or an award-winning dissertation. I am not suggesting lowering your standards. Rather, I encourage you to recognize (1) that your dissertation will not be without limitations; (2) that given unlimited time, it could be revised ad nauseum; and (3) that it will be challenged by scholars. Be prepared to address these points. Also, remember the advice of my mentor: "A good dissertation is a defended dissertation." You will have time after graduation to craft your magnum opus.

28.3   SELECTING A DISSERTATION CHAIR AND COMMITTEE

Just as selecting a dissertation topic was challenging, so too was selecting my final dissertation chair and committee. I was assigned an advisor (Dr. Northe*) when I matriculated in the EdD program. We were matched by degree earned; since I had recently obtained a master's degree in Special Education, I was paired with the coordinator of the Special Education Department. Dr. Northe and I "fit" well as advisor–advisee during coursework and my first two dissertation proposals. She was highly regarded in her field and knowledgeable about Native American education. Yet as I moved farther away from the areas of special education and Native American education, our "fit" was no longer snug.

Matching expertise and personalities is important. I was anxious to ask Dr. Northe to step down as my dissertation chair. After all, we had worked closely together for four years, and I did not want to offend or disappoint her. Again, my mentor offered advice. She recommended I identify faculty members who could contribute to my dissertation in regard to content, methodology, and mechanics. She also suggested I consider the group dynamics among committee members. Once I closely examined these factors, I realized that I wanted my advisor on my dissertation committee, but in a new role. I would ask her to serve as a committee member who would scrutinize my methodology and mechanics. This allowed me to invite a new faculty member as my dissertation chair. As coordinator of the educational leadership program, my new chair (Dr. Oliver*) would "fit" a dissertation in educational leadership quite well. In my head, this shift in committee membership seemed logical. I spoke with Dr. Northe, who was receptive of the idea. Then I spoke with Dr. Oliver. I had another hurdle to overcome: convincing her to become my dissertation chair.

Dr. Oliver had clear expectations, which she explained at our first meeting. She required a 40-page proposal that would help her determine if she would assume the role of dissertation chair. After that, she required I submit the first three chapters of my dissertation before entering the field (to collect data). She also suggested that I design a strictly qualitative or quantitative dissertation, saving mixed methods or arts-based methods (methods that are less

---

*Pseudonyms were used to protect privacy.

traditional and sometimes harder to pass through the dissertation committee) for future work. Initially, this seemed overwhelming. But Dr. Oliver's transparency and requests made the next phase of the dissertation feasible. I submitted the proposal followed by the first three chapters. She became my new chair. And my dissertation commenced. Compared to selecting a topic, chair, and committee, collecting, analyzing, and presenting data for my dissertation was straightforward. Dr. Oliver continued to support me through the rest of the dissertation process. This, too, is a story for another time.

Tips.

Tip #7: Take multiple courses with multiple professors. Attend colloquia, seminars, and office hours where you can interact with professors outside of class. Get to know as many professors as possible and let them get to know you. Learn about each other's research interests and approach to work. This information will help you design the best committee for you.

Tip #8: Talk with graduates and doctoral candidates who are farther along than you. They can provide insight on what to do and what to avoid as you craft your dissertation committee and move into and through candidacy.

Tip #9: Have a backup plan. Consider ways to reposition faculty members or identify other faculty members to invite to the committee. My initial chair no longer fit because I changed topics. Sometimes committee members go on sabbatical, retire, or have medical issues that prevent them from fully participating. These are all legitimate reasons why you may want or need to restructure your committee.

Tip #10: Select committee members based on expertise and work relationships. Each member should substantially contribute to your dissertation in terms of content, methodology, or mechanics. Ideally, they would have similar expectations and philosophies to facilitate collaboration and move the dissertation forward.

28.4   SURVIVING CANDIDACY

Selecting, and committing to, a dissertation topic, chair, and committee is not necessarily easy, even if you have been contemplating these ideas from the beginning of your program. These are decisions that deserve a great deal of consideration. Be passionate about your dissertation topic, but not overly attached. Prepare to change research directions and/or committee membership and open to new paths. Be content with defending a rigorous and doable dissertation. Capitalize on faculty support (from mentors, advisors, and chairs). Would I do this all again? Yes, with modifications. Particularly, I would not attempt to design the perfect, most novel dissertation. Nor would I try to survive the doctoral experience single-handedly, as if proving that I was strong enough and capable enough to handle the work on my own. Such self-imposed social isolation is not productive. I would seek out and trust the advice of those farther advanced in candidacy and of my chair. I would regard the words of my mentor: "A good dissertation is a defended dissertation."

REFERENCES

Ali, A.; Kohun, F. (2007). Dealing with social isolation to minimize doctoral attrition—a four stage framework. *International Journal of Doctoral Studies, 2,* 33–49. Retrieved from: http://www.informingscience.org/Journals/IJDS/Articles?Volume=2-2007&Search.

Foster, M. (1997). *Black Teachers on Teaching.* New York, NY: New Press.

Jairam, D., & Kahl, D. H., Jr.(2012). Navigating the doctoral experience: The role of social support in successful degree completion. *International Journal of Doctoral Studies, 7,* 311–329.

U.S. Department of Education (USDOE). (2013). *Table 209.10: Number and percentage distribution of teachers in public and private elementary and secondary schools, by selected teacher characteristics: Selected years, 1987–1988 through 2011–2012.* National Center for Education Statistics. Washington, DC: U.S. Government Printing Office. https://nces.ed.gov/programs/digest/d13/tables/dt13_209.10.asp.

CHAPTER 29

WHEN MOTHERHOOD AND PhD COLLIDE: THE POWER OF POSITIVE MESSAGES

KATE BRESONIS MCKEE, MAT, MSEd, Doctoral Candidate

Massachusetts College of Pharmacy and Health Sciences, Boston, MA, USA

During my interview process at the institution where I ultimately chose to pursue my doctoral degree, a professor who was on my interview panel made what might have seemed to him like an innocuous statement, but it had a profound impact on me. He said that some faculty recommended to their students to minimize or delay any major life changes while pursuing a degree. Although I remained outwardly unfazed at his statement, on the inside I was equally astounded and unsurprised to hear this. My mind scrolled through the pages of literature I had read about doctoral attrition rates and the disproportionate challenges and differential socialization experiences women have been known to encounter in academia compared with their male counterparts. A surprise came, however, as he quickly followed his initial statement by saying with a grin and a chuckle that the majority of the doctoral students he advised went through at least three major life events while in the program (moving, getting married or divorced, changing jobs, having children) and still managed to finish successfully. I let out the breath I was holding in and embraced the sincerity of his statement. This might be the right program for me, I thought.

I revisited his words many times over the years, and they have operated as a source of strength for me. In the few short months after accepting that institution's offer of admission, I said goodbye to my colleagues, friends, and family in Albany, NY, moved with my two cats into my then fiancée's, (now husband's) apartment in Boston, started my first semester of doctoral coursework with my new cohort, began a full-time job at a Boston-based college, and started planning a wedding.

His message became reinforced as more life events continued to emerge over the various stages of the program. What I appreciated most about his sly admission is that by saying it, he sent an important message that moving through life and moving through a PhD are not mutually exclusive. In fact, as he and I would discuss later, life events can and do serve as great motivators, shifting our worldview just enough (and sometimes dramatically) to crystalize what is important to us. And, more often than not, what is important to us often connects us to what we believe is important to examine in research contexts. In other words, who we are and what we care about shapes how we conceive of, conceptualize, and interpret our research.

Writing this chapter provides a reflective opportunity to look back over the social and academic successes and challenges along the road to obtain the PhD. The PhD program I have been traversing is marked by some special features, both challenging and supportive, that are important to the context in which I discuss my degree experience. Some of these include

- A focus on underrepresented populations and issues of social justice in higher education.
- 72 credits of coursework over three full-time semesters a year, including a rather grueling summer session where students take two three-credit courses over three weeks—attending classes Monday–Thursday from 9 am to 4 pm (with additional weeks before and after devoted to pre-reading and final exams/papers).
- A cohort model where you travel through the bulk of your coursework with the same group of students, who become learning partners and, in my experience, a close-knit community of supportive friends with whom the doctoral experience is shared.
- The expectation that students are pursuing the degree while simultaneously employed in the field.
- Limited or no funding for research or teaching assistantships.
- A race- and gender-diverse faculty who are highly dedicated to the student population and who are willing to engage in co-scholarship experiences that demystify the processes of peer reviewed publishing and presenting.
- Invited student participation and input in many facets of the department and program, including assessment, mission statement review and revision, new faculty hiring, and other similar initiatives.

Within and across these and other structural and cultural features of the program, messages are explicitly and tacitly embedded. Today, as I write, my infant daughter naps next to me. Becoming a first-time mother at the age of 43 has sharpened the lens of my retrospective meaning-making on the nuances of my PhD program, illuminating socialization experiences and messages that have shaped me as a scholar-practitioner, and now shape me as a mother-scholar-practitioner.

Becoming a scholar while also becoming a mother has underscored the significance of peer and faculty support. I think of the critical importance of the cohort model that is a core structural feature of my PhD program. I consider how many of my cohort mates, in addition to working full-time, were parents (or perhaps caregivers in some other way) themselves as they moved through the program and how heavily I am drawing from what they taught me about parallel processing of work, family, and PhD. I think of my advisor and dissertation chair, a highly accomplished early career scholar, who gave birth to her two daughters while I was her research assistant. I remember feeling somewhat puzzled when she told me that having her daughters was "the best thing she has ever done" despite her inspiring record of scholarship that I saw as an immutable accomplishment. Now that I am a new mother, her stories and experiences have come alive for me in a different way. I think about how she carried her first born on her hip when she accepted an award for her dissertation work from our most prestigious scholarly association. I think about how she was in the throes of caring for her growing family while moving through her early tenure years. I think about all the research projects, co-authorships, and conference activities we navigated during that time and how our working dynamic morphed from long sense-making discussions and literature searches that resulted in fun deliberations to short but highly productive bursts of scholarly production. It was so impactful for me to see that, in fact, both approaches were equally successful in carrying out and publishing innovative and creative research.

I draw now from what she modeled for me then—how we should make our mother-scholar roles visible and not "hide" our children from academe, how efficiently scholarship could move forward in short bursts, and how boundaries could be redrawn and deadlines renegotiated—although I had to wade through a bit of uncertainty to reach my current comfort level with this new way of being.

The end of my first trimester of pregnancy coincided with my dissertation proposal defense. The proposal defense is a pivotal milestone on the road to degree completion; it is when you formally present your first three dissertation chapters to your committee. At that presentation, the committee provides feedback, asks clarifying questions, and ultimately decides if your research is designed and framed soundly enough to seek Institutional Review

Board (IRB) approval and begin data collection. Although my committee chair knew that I was expecting a baby (and was very excited about it), I was trying to decide when and how to share this news with my other two committee members as it was still fairly early in the first trimester and my husband and I had only just shared the news with our close family. All too familiar with the well-documented challenges faced by women in academia as a whole and, more specifically, the added challenges of women who also must contend with family care-taking responsibilities, I was negotiating a combination of anxiety and self-doubt. What will be their outward and inward response to my news? Will I find the time to finish this degree? If so, how? Will I become an attrition statistic?

I chose to share the news with them just after I had successfully defended my dissertation proposal. I also began sharing the news with other faculty in the program. I was met with overwhelmingly supportive and encouraging responses from male and female faculty alike. Several women faculty members shared stories about how they wrote dissertations with their newborns strapped to them, assuring me that making progress was possible but not an imperative and encouraging me to focus on the baby, health, and family. Ultimately, the best route for me was to be in the moment with my newborn and family while re-envisioning my new timeline for dissertation completion. Now that my daughter is four-and-a-half-months old, I am beginning to activate my new mother-scholar timeline—in short productive bursts as I was fortunate to have modeled for me by my advisor and committee chair.

In providing this glimpse into my story, my hope was to illuminate how positive messages transmitted by my PhD program allowed me to reimagine and reposition myself as mother-scholar. In sharing this perspective, I am not suggesting that other less positive messages were absent. They were there too, unspoken perhaps, but there. The competing messages I wrestled with told me that the PhD should be my sole focus. Competing messages suggested to me that having children while in pursuit of a PhD made me a less serious or committed scholar, which in turn, would result in fewer scholarly accomplishments, career stagnation, or worse. The option to "stop the clock" is not available for PhD students or mid-career professionals. And, even when such an option is available, like it was for my advisor, I observed her sifting through a mire of mixed cultural and institutional messages and advice, both solicited and unsolicited. She chose to keep the clock running. I often wonder what I would have done if I had been in her shoes. The complex and potentially damaging messages were present, but they were unable to withstand the torque and frequency of the positive messages I received.

Today, despite the major life change that accompanies motherhood, I can confidently envision a successful dissertation defense and degree completion in the coming twelve months. What could be a very isolating and uncertain time in a PhD program has been made less uncertain by the many supportive and reinforcing messages I have received from faculty, committee members, and peers. So although an approved IRB has been waiting patiently for me to start my data collection, it has been the greatest pleasure to choose to let it wait and to fully enjoy my new daughter and priceless family moments during this special and fleeting time. And now I cannot imagine my doctoral journey without my daughter.

CHAPTER 30

PROMISE AND POTENTIAL: HOW I LOST AND FOUND MY SCHOLARLY COUNSELING SELF

KAREN L. MACKIE, PhD

Warner School of Education, Rochester University, Rochester, NY, USA

The story I will tell about the doctoral journey concerns moving from the comprehensive exams to the dissertation process. For me, this was a vulnerable moment in my development as a person, as a researcher, and as a future counselor educator. In retrospect, it appears there were a number of things that made me lose confidence in my ability to cross the threshold to the scholarly life from my pre-dissertation location as a practicing counselor and as a woman. Perhaps my story and reflections will resonate with your own.

In constructing my comprehensive exam questions, I had chosen to work with a faculty committee of the three people I had learned a lot from during my coursework and whom I perceived to be the best theoreticians available in my program. Only later did I learn that I had made a classic, doctoral student mistake. In reflecting back from my current feminist understandings, I would submit that this is the mistake of bright young women in many academic disciplines who misunderstand that being able to hold your own in discussion and debate with leading faculty will make you attractive to them, but that their attention to your project and their ability to mentor you into your own work will likely remain limited. It is not that established faculty members don't have important ideas and guidance to share or that they deliberately withhold this from you. Usually, their expertise is on point and they do help with the intellectual contours of your work. I always felt that my male advisor gave me excellent tutoring in how to make academic products like the dissertation, and I learned a great deal about structuring arguments and crafting a good qualitative account of data from him. The other faculty committee members were also astute in their thinking and analysis of my ideas. But still, I hit a major psychological snag and lost momentum for a long while between the oral comprehensive exams and the completion of my dissertation.

In considering what happened, I eventually recognized that my committee was brilliant at dissecting argument but poor at midwifery when it came to generating new scholars through sustained attention. The members of my committee were personally consumed by their own intellectual pursuits and had their own prestige to continue to successfully steward. They didn't really have patience or investment in the project of "birthing" the success of very junior scholars like me, no matter how highly they regarded me personally. Ironically, their high regard for how I might at some point become a member of the academy in their own mold was actually the biggest contributor to my confidence problem. I found myself laboring under the mantle of that old quip "there is nothing as heavy as the burden of a great potential", and certainly I feared disappointing those high expectations. Yet simultaneously, I had the realization that I might not really want to emulate my committee's example of living the scholarly life. I couldn't articulate it at the time, but what I think happened is that during my oral exam and shortly thereafter, I came to consciousness. I suddenly knew that I would never be able to move through the scholarly world as a privileged White male would. What I wanted to study—the lives of feminist women who were also therapists and counselors—was not going to position me for a smooth transit through an academic career. My committee thought my proposed work was interesting and academically sound, but it was clear I was going to be on my own with it. Having been vetted as capable of conducting independent scholarship through the comprehensive exam process, I could now go forth, and they would, for the most part, not see me again until closer to my final disserta-tion defense. Perhaps they didn't realize that their confidence in me also conveyed a definite lack of interest in investing time into mentoring my developing ideas for the study of women's lives. The midwife role is not common to men in our culture, yet intellectual production is not actually a lone endeavor. It requires time and attention. Scholars routinely attend conferences and hold long conversations together in order to advance their thinking and research. My committee just didn't seem to think to extend such invitations. It may have been an oversight, but it felt more like a dismissal. Having recognized that I was not really going to be able to take up the same path, or inhabit the same privileged identity, I was initially at a bit of a loss. How was I to connect the academic life of a researcher and scholarly writer with my lived professional story of being a counselor-therapist? How was I, as a woman and feminist thinker, to relate my thoughts and experiences to the modes of critical analysis and deconstructive discourse that my faculty committee was so immersed in? To be successful, did I have to become as they were even though this meant not speaking to other parts of myself as a woman and therapeutic professional? Could I even? Psychologically, I was stranded.

Looking back from quite a few years hence, it seems to me that I was inexperienced in understanding gender politics and the dynamics of power and privilege within academia. Brilliant faculty members—who traditionally are often, but not always, male—simply don't appreciate their own institutional privilege and have little idea about how to mentor smart women except in their own mold which, *de facto,* is not a perfect fit. Initially, to students, their offer sounds appealing on some level; after all, why not learn to be successful on the same terms that have worked for well-regarded faculty? However, the belated discovery for most doctoral students is to find that things don't quite go according to plan or work that way if you are a female rather than a male doctoral student or are not a Caucasian/European–American person.

My very successful faculty models weren't of much use in helping me disentangle the puzzle of why my work had stalled or why I had lost confidence in my ability to belong to the academy. It took me quite a while to find experienced female faculty who could help me understand what was going on and work with me to reconstruct my project in such a way that I had my own scholarly voice within it. The female faculty members were, in fact, more junior in rank and not as well recognized by the institution, but they were amazingly wise and insightful in both scholarly and human ways. I learned, up close and personally, that academic research and writing is a process of production by embodied people with a social location that matters in how they approach the work, see the world, and pose research questions. Until that point, I think I thought of a dissertation as a mental exercise in the abstract, and so it made sense to be tutored by those who were best at solving mental challenges through discussion and debate. I didn't think intellectual practices were intimately connected to personhood. Today I would identify my problem as one of recovering from false consciousness while finding my way as an intellectual in terms that fit with the history I brought, my social location as a woman, and the kind of research work I was meant to do.

When it comes to relations of power and privilege, it is easy for those new to doctoral study or to the workings of higher education institutions to become mystified by the hidden curriculum and by the masculinist dynamics of prestige and power that are operating in academia. In contrast, it takes considerable work with oneself and in relation to a community of people who have worked through these dynamics, as raced, classed, gendered, and cultural beings to finally see what is going on in terms of the social dynamics of knowledge production and how, more critically and specifically, "it is happening to you."

Young women in doctoral programs may see themselves as entirely capable and no different in terms of academic or professional potential than their male counterparts, which of course is true. In some cases, they may even be stronger academically and intellectually than some of their male peers, but what they may not see are the intractable ways in which they are relatively disadvantaged structurally, by the taken-for-granted norms and practices of the academy itself. Even aside from sexist slights and microaggressions that disempower in the moment, there are complex but unspoken negotiations about who can speak with authority, how often, and to whom. This extends to writing for academic publication and the authorial "voice" of one's dissertation as well as to oral presentation and group participation. I don't believe there is intentional and deliberate discrimination by faculty toward female and ethnic–racial minority students for the most part (although undoubtedly notable exceptions continue). Rather, the structures and norms of colleges and universities have only slowly evolved from their historical moorings in the (male) nobility and monastery while still holding, intact, distinct values and privileging certain ways of knowing and of operating which are not entirely consonant with the experiences of most nondominant groups. We probably have greater appreciation of the located nature of higher education norms and practices today than was true in the 1990s when I was starting my doctoral work, so perhaps my experience of losing confidence in my abilities and fit within the academy would be less likely today; but I do not think we are out of the woods yet. There are always newcomers to higher education from underrepresented groups or other nations, who also need to be mentored in ways that help them find their intellectual path, their own authoritative voice, and their own purpose for continued participation in the arduous process of becoming a researcher through the dissertation experience.

My discouragement and resulting "time in the wilderness" in terms of finding traction for my doctoral dissertation project after passing my comprehensive exams proved to be a two-edged sword. On the one hand, I went through emotional angst and self-recrimination for not making sufficient progress for far too long without finding myself able to seek help. I continued to meet with my advisor, who responded as best he could, given that he couldn't fully comprehend my dilemma. I was not good at first at finding my own external sources of support, until with enough conversations with just the right group of trusted friends and colleagues in the arts and humanities and in neighboring professions, such as ministry, I was able to form what I came to think of as my "discernment committee." This was a group of women in and out of the academy who shared my interests and valued my voice. They reflected back to me the version of myself and my intellectual aspirations to complete my doctorate consistently enough that I grew the narrative I needed to develop in order to continue my research work and the confidence to speak about it with my all-male faculty committee. The other side of the "two-edged sword" time was that I came to know, first-hand, all the ways in which a doctoral dissertation journey is a transforming and identity-defining undertaking. I stumbled into many of the roadblocks and psychological swamps familiar to any difficult journey, and I think, as a result, I have come to appreciate that even long and winding paths to finish one's doctoral program can ultimately be successful. And so, I find it easy to keep compassionately supporting my own advisees, knowing that in its own strange way, the dissertation process is doing its defining work, molding a person different from the one who started out naively at the beginning. I stay attentive to the social dynamics of race, class, and gender in the production of knowledge for the counseling field, and I appreciate that there is still much to demystify for students today, to make the doctoral experience sustainable and successful for all those who attempt the process.

CHAPTER 31

A GREATER PURPOSE

WANDA I. MONTAÑEZ, EdD

Massachusetts Charter Public School Association, Hudson, MA, USA

E-mail: montanez_w@yahoo.com

At about 1:20 pm, the bell rings. I was one college preparatory class away from the weekend. I run downstairs, stop in the faculty room, pick up class materials on my desk. Bell rings. I am late for class. In heels, I sprint across the multipurpose space, open the classroom door anticipating the complaints of a classroom full of high-school juniors about their previous homework assignment—completion of their college essay. I enter to a barrage of applause and whistles. *"Congratulations, Dr. Montañez!"* was written on the dry erase board in red ink. It was then that I felt what I knew all along, that my obtaining a doctoral degree served a greater purpose beyond myself.

During the final three years of the pursuit of my doctoral degree, I worked as a college counselor at a Boston charter public high school whose population of students was predominantly low-income students of color. Fifteen years prior, as my first job out of high school, college counseling served as an introduction to the challenges associated with access to higher education. In many ways, I had come full circle, again working with students to access some of the best colleges and universities across the country. For all of the students in the junior class, and probably most students in the high school, this was the first time they knew and were taught by someone who looked like them and grew up in similar circumstances and held a terminal degree. That, to me, was the most fulfilling feeling and the best gift I could give to any of them.

As a personal decision not driven by future employment opportunities, I entered the Higher Education Administration program with 12 superhuman higher education administrators who, today, are more like family than classmates. The cohort model served its intended purpose of building camaraderie and creating a system of support. I knew rather quickly that I was blessed to walk with them through this process as the challenges came immediately, both personally and professionally. I have vivid memories of sitting in my advisor's office with tears streaming down my face on more than one occasion because things had become too difficult. Ironically, she never knew what to say to make me feel better, but she always knew what to say to make me *want* it again. Through the program, each stage was seemingly harder than the next.

When I entered the phase of choosing a dissertation topic that resonated with me, I explored some of the themes in higher education that I was particularly drawn to and eventually settled on a subject that, I later learned, was outside of the expertise of the faculty in my program. This was a particularly difficult time for me. I second-guessed my decisions constantly. I was overwhelmed by the very nature of writing and finding the time to write. I struggled with articulating the reasons why this research was important and rightfully was met with some contention from faculty as I moved through various steps of developing a justification for exploring this work. Two months later, I had developed an argument for a proposed research topic that had absolutely nothing to do with what I wanted to research.

I set up a meeting with my advisor. I once again sat in her office wiping away tears of frustration. After much discussion, she said, "Wanda, you need to do your research on what you really want to study; you need to love your work." In one statement, she made me *want* it again. My topic, *The Role of Identity Development in Multiethnic Latino Students' Sense of Belonging in College*, was the reason why I needed to complete my work. This was the first time that the experience of multiethnic Latino students was to be explored in the way that I had suggested it needed to be. I strongly felt that these students' experiences needed to be heard as they were a demographic of students who had been overlooked for quite some time in academia.

As I developed my problem statement and explored literature to review, I was encouraged by my faculty to reach out to several Latina researchers across the country whose work was well-renowned in higher education. What a fantastic idea, I thought! After reading much of their work over the last couple of years, I thought for sure that these inspiring Latinas could serve as sources of information for my work and great personal connections for me. Surely, I thought, they would be able to point me in a direction that would improve my work and expand my thinking on my topic. After sending several emails and several weeks passed, I was extremely disheartened and to some degree angry by the lack of responses I received to support not only my work but also me as a fellow Latina. I felt, and still do, that as a woman of color, as a Latina, I have a responsibility toward those who follow behind me. If I can help, I will. Only two responded, out of the half dozen women to whom I had reached out.

By the time I reached the dissertation phase, I had gone through numerous iterations of my proposal draft. I was unsure if I had enough energy left to continue to pursue what, by that time, seemed more like a burden rather than an exhilarating pursuit of a degree. But, I found true champions of my work through my committee who allowed me to explore this complex topic in a very nontraditional way and supported my growth from inception to completion. I had heard terrible stories of others succumbing to increasing challenges because of a committee that was less than useful. I, on the other hand, had a very different experience. My committee could not have worked better together! They built on each other's ideas, steered me toward resources, and pushed my thinking on the topic beyond what I could have imagined. I, for the first time, felt validated in my writing, my topic, and my path toward my degree. I questioned less and made decisions with my work that I knew I could defend.

It was hard. It was so hard. I continued to push through with incredible support from my committee, cohort, family, and friends ... and wine. Wine helped a lot! I often used a glass of wine (or two) as my reward for writing or as the impetus to begin the process on particular days. In conjunction with my advisor, I created a timeline of completion that was very ambitious, particularly since my advisor had recently announced her pregnancy and the plan allowed for very little room for missteps. However, my advisor and I agreed to work on meeting pertinent deadlines to reach my goal of defending in spring 2014. I believe that this step was crucial to my success. I had semi-firm deadlines for everything and someone to hold me accountable in meeting those goals. More importantly, my advisor held true to her end of the agreement even while taking care of a growing family and balancing her own career. I am forever thankful that she wanted me to succeed just as much as I wanted to.

The summer before my spring defense, through the power of the universe aligning perfectly, I had five weeks of vacation before the new school year began and I returned to my college counselor duties. On most days that summer, while others were taking relaxing vacations, I would sit on my couch with the television on in the background and forced myself to write. As a young kid, I would sit at the kitchen table while my mother cooked dinner, and I always did my homework with the television on. The television never served as a distraction, except that this time I was binge watching episodes of *Breaking Bad* rather than *The Reading Rainbow*. There were some days when I wrote for 14 hours straight and only took breaks that I deemed as absolutely necessary.

Having the time to write was a luxury; having the stamina to continue to write was a real challenge that often led to real tears. Chapter 4. Submit. Obtain feedback. Review feedback. Revise. Resubmit. Chapters 5–7. Repeat …. Full draft. Submit. Obtain feedback. Review feedback. Revise. Resubmit. The rest, as they say, is history. My history. My story of pursuing something that very few people attempt and even fewer complete, especially in the immigrant Puerto Rican community from which I come.

A month after defending my dissertation I was chosen by the senior class to deliver their faculty speech at their high school commencement. I worked on my speech for weeks! You would have thought that I was delivering a speech to the President of the United of States. At graduation, I walked on stage, wearing my doctoral regalia, and spoke to the families, friends, and loved ones of my students. Most of the families were families of color, spoke a second language other than English, and had, like my family, immigrated to the United States for better opportunities. And, it was to this crowd that I, for the first time, publicly introduced myself as Dr. Wanda Montañez.

PART IV:
Stage 4: The Dissertation Stage

During this stage, coursework has been completed and the focus is on independent research guided by the dissertation advisor (and, perhaps, committee). The increased independence of this stage is generally characterized by less structure and more pressure. This stage culminates in the successful defense of the dissertation research (Ali & Kohun, 2007).

DISSERTATION STRATEGIES

After completing the comprehensive exams, students usually feel exhausted, and inertia can set in. It is important to set goals and give yourself meaningful rewards for meeting those goals. Every student will find (or create) her own most effective way of completing the work of the dissertation. The following are some considerations that will help you in developing your best strategy:

1. *Create a workspace in your home:* This should be a place where you can study, read, and write. Think about what you will need to make this your haven. If you don't have a spot at home, then you might consider a study carrel space at the college's library or your local public library. Think about how you work—are you an early riser, or a late nighter? How will that impact the space where you need to work? Discuss with your family the boundaries of this space—who can come in, when (if ever), and so forth.
2. *Acquire a portable workstation:* Consider moving from a desktop to a laptop or tablet to help with time management. There may be times when you need to make your work more portable. If you don't already use a laptop this may be a time to invest. Being able to work at multiple locations on your projects can help you manage your time.
3. *Save yourself from becoming overwhelmed by the idea of writing a dissertation:* Envision the dissertation as a series of 5–10-page

papers that are woven together to create the whole document. It can be hard at first to see that it can be broken into small chunks to work on. It does not have to be written all at once. Waiting to do all your work in big blocks of time may not be realistic. There may be times when you can tuck work into smaller scraps of time. It can be surprising what can be accomplished in a 20–40-minute chunk (i.e., read an article and highlight, write an annotation for an article you are reading, and so forth). Pace yourself and, daily, make time to work on projects/papers; this will keep ideas fresh and flowing. Use your time: waiting at the doctor's office, riding the bus or train, listening in the car to self-made notes—there are little places everywhere.

4. *Create a briefcase, Courier bag, or backpack that has all your basic supplies:* Think of it as a portable desk with highlighters, tape, scissors, stapler, (and extra staples), pens/pencils, charger, and so forth. Also think about personal needs—a granola bar, water bottle, extra cash, aspirin or ibuprofen, and an umbrella.

5. *Keeping track of dates is important:* Haven't used the calendar function on your smartphone? Never used a planner? Consider how you will map out each month. What tools can you use to look at the big picture, create small goals, and keep up with your deadlines? Some people find using multiple tools helps—consider: a big whiteboard calendar on the wall, settings on the smartphone, a planner. Use different colors, if that works for you, for home/family dates, school deadlines, work schedule.

6. *Remember everything we told you in Part III.*

STAGE 4 NARRATIVES

Our authors share stories that affirm that this stage of the doctoral journey is characterized by independence, isolation, pressure (of time and of deadlines), and a "crappy" work-life balance. Each doctoral student has to make her own space and time and set up her own workspace and structure for doing the work and getting each portion of the dissertation completed. There is no pre-existing structure, though there are plenty of advice, tips, and strategies. As our authors here and elsewhere have emphasized, what works is what will work for you; the goal is to get it done.

REFERENCE

Ali, A.; Kohun, F. (2007). Dealing with social isolation to minimize doctoral attrition—a four stage framework. International Journal of Doctoral Studies, 2, 33–49. Retrieved from: http://www.informingscience.org/Journals/IJDS/Articles?Volume=2–2007&Search.

CHAPTER 32

MONSTERS

SILVIA MEJÍA, PhD

The College of Saint Rose, Albany, NY, USA

E-mail: mejias@strose.edu

> *To my mom, who did not have access to higher education, but who would have loved to become a teacher…or a psychologist.*

I had not set foot outside the airport yet when my mom took a long look at me and embraced me, saying the loving words that only a mother could blurt out like that, in cold blood: "Mija, what's happened to you? You're so fat!" Gloria, my mom—who, for the record, is not that thin herself—could hardly wait to begin fixing me. It was late May and I was coming back to my country, Ecuador, after having eaten my way through the comprehensive doctoral exams, the oral defense of my dissertation proposal in comparative literature, and a painful breakup with the man who, I had convinced myself, was going to stay with me for the long run.

Matt and I had lived together for about a year and a half, in a small studio apartment in Washington, DC. Truth be told, this arrangement had been more of a strategy to afford living in DC than a decision brought about by the maturity of our relationship. Nevertheless, we seemed to function well together. He worked for an NGO that specialized in Guatemalan affairs, spoke almost perfect Spanish with a cute Guatemalan accent, enthusiastically attempted to dance, and succeeded to drink like a regular Latin American guy. *La familia*—a group of Latin American graduate students and my closest friends—loved Matt's easy-going approach to life as much as I did. But one spring day this Jewish boy with a Latin American soul went on a one-week trip to Israel and, I never knew exactly why or how, came back with a couple of decisions made: he was to quit his job and our relationship, since he was not feeling really committed to either of them. On an April morning, heartbroken, I saw him drive away in a station wagon, headed to his parents' home in Boston.

Thus, I headed home too, as a sort of refugee, with a mangled self-esteem that did not feel like the best state to begin working on a doctoral dissertation. A backpack full of equipment to shoot the video part of my research traveled with me. I had an extremely vague idea of where to start, two months to complete whatever video work I was going to do in Ecuador, and a graduate student bank account depleted by the expenses made in equipment and traveling. Luckily, my mom, who had married my dad in her mid-twenties and left her village in Northern Ecuador to begin a family in Quito, the capital, always had shelter for my younger brother and for me, her prodigal daughter. Staying with my mom I would feel unconditionally loved and protected. And while under her wing, a creature whose existence I had only noticed in passing, when younger, would begin to take hold of me. She was stubborn. She seemed to be powered by her wounds. She was a monster in survival mode.

By June 1st, a Monday, my mom and I were sitting in front of a nutritionist in a weight loss center. The survivor of a bad marriage who fell into the worst of depressions when my dad died, six years earlier, Gloria had become (or had always been?) a force of nature since then. She had pressured me into making the appointment, and now we were committing to a special offer program, two people for the price of one. We had to show up at the center three days per week, to be weighed and measured, as well as to receive instructions on what we were to eat the following two days. According to their calculations, to reach her ideal weight, my mom had to lose 40 pounds. I needed to shed 60. By the first checkup, on Wednesday, I had lost three pounds. Maybe because I did not know that losing weight is easier at the beginning, or that those three pounds were most likely fluids, the unexpected number filled me with hope. At that rate, I could reach my ideal weight in less than two months, right?!

Well, I did not know it then, but the whole process was going to take nine months. Nevertheless, that Wednesday afternoon, while stepping down from the scale, something clicked in me: I had always thought that being overweight was, like being loved or dumped, something over which I had no control. People in my family tend to gain weight easily; it is in my genes, no doubt. But I suddenly realized that I was really doing it to myself too, with my unbounded devotion for bread, cookies, and stashes of sweets. I may have no control over who stops loving me all of a sudden—I thought to myself, but I can certainly take the reins of how I feed my body. So, I did, and with such ferocity that, I believe, at some point, my mom regretted having joined the weight-loss venture with such an inflexible partner. The pig-headed monster that had possessed me did not make exceptions. Around that time, in between daily scuffles over avoiding an extra bran cracker, or not eating more than a tiny mandarin orange as dessert at lunch, things began to take shape, so to speak.

One fateful day in Quito, as soon as I woke up, I began fretting about running out of time to shoot video material in Ecuador. In truth, I knew that I was in the right place but had no idea of where to start. My dissertation proposal had promised to focus on the case of Ecuadorian emigrants, to demonstrate that nostalgia was being transformed by new technologies that had shrunk space and time, placing migrants and exiles "just a click away" from home. In contrast with the lofty theories about nostalgia, digital technology, and immigration that I had examined for my dissertation proposal, the documentary video was meant to be a candid representation of how regular people experienced—or not—that theory in their daily life.

Wide awake but still in bed, I figured that my documentary needed to tell three stories, very different from each other but also representative of distinct moments in the history of migration from Ecuadorians abroad: the traditional stream of undocumented emigrants from Southern Ecuador to the United States had to be addressed in one of the stories, whereas the other two could be centered around the more recent waves of migration toward Spain and Italy. I had begun brainstorming possible ways to meet migrants who would allow me to film them, when a fleeting thought crossed my mind, quick as a ghost: this was the very first morning in months when opening my eyes had not been immediately followed by the dread of rejection. I had not dedicated a split second to my tiresome broken heart (read: ego). The monster was too busy for the customary morning weep over the drama of having been dumped. Hallelujah! I must be getting over it, I thought, and triumphantly got out of bed.

That same week, I happened to mention to my mom how worried I was about not having a single contact or a place to stay in Cuenca, the third largest city in Ecuador, where I needed to go in order to find the central piece of my documentary video: a true story of undocumented migration from Southern Ecuador to New York. In fact, the previous spring I had traveled from DC to Queens twice, and parked myself and my camera in the local "videoconference center," naively thinking that at least one of the customers—most of them male, undocumented male Ecuadorian immigrants who spent fortunes just to see their loved ones through the videoconference screens—would open up to me, let me film him, and even put me in touch with his family back in Cuenca. Naturally, not a single of these men—perpetually frightened that any false step could bring about their deportation—agreed to talk with me. I would not have talked to me either, had I been in their situation. The only possibility of finding a path to their experience, I told my mom, lay in trying the other side of the story, the side of the family left behind.

My mom nodded, told me not to worry and to leave it in her hands, as she left the house mumbling something about "*doña* Lolita's niece, who might be living in Cuenca." While I wasted time scoffing at my mom's self-assurance ("as if she could do anything that I had not tried already ...") and begging via email for support from NGOs in Cuenca, she was busy convincing her neighbor of decades to give the niece a call and talk her into receiving me in her house. A couple of days later, I landed in Cuenca, where *doña* Lolita's relatives had agreed to have me for two weeks. Single-handedly, my mom had removed what I perceived as a huge obstacle for my research, while buying herself no more and no less than 14 days of freedom from whom she perceived as a huge obstacle for her well-being: me, the food police, the obstinate monster that she had, also single-handedly, woken up.

It has been almost 12 years since that third Sunday in June, Father's Day, when I found myself with camera in my hand, waiting again in the lobby of a videoconference center. Only this time I was not in New York, but in Cuenca. I approached a young woman, clearly a customer, explained my project as quickly as I could, and asked if it would be okay that I film parts of the videoconference that she was about to have. I knew that I was intruding, so I promised to stop filming and leave the room whenever she asked me to. She went inside the conference room to consult with the rest of the family, and came back wearing a big smile: "Come in, come in.... We are going to have a videoconference with my brothers who live in Queens, but my dad does not know; it's a surprise." A lot more filming would come afterward, first in Southern Ecuador and Quito, and then in New York, Madrid, and Milan—the other side of the three stories, the perspectives of those who had left. Over 70 hours of video in total. However, even now, no scene in the documentary touches me as much as that very first one, when Arturo and Mercedes gasp, speechless, at the sight of their kids talking from a big screen, after 11 years of separation.

Speechless too, and shedding tears as always, my mom draws an invisible cross over my forehead, chest, and shoulders, and gives me her blessing. We are at the airport again, feeling sad but also, literally, lighter than two months earlier. Yes, she has lost 20 pounds and I have lost 30 as of that moment, but to me this lightness feels more like the quiet happiness after an honest day's work, like the thrill and expectation of a road wide open in front of me. Unlike a few weeks earlier, now I have a sense of the direction that I want to take—at least for my dissertation work.

After not having heard from Matt in months, he sends me a postcard from some mountain range in California. Of course, I make sure to be back from Europe to "coincide" with a brief visit to DC that he has planned for November. About two months later, after having spent the holidays together, he breaks up with me again, this time on the phone. I wish I could report that this second rejection did not break me. I wish I knew then, like I know now, that in the big picture of life, that was just a minor scratch.... Do not worry, though. My *familia*—both of blood and of friendship—was still there. And the resilient twin monster that my mom had uncovered and nurtured, the one who is at her strongest when hurt, has not gone away either.

CHAPTER 33

THE IMPORTANCE OF SOCIAL CAPITAL AND INTERNAL DETERMINATION

TERRI WARD, EdD

The College of Saint Rose, Albany, NY, USA

My journey in a doctoral program cannot be isolated to the four years of courses, study groups, qualifying exams, and dissertation committee struggles. I brought to my final degree all that came before I sat in my first doctoral course. For good or bad, the acquisition of the degree was merely the culmination of an odyssey of passionate curiosity and deep regard for a single topic of interest, unstable self-efficacy during a four-year-long triathlon, and reliance on social capital, both human and resource, built over the years.

33.1 A HISTORY OF EDUCATED WOMEN

Growing up, formal education was held in high esteem in my household. Each generation before me had at least one family member who attended some form of postsecondary training, whether it was tailoring, dental hygiene, comptometer operator, or that of a more formal four-year degree in liberal arts or a professional area such as accounting. Interestingly, this was true for both males and females on both sides of the family, many of whom are now nonagenarians. My grandfather received a bachelor's degree in accounting prior to World War II, my great aunt has a nursing degree, and my own mother pursued a bachelor's and master's degree on a part-time basis, whereas my father cooked evening dinners. Perhaps that was one of the first supports that blessed my own educational pursuits, a long line of educated women working outside the home while raising children in nuclear families, and often relying on extended family supports. I was provided a foundation of educated females serving as a silent springboard for my own academic interests. I cannot overstate how fortunate I was to be surrounded by nine of twelve female relatives, spanning three generations, who attended postsecondary training prior to 1960. We were not a wealthy family, but we spoke the language of higher education. Somehow I think this culture secretly hovered over my spirit as a young child, paving a path for my own adventure.

Another blessing was having a mother who was a staunch advocate for her children when it involved educational endeavors. For whatever reason, supplied in another writing outside the scope of this publication (Ward, 2008-2009), I was formally identified as borderline mentally retarded in 1968, the fall of my first grade year in public school. Although there were no formal special education services at the time, if a child performed poorly on a group-administered intelligence or achievement test, he or she was informally classified as intellectually deficient based on standard deviations from the mean score. The term "retarded" is not used as a pejorative, rather as the language of the time period. My father, a salesman for the General Electric Corporation, and my mother, finishing her master's degree at the time, were requested to meet with the principal and told of my inadequate intellectual capabilities. Within one week, my brother and I were removed from the public school and educated in the private school where my mother was employed as a teacher. Neither of my parents told me of my perceived intellectual status; they continued to support my schooling much as they had. Although I knew that something was different about my education than that of my peers, I was not aware of any formal label. Conversations with my mother much later in my life revealed her frustration with the school system's hasty findings and her fear that expectations for me were set too low. She was a one-woman advocate, editor, cheerleader, and guide throughout my k-12 education and college acceptance. I often wonder what might have become of me if my mother had left the school system to follow the label so casually tossed onto my shoulders. It could have been a classic case of sociological labeling theory (Becker, 1963); one becomes the label of deviance placed upon him or her. I did not know the term but knew that being educated in the basement of the school near the boiler was not "normal."

As the story of my educational career continued, I found myself lost, troubled, and in danger of failing out of high school. There were two reasons for this. First, I knew many were aware of my educational struggles and expected little of me, and, secondly, I began to question my own sexuality. Again, women stepped in to guide, punish, and mentor. Mathematics, English, and art teachers revealed possibilities of further pursuit such as art therapy, creative writing, and architecture. Those educated women helped shape my future as I left high school after my junior year, succeeded in junior college, and ultimately majored in secondary english education. I then pursued a master's degree in special education, certification in school leadership, and finally, a doctoral degree in education that focused on the inclusion of learners with severe disabilities in typical classrooms. I was 34 years old at the awarding of the doctoral degree, one month prior to my 35th birthday, and just within my personally established timeline goal.

The glimpse of my early educational years and the strength of my family provide historical context for the true purpose of this essay: a recounting of the doctoral experience. A decade or more of middle, high school, and undergraduate degrees are glossed over in order to concentrate on the doctoral experience and all it entailed. However, it is remiss to ignore the tremendous impact of others on my personal and educational successes and failures. Perhaps the first bit of wisdom is to understand who you are, how early influences shape our self-efficacy, physical stamina, and the critical skills needed to build social capital. I was not a strong early learner, but I began to believe that I could do well pursuing my doctoral degree.

33.2 STRONG FEMALE MENTORSHIP AND COLLEGIALITY

The University of Central Florida (UCF) is a thriving campus just outside the heart of Orlando. It opened in 1963 and is considered an infant of an institution in many circles. Over the years, like many institutions of higher education, it became a large campus with diverse majors serving the military, high-tech industries, and education. I had an opportunity to attend another university further north, but my employment as a regional facilitator of inclusive education in the state kept me tied to central Florida. Moreover, the doctoral program did not require a residency, which helped support my desire to conduct original research in schools with which I currently worked. So, I accepted UCF's offer and began my studies under the critical mind of Dr. Marcella Kysilka. Dr. K was a middle-aged, plump, dress-wearing, intellectual powerhouse. She reminded me of John Houseman who played the role of Professor Charles Kingsfield in the movie *The Paper Chase* (1973). She required deep reading, clear written skills, and cogent arguments formed during the spontaneous verbal debate. Somehow, at the end of every class, one left more curious than when he or she entered, which led to reading and investigating topics far beyond what was required in the syllabus. It was exhilarating. Fortunately, I was blessed with her presence for three classes.

At the time my doctoral program began, I was employed as a regional facilitator for the Florida Department of Education, serving an eleven-county geographical area in central Florida. Originally, there were four of us in the state, three of whom were women. The work required two or three nights out of the house per week, travel across the state to meetings in Tampa, and travel to the state capital in Tallahassee. The job was timely, focused on inclusive education in public schools by supporting and conducting professional development for teachers and administrators so children with disabilities gained access to general education curriculum and environments. This position was a dream job. I was supporting students with disabilities, involved in the deep study of schools with like professionals, and all the while I was continuing to build social capital through my work ethic. I was in class at night focusing on inclusive education, and during the day, I was collaborating with my colleagues on the very same topic. As I delved into both worlds, it seemed that the harder I worked, the luckier I became.

33.3   THE SOCIAL CAPITAL OF FEMALES

The first point of this essay, realizing we all bring to doctoral studies our own historical educational experiences and self-efficacy in the pursuit of a formal education, brings me to my second point: social capital is a necessary component in doctoral study. In case this term is unfamiliar, social capital refers to the relationships, or the banks of social trust, norms, and networks, between people that enable productive outcomes (Szreter, 2000). My work in a model school for inclusive education in the early to mid-1990s nurtured relationships with professionals and academics across the country. Though I did not know the term for it at the time, it was clear that I had developed social capital, a network of professionals who shared my passion for inclusive education and the drive to deeply study the factors that led to the success or failure of students with disabilities in general education classrooms and environments.

At one point in my studies, I remember holding day-long meetings in Tampa, driving to Orlando for an evening class, then driving back to Tampa in order to conduct meetings the following morning. I relied on coworkers to set up materials the night before and classmates to schedule presentations for later in class, just in case the traffic on Interstate 4 was backed up. If one has ever been on that highway, it is often known as a great big parking lot! I also remember traveling from my home along the east coast to advanced statistics study groups at a classmate's home outside Orlando. This occurred for two or three hours each Sunday during most of our time in the quantitative and qualitative research coursework that spanned four semesters. What's interesting about all this is that all those upon whom I relied were women. There were males in the doctoral cohort, and we invited them to study with us, but none accepted. I was the youngest and only lesbian in the group of 17 in the academic cohort, but all in our study group were women. Of the wonderfully brilliant women in the study group, two were married with children out of the house, two single middle-aged African–American females, and one a single woman who was a softball coach at a coastal college south of Orlando. We were diverse in culture, marital status, age, religion, and career trajectory but all dedicated to being a woman with a doctoral degree. My colleagues at work, at least the ones upon whom I relied, were also female. My boss served as mentor and role model, while a colleague on the west coast of the state helped setup rooms, take notes at the last minutes of a meeting, or provided related readings and connections for my academic studies. My networks came in handy more than once, but I remember the support I received on those heavy travel nights.

33.4   THE SELF-EFFICACY OF EXHAUSTED FEMALES

A doctoral program is not only a test of your ability to analyze discrete elements within a whole, it is also a test of your physical endurance. Earlier I stated that the four years felt like a triathlon. The physical exhaustion that comes from balancing so many demands is accompanied by a mental struggle to convince yourself that "this too shall pass" and self-doubt is your worst enemy. At one point, I remember sitting at the beauty shop waiting for the stylist while reading some historical account of the foundations of educational models. I fell asleep. She took another client before my scheduled time, thinking that the nap probably did me some good. I was exhausted and, yes, that nap helped. I went home after my appointment and flopped on the bed, sleeping soundly until the following morning.

Over the four years, a patterned developed. When I was tired physically, the waves of self-doubt crushed me. After high school, I received stellar grades in my undergraduate program, master's program, and my certificate of advanced study in educational leadership. However, the history of borderline intellectual abilities and knowledge of low expectations earlier in my schooling impacted my own belief that I was worthy of a seat in any doctoral class. In my studies, I came across the term "self-efficacy", one I'd not heard before. As defined by Bandura, self-efficacy is one's belief in one's ability to accomplish a task and how to approach goals, tasks, and challenges. It seems unimaginable that anyone experiences a doctoral program without questioning his or her personal abilities. The critical factor is moving through those doubts and returning to a more healthy state of positive self-efficacy. Often, in those mentally exhausting moments, a break from everyone and everything just to walk on the beach along the Atlantic Ocean was the perfect tonic for low self-efficacy. It was a constant reminder of the strength, beauty, and the power of nature. It provided a few moments of distance from demands of work and study. I loved my work, my studies, my classmates, and colleagues. I was a respected scholar, coworker, and friend to a precious few. In order to remember that, once in a while, distance and time away from it all was absolutely necessary.

The final phase of most doctoral programs is the dissertation. Once qualifying exams are complete and the green light for the proposal is given, the hard work begins. This is probably the loneliest work, when you are engaged in the deep study and the pursuit of original research, usually as the sole investigator. Careful selection of the dissertation chair and the members of the committee is an arduous process. Fortunately there were no hidden agendas, political minefields, or sabbaticals during my ten-month dissertation process. In fact, the professors were all very helpful and timely with feedback. Perhaps my topic was so unknown to many that there was little argument. It seemed that, at the point of the dissertation, we all split into our separate silos with our dissertation chairs. The study group, so close for nearly three years, was meeting only at holidays to laugh, commiserate, and share our progress. Now it was sheer determination and stamina.

The dissertation committee approved my study without delay. I spent the next six months traveling between schools, conducting observations, analyzing data, and transcribing field notes for my mixed methods investigation into inclusion. As the public school year drew to a close, my study called for a series of focus group interviews, all of which would occur on the same day. Once again, I relied on my social capital as I recruited and trained my colleagues and old study group members to conduct the final field interviews. The study was massive, as it required five focus groups with at least seven people in each group who were asked to answer a series of eleven questions regarding the impact of inclusion. The groups lasted nearly two hours. That was a heap of transcription. My former secretary, who is still a close friend today, offered to transcribe all the recordings for a reasonable fee and in a short period of time. When she was not transcribing,

I was listening to the recordings while driving the car. I made use of my time stuck on I4 between Orlando and Tampa.

The last hurdle was hiring an editor for each chapter of the dissertation. I suppose that some feel an editor is not necessary. Looking back, I believe it was one of the best investments I made. The pages came back filled with corrections, things I never noticed because I was too close to my own work. It was also helpful that the editor was someone unknown to me but highly recommended. Some classmates used spouses or friends to edit, but I could not think of placing such an emotionally charged responsibility on someone I loved. This was the first time I relied on my bank account for support rather than my network. It was the best decision for everyone involved.

At the end of a doctoral program, there is a mix of exhilaration, anxiety, self-doubt, and just a little bit of confidence. After all, I was the person most familiar with every piece of the study. I worked closely with each professor on my dissertation committee as I developed the literature review, the overall design, and methods of analysis. At one moment, I was confident, and at another point I remembered that I chose the people on my committee because of their excellence, so it was not in my best interest to be overly assured of successfully defending my dissertation. I would face questions regarding the results, the application of a chi-square test, or data triangulation. Confidence is needed but caution is also necessary. The range of emotion is staggering the closer the dissertation defense date.

On the day of the defense, I was surrounded by positive energy. I designed it that way. I knew that it was a small group of strong women that had supported me to that point, so I was careful not to change what worked. Outside the conference room of my defense stood one colleague, my best friend and secretary/transcriptionist (all-in-one), a study-group member (with whom I remain in contact), and my partner of nearly seven years at that time. One of the committee members stated that they had not seen so many friends in attendance at a dissertation defense. I couldn't think of doing it any other way.

That's it. A little over an hour after the final dissertation defense began, it was over. The door to the conference room opened and my chair welcomed, "Dr. Ward." I sat at the conference table and told the committee of my educational background, which I had never shared. Stunned by the story, the statistics professor sat in silence with his mouth agape, the chair cried, and Dr. Kysilka smiled, gave me a hug and said, "well done, you will do well." Those words, from the professor I admired most, remain the most treasured over the last two decades.

REFERENCES

Becker, H. S. (1963). *Outsiders: Studies in the sociology of deviance.* New York, NY: Free Press.

Szreter, S. (2000). Social capital, the economy, and education in historical perspective. In T. Schuller (Ed.). *Social capital: Critical* perspectives (pp. 56 – 77). Oxford, U.K.: Oxford University Press.

Paul, R., & Thompson, R. C. (Producers); & Bridges, J. (Director). (1973). *The paper chase* (Motion Picture). United States: 20th Century Fox.

Ward, T. (2008-2009). Voice, vision, and the journey ahead: Redefining access to the general curriculum and outcomes for learners with significant support needs. *Research and Practice for Persons with Severe Disabilities, 33–34*(4–1), 241–248.

CHAPTER 34

MRS. MOMMY, DOCTOR: THE DISSERTATION PHASE

CHERIE L. KING, ScD

Central Connecticut State University, New Britain, CT, USA

E-mail: kingche@ccsu.edu

The dissertation phase is usually the most stressful phase of a doctoral program. Picking a topic and committee, designing a study, dealing with the Institutional Review Board (IRB), collecting and analyzing data, and writing, writing, and more writing. For me, this phase was what I had been waiting to do. Although it was all consuming, I was invigorated. My topic was very clear to me given my experience with the comprehensive exam phase. I chose to investigate clinical supervision in a specific setting of private rehabilitation counseling.

I chose my dissertation committee very carefully and strategically. I had developed excellent relationships with the program faculty as well as with other professors in related programs. I had heard "horror" stories from other doctoral students about nightmare dissertation committees. I knew if I was to complete the dissertation, I would need to choose members who worked well with each other and were reliable, and "drama free." My members consisted of my mentor, a primary faculty member in my program who understood private rehabilitation, and a faculty member in another department with expertise in qualitative research. I also had to choose an outside subject matter expert. It was a terrific group that was supportive and reliable.

I proposed a mixed methods study on the clinical supervision experiences of private rehabilitation counselors and supervisors. I gained permission to use an existing survey modified by my outside subject matter expert. He proved to be extremely helpful in my research design. I also felt that the voices of the rehabilitation counselors and supervisors were important due to the unique setting of private rehabilitation. My qualitative research expert committee member taught me so much about the development of strong objective interview questions.

One aspect of the dissertation phase that sometimes was not clear is that I was in control of how fast or how slow I moved the project along. No one set a timeline for me to get anything done. I had to be entirely self-motivated. Even on days when I was preoccupied or had a mountain of laundry to do or did not feel like writing, I set a very structured schedule for getting research tasks done and for writing. The days when I did not feel I could write, I would revise my references and be obsessive with American Psychological Association (APA) formatting. I could at least feel like I was productive. I used my time wisely to write and revise on days I was not teaching. I also met with my mentor once every few weeks to review what I had accomplished, which led to the final proposal of the first three chapters of my dissertation, including the methodology. I had to be patient and wait for my two other committee members to read the proposal. They were surprisingly timely and gave me the green light to start data collection. I was ready to go.

I conducted an online survey and recruited several rehabilitation counselors and supervisors to conduct interviews. The survey was easy to implement and analyze. I used an online survey platform, which I paid for myself. The survey results were straightforward. For collection of my qualitative data, I hit the road to conduct face-to-face interviews in my region. On one trip, I brought my daughter who, by then, was 13. While my task was collecting data, she and I had a great time driving through Upstate New York and New England, staying in hotels, getting room service, and drinking Starbucks on the road. She felt she was helping me finish my degree.

Analysis of the interviews was time consuming but the most energizing part of my dissertation process. Though I put a lot of pressure on myself to finish and successfully defend, I wanted to be mindful and not rush my analysis. I utilized qualitative data software for analysis but had huge Post-it Notes all over the walls of my home office, which helped me visualize the themes emerging from my data. My committee members were always available to meet and consult as I worked on the analysis. My qualitative research expert helped me tremendously in conducting a rich analysis of the qualitative data. I was in heaven! I spent the entire summer carting kids to day camp and writing chapters four and five. I was fortunate that the chapters came easily to me. I spent the lazy days of August watching my kids play and swim at the town lake, whereas I read and edited my writing. As I finished each revision, I would forward them to my committee members. I received constructive and timely feedback and spent another month refining the chapters. By the time the school year began, I was ready for defense. My committee agreed, so a date was set.

My defense came six years after I had started my program. Preparing for the defense was anxiety-provoking as I tried to anticipate the range of possible questions from committee members. I knew my topic and I knew I was supported by my committee. The defense was straightforward. I presented the background of the topic, gaps in the research, my research questions, methodology, data collection, limitations, and results. I was prepared for anything. My committee members posed some tough questions, but I managed them thoroughly and competently. I was asked to leave the room for about 30 minutes while the committee discussed my presentation. My mentor emerged with a smile on his face and said, "Congratulations, Dr. King." It was a huge relief and one of the proudest moments of my life.

There is a period after the defense when signatures are required on paperwork and the committee completes the administrative tasks. Once this was completed, my committee asked how I was going to celebrate. I looked at my watch and said I had to get on the road home to meet the school bus and get kids to dance lessons and Tae Kwon Do. It seems that this was an anticlimactic conclusion to successfully defending and being approved for a doctorate degree, but in my life, it was in all in the day of a Doctoral Student Mother.

CHAPTER 35

MAKING THE PhD HAPPEN: STAGE 4

ANNE TOOLAN ROWLEY, PhD

The College of Saint Rose, Albany, NY, USA

As the daunting dissertation stage arrived, the light at the end of the tunnel only glowed slightly. Ali & Kohun (2006) described the need for an organizational plan for meetings with the chair, submission of chapter drafts, the frequency of committee meetings, and a reasonable timeframe for feedback of submissions. For both the candidate and the committee members, the commitment to the plan is essential for completion in a prescribed time.

35.1 STAGE IV: THE DISSERTATION STAGE

Now, with the proposal accepted, the next two and a half years of dissertation work were ahead of me. When colleagues and doctoral peers heard of my milestone, they frequently felt the need to tell me about their experiences, from genuine committee support to unusual and unprofessional demands. Since the individuals had felt locked in at this stage of the journey, they went along with the demands to complete the degree. I have to say that I had a professional experience with my committee, but bumps in the road did occur. Social isolation prevailed as academic contact with peers had all but disappeared. Some colleagues had given up if their proposal had not been accepted, and others had begun their own dissertation work. The primary contact begins with the committee chair and, later, with the chair's approval, submission of drafts to the other committee members. In this section, I will discuss some high and low points in the process and offer suggestions to help a candidate progress successfully through this stage.

First, check the department policies regarding the dissertation process. Some provide guidelines on committee selection and reasonable time frames for the turnaround of chapters and documents. For example, one of my colleagues was guaranteed that all submissions would be reviewed and returned within a two-week period. This was adhered to faithfully. In some programs, it is left to the committee chair and no specific time frame is established. Several colleagues reported waiting up to two or more months before any feedback was provided.

Once the committee is established, it is important to create a plan with the chair that reflects her/his expectations regarding the timing of chapter submissions and turnaround time. This should be put in a document for later referencing. It is wise to summarize each meeting in an email and send it to the chair for confirmation. In my case, the chair read each draft first and signaled when chapters could be forwarded to the full committee. When full committee meetings take place, the same type of summation should be made and forwarded to all committee members with a request for confirmation. I always took notes at individual meetings and reserved them for future discussions. Although I did summarize the discussion in emails and requested a confirmation of the topics, verification was not always forthcoming.

My study began with an extensive review of the literature relevant to my topic. I submitted drafts as required. The turnaround time was reasonable, with feedback sent by the committee chair within a week to ten days. When the literature review was completed, the other members of the committee were permitted to review the chapter and offer suggestions. Some members gave specific suggestions within two days, whereas others took longer or just added to or agreed with the chair's suggestions. This changed later in the process when the committee chair took an out-of-state assignment. She designated the role of chair to another member of the committee whose feedback on submissions was brief and slow in coming.

As the chapters are developed, the candidate may be asked to add theories or concepts that do not fit with the original intent. If the committee is open to a discussion on how relevant the change is to the study, it is worth attempting to dissuade the committee on the change. However, the candidate may need to be flexible and make the change in order to move forward. This did occur with my committee and I argued against the theory that was suggested. It did not seem to fit the research concept. Eventually, I gave in and spent many hours developing the concept and folding it into my paper, only to have it removed later. Similar demands were described by colleagues in the process of completing their dissertations. Needless to say, as mentioned earlier, this can be a very stressful time until the candidate and committee are working in unison.

With the topic established and my research questions developed, it was time to work on methodology. My research required the creation of a quantitative assessment tool and a qualitative survey. The chair and committee members approved the tools and, as required in a quantitative study, I needed to pilot the assessment and the survey. I did so successfully and made the adjustments determined by the piloted research. One issue arose when one of the committee members suggested a change in the format after the piloted results were confirmed. The reason did not make sense so I rejected the suggestions. I heard one member of the committee comment, "I told you that she would not change." When I justified the value of the tools as is, the committee accepted the rationale and gave the go-ahead to begin recruiting participants.

As the data began to come in, I hired a statistician to help me with the statistical analysis. He completely understood the purpose and goals of the study and consistently reviewed the data as they came in. At one point, there was a discrepancy between the committee chair's interpretation and the statistician's view. Without me knowing it, a few heated emails were sent between them, and I was obligated to smooth things over and not lose my statistician. A compromise was met, and I incorporated suggestions from both viewpoints as I interpreted the data outcomes.

Other glitches occurred, such as when the fourth member, a professional colleague, was not on the faculty of the college and lived out of state. This member was selected for her valuable expertise related to the topic of the dissertation. However, at times she was left out of meetings, which should have been arranged via conference calls or left for me to arrange when no equipment was available. When she stated that she had not received emails summarizing the topics discussed, I felt again in an awkward position to keep the committee running smoothly.

At any point in the process, a network of support from colleagues, doctoral peers, and family members can make the journey more bearable. My family was my 'go to' support throughout the process. Stress can be heightened by any number of events. These could include the time spent waiting for feedback after a chapter submission; the appearance of numerous tracking notes as document feedback; or a reversed decision without any rationale that had been finalized with prior approval. Also, promises of a completion date that are not upheld can be devastating. The peak of the stress comes with the dissertation defense.

My committee offered me a reasonable defense date that was manageable for my preparation. This would have left sufficient time to meet the promised completion date at the end of the semester. Typically, the candidate expects the dissertation to be approved, usually with only minor editing changes to be completed. However, if the defense is accepted, but major changes to the dissertation theory or organization are expected, program completion can be extended for another semester. Sometimes only the smallest change is needed to meet precise APA format. Patience and stamina are the keys to completion at this point.

After the defense is presented and the committee questions are answered, the candidate is asked to wait outside as the committee makes its final decision. Usually, the candidate is welcomed back with congratulatory remarks. In my situation, I was invited back to a solemn group. I interpreted the atmosphere as one of failure. When I directly asked if I had passed, the committee members overwhelmingly responded that I had done a successful presentation and certainly had passed. However, the members suggested a major change to one of the theories that I had incorporated. It was the theory that had been required by the committee that I had stated would be irrelevant to the topic. Moreover, the final upset was that the committee would not be available to help me finish by the end of the semester, thus, adding another semester to the program. I felt devastated and isolated. It was difficult to discuss the outcome with my peers and family as my graduation had been anticipated by all.

I prepared the changes as required, submitted each chapter again for final approval, made the necessary APA format changes, and presented my manuscript to the college. Although I was numb after the nine-year commitment came to an end, I was ecstatic to attend my commencement ceremony and be hooded as a Doctor of Philosophy (PhD)!

The best advice for anyone considering pursuit of a doctoral degree would be to stay in good health and pace oneself. It is important to seek support and accept help with a smile. If possible, get family members to take over some of the home responsibilities. My family was wonderful during the nine years. When the pressure was high, I found that I needed to walk away from the reading or typing. I took time for myself to meet with friends or family, as social interactions were valuable distractions from the stressful situation. I regret to say that there will be tearful moments, points of frustration, feelings of defeat, and episodes of almost quitting. A semester break or a request for an Incomplete (I) grade in a course to use the extra time to complete may help. It was worth the journey, ultimately, for me to write my signature with the three coveted letters—PhD!

35.2 RETROSPECT

Many years have passed since I completed my doctoral degree. I felt the stress and strain of the process for almost a year. I often thought about how the experience could have been easier to complete. Although some of the pressure of my timeframe was related to my need to continue full-time employment and some personal concerns, I was under the impression that part-time study would not take me close to the ten-year limitation.

I would advise anyone interested in pursuing a doctoral degree to investigate the various programs that are related to one's interest and schedule a meeting with a department chair prior to making a commitment to the program. Get specific department policies in writing and confirmation on how program changes could affect current students over the years. Be sure that the program is the perfect fit before making a time and financial commitment. If it is not the right choice, address that early and make a change before getting too deeply immersed in the process. It is not a reflection on an individual if she/he decides to pursue a different path.

Be aware that 'bumps in the road' will occur and can be handled with patience and professionalism. The achievement of the doctoral degree is a collaborative process among the faculty who prepare the student, the committee members guiding the process, and the determined candidate eager to achieve the goal—the doctoral degree.

"The harder the conflict, the more glorious the triumph."

Thomas Paine (1737–1809, cited in Foner, 2001)

REFERENCES

Ali, S., & Kohun, F. (2006).Dealing with isolation feelings at IS doctoral programs. *International Journal of Doctoral Studies, 1,* 21–33. http://ijds.org/Volume 1/IJDSv1p021-033Ali13.pdf.

Foner, E. (2001). *Thomas Paine: Collected writings.* Penguin Random House. Retrieved from: https://loa.org/books/95-collected-writings?gclid=CjwKEAiAoa XFBRCNhauti Pvnqzo SJABzH d6hDSh_bNd2VmM.

CHAPTER 36

TALKING ME OFF THE LEDGE

WENDY NEIFELD WHEELER, PhD

Albany College of Pharmacy and Health Sciences, Albany, NY, USA

E-mail: wnwheeler1991@gmail.com

One could not imagine that it was a crisis-oriented, emotionally filled phone conversation that turned everything right-side up again. I am really not sure what would have happened if it hadn't been for that one phone exchange.

It is my belief that everyone anticipates challenges during the dissertation journey. We have heard the stories of unsupportive or unavailable committee members, data that have been lost, participants no longer willing to be interviewed, not enough data collected, and so forth, but I was more than unprepared for the challenge that came from the institution where I had been employed for 20+ years. I will refer to my "employment institution" as my home institution, because that is where I grew into the professional I am today. My home institution's IRB balked at my research questions and methodology. Yes, I said my home institution—not the institution where I was studying—but where I was employed.

As the story goes, I successfully built a powerhouse committee. Not only does the Dean of the School of Education agree to be my chair, I am well supported by a highly respected (female) faculty statistician and a (female) content expert. Both are enthusiastic about joining the dissertation committee. We meet as a team very regularly, and I receive helpful feedback that continues to push me forward. I effectively defend my proposal (with some minor tweaking of the research questions), sail through all IRB protocols, and have one final hoop to pass through before I can begin collecting data, which is tentatively scheduled for two months away.

While I was a doctoral candidate enrolled in a large local university, I was also a full-time student affairs professional at a smaller college in the same city. My proposal had been designed so that my sample would be drawn from my home college—the place of my employment. I had taken all aspects into consideration in making sure that no participant felt pressured into participating and that there would be no consequences for choosing not to participate or for withdrawing at any time during the process. And, as is typical, the survey responses were completely anonymous. I had secured a peer colleague to administer the paper and pencil survey, so that I was not present at the time of distribution and collection of the data. I had prepared a statement about the ability to participate or not, as well as how the entire study had been reviewed by the teaching institution's IRB and had met all approvals.

What I did not anticipate was that the chair of the IRB at my home institution had a personal bias against the research topic and questions. Due to that bias, when my request was being reviewed by the IRB committee, she made it clear that she was not in support of approval from IRB. This faculty member was a tenured, long-time teacher. As it turns out, her IRB colleagues did not agree and felt that the research project should be supported. I was in the clear to move ahead…I thought. That was until I received a phone call from the Provost of my home institution requesting a meeting with me and my supervisor, the Vice President for Student Affairs. The chair of the IRB had chosen to take it upon herself to contact the Provost (who was not directly or indirectly responsible for the decisions of the IRB) and communicate that she thought my research and data collection should not be permitted to occur.

This was an awkward and extremely stressful discussion on many levels. In summary, I was astounded: I was astounded that an individual faculty member's "opinion" of a research proposal could be taken under consideration, even though all IRB policies, procedures, and practices had resulted in an approval during the review; I was astounded that the Provost actually requested a meeting based solely on this faculty member's opinion, despite approval from the IRB; I was astounded that the Provost included my supervisor in the meeting request, as my academic pursuit of my doctoral degree was not the business of my employment supervisor; I was astounded that my dissertation committee was not included or consulted on this matter; I was astounded that I was required to answer questions proposed by the Provost, despite the fact that he had no jurisdiction over the decisions of the IRB; and, mostly, I was astounded that following the meeting, I was not given an immediate response permitting me to move forward with the research. I was asked to wait. Wait for what? I do not know.

It was at that moment that I called my dissertation chair and said I was done. I was no longer emotionally, physically, psychologically, or mentally able to withstand this unprofessional "hoop" that I was being asked to jump through. Every detail, angle, lens, policy, practice, and procedure had been followed with great care. Data collection was scheduled for approximately two months away. There was no other sample of participants that would be easily available. This was a barrier I did not understand and one for which I had no resources to overcome.

The phone call with my dissertation chair lasted about one-half hour. He reminded me of all that I had already accomplished. He reminded me of how meaningful the work I was doing would be—how it would fill a gap in the literature. He reminded me that there are always unexpected hoops and that I had already passed through several successfully. He said this was an unexpected but not unmanageable part of the challenge. He told me to think positively and take deep breaths. He talked me off the ledge. I had already taken one step off and the other foot was just barely holding on.

We ended the phone conversation and I cried. I cried out of frustration, confusion, and insecurity. I became immobilized and was not sure how to proceed. For a brief few moments, there was a sense of relief that it was over. I could close my computer, shred the articles that took up binder after binder on my shelves, cancel arrangements for the distribution of my survey, and let it go. But really, that only lasted a few brief moments, because what I realized was that the light at the end of the tunnel was getting brighter and brighter, and I would not let this nuisance barrier stop me from completing work that I valued and cared deeply about. I would become resistant to the challenges and take control of the situation. The voice in my head was that of my committee chair's—encouraging me, persuading me, coaxing me, and congratulating me on what I had already accomplished. I would not let myself down. Not this time and not in the future.

And so, I waited to hear the outcome. For about a week, I heard nothing and was unsure how to proceed, but starting to consider a Plan B for alternate samples. Finally, I received an email indicating that I could move forward with my data collection. I cried then too. Out of frustration, confusion, anger, and a small part of joy. None of what occurred was appropriate or professional. What happened did not particularly "make me stronger" or "build character," but it better prepared me to expect the unexpected and face it head on. It also became another story to be told.

CHAPTER 37

A PLACE FOR ME

AJA E. LADUKE, PhD

Sonoma State University, Rohnert Park, CA, USA

I entered my first day at Rana High School (RHS) excited about embarking on a new journey with a group of Latino/a high school students. My doctoral advisor, a Puerto Rican male university professor in his mid-thirties whom the students eventually called "Doc," had piloted a Youth Participatory Action Research (YPAR) (Cammarota and Fine, 2008) collective project the previous year. I had played an important but secondary role during the pilot year, working as a graduate assistant, but this new iteration of the project would serve as the source of my dissertation research, and I would have a more prominent role and increased interactions with the students. The core of the program, an elective course, titled "Action Research and Social Change," was well-received by the students the previous year at the magnet school, where the project originated. The projects they developed were inspiring, impressing hundreds of audience members at the numerous conferences and professional meetings where they presented their work. After the customary introductions, my advisor began to share with this new group of students some of the background of the course and several of the accomplishments of the previous cohort. While he was speaking, a student fidgeted in her chair staring at the floor and occasionally shaking her head disapprovingly.

Tania, a 15-year old Puerto Rican girl, looked up from the floor and stared at him. "Mister, what are you doing this for? Latinos are not smart; we are just not smart!" she responded. Several of her classmates nodded along, defending her claim and asserting their alleged genetically predisposed lack of intellect. Struck by the sweeping proclamation about the academic abilities of the class, Doc challenged them to provide evidence to support their case. "We are in the lowest classes," and "We are not like the White kids," were common responses in a threaded conversation that would span an innumerable number of classes, reemerging at various points throughout the year. The fact that Tania and her classmates were asserting the intellectual inferiority of Latinos to a Latino university professor with a doctorate was inconsequential to them. Their years in public schools had taught them one thing—"Latinos are not smart."

This was both shocking and logical to me at this point in my life. Hearing Tania's words being said so convincingly, surrounded by both verbal and nonverbal signs of agreement from her peers—even in the face of a successful, highly educated Latino adult example—was heartbreaking. As all of the students were juniors and seniors, it was clear that instead of challenging this belief, schooling had aided in it being deeply internalized and accepted as truth by these students. However, Tania's claims aligned with what I had read in my education courses—statistics about students of color being grossly underrepresented in honors and AP classes, and overrepresented in lower-tiered classes, critiques of an overly Eurocentric curriculum, and schools' practices in general being normed to a White, suburban, English-only standard that matched the demographics of the majority of their teachers. What I realized as I reflected on the day, my thoughts and emotions swimming, was that unlike last year's students who had attributed at least some of these patterns to flaws in the educational system, this group's explanations fell on the other end of the spectrum. In other words, these predicaments were to be attributed to Latinos themselves.

I knew of the segregated worlds of urban schools through texts, and I had been a visitor in urban schools as a teacher candidate, but I had never been immersed in this environment fully until this unique role. To clarify, I was not a student teacher, an intern, or the instructor of record for the action research course, so I was able to observe the student-researchers from a unique standpoint. I watched them navigate through contexts and decide which identities to perform and which languages they used to enact them. I respected the literacy they had to "read the world" (Freire & Macedo, 1987), to read situations, to know which roles to play and when. To be literate in a way that I had never been. This was a literacy that I had never had to develop nor did I need it to survive, and certainly not when at school. I had never had to show anyone that they were "wrong about White kids" and were underestimating what I was capable of. These personal and psychological struggles were never part of my life, or my schooling. I never had to learn how to survive in the "White man's world." To me it was just "the world." I was building a deeper and more sophisticated understanding of it being "a man's world" around the same stage when I was undergoing my studies, looking ahead to being on the job market and reading enlightening research on salary negotiation and other parts of the hiring process. This made me think deeply about how, what I knew from books about educational inequity, these students knew from their day-to-day experience. Though I could cite researchers and use scholarly terms to describe what I saw, they had more knowledge than I ever could.

As our meetings progressed, the students learned these terms as well and came to life in reading works by Latino/a scholars who wrote about injustice in schools like theirs. They began to become scholars themselves, blending the work with what they knew from their lives in public schools. We all found out more about each other, which included Doc sharing stories of his own childhood in New York City, music that his family listened to, and other traditions. These stories, often told in a mix of Spanish and English, resonated with the students' own experiences. For the first time, I was sitting in a school, in this unique space created within it, and feeling like "the other."

As the project progressed, the students were involved in similar research and academic endeavors as their previous cohort. Their perspectives began to shift about schools and themselves. A pivotal point in the year came when students chose to investigate how prepared their teachers felt to work with Latino students. Had they had any courses or professional development, or even life experiences (travel or otherwise), that had addressed aspects of the many Latino cultures—Mexican, Puerto Rican, Dominican, and so forth, that were represented at their school? The students, with our support, designed and administered the survey to the RHS faculty at one of their staff meetings, explaining how the survey was situated within the greater research project. The results were, similarly to Tania's argument on Day 1, equally shocking and at the same time not surprising. The responses were fraught with deficit perspectives on Latino students, families, communities—making blanket generalizations about the presence of Spanish, as well as the absence of parents, in their homes. Only seven or eight teachers out of 90 made comments such as "maybe I don't do enough to connect with this population."

Doc and I were the initial readers of the responses, and our stomachs sank. We expected this to some degree but were also overwhelmed at reading these sentiments over and over, and knowing that our students—being the researchers and creators of the survey—would also have to read these statements. Their reactions ranged from dismissal, "This is what we already knew, you guys" to tears, to anger, and back again.

Some of the highest points of the project, making much of this anguish worth it, were the students' presentations of their research at education conferences. Suddenly, a group of students, whose voices had been largely silenced at their own school, were presenting alongside experienced teachers, advanced college students, professors, and other scholars—and were often the "hit of the party" so to speak, with audience members filling seats and approaching them like paparazzi at the end of the presentation.

Shortly after one of these many presentations, as per our routine, we were going to spend class time talking with the student-researchers about the presentation they had just given the week prior. This was a pretty routine occurrence for everyone at this point in the year. A large part of the overall project was to check in with students after these experiences. Do they feel any difference? How does it make them feel to be up in front of a room of practicing and preservice teachers who are looking to them for advice on how to improve their instruction and interactions with students? But this day was slightly different. Students responded to our prompts for about 30 minutes of the hour-long class period. During a pause in the conversation, they shifted the camera onto the adults, coming up with their own discussion questions to ask us. To me, it was a sign that they had truly adopted their new "researcher identities." They took the skills they had developed as a result of being interviewed several times by the university researchers and through conducting their own interviews for their research, and applied them in this real-world context.

As a White, monolingual female from a suburban community, I shared many identity characteristics of the teachers at RHS and in schools across the nation. However, unlike many teachers, I had the opportunity to immerse myself in a research project where I was thrust into learning with and from Latina youth. In contrast to traditional teacher preparation, where you are there to try new methods out on students, we were all vulnerable (although I acknowledge my adult identity and status as graduate student afforded me power), albeit in different ways. As the only White member of the research collaborative, I was constantly confronted with my White identity and aware of how my racial identity might impact the group and my interactions with students. While I had taught in public schools before, this was fundamentally different. As a teacher, there was no ambiguity about who was in charge and who held the power in those relationships. Working within this research collaborative, power was distributed differently.

Thinking back, I am flooded with moments in which I felt powerfully interconnected with my student-researcher colleagues. For example, I did not predict the surprise and sadness I would feel from hearing our student-researchers passionately insist that they were not smart. I did not know that months later this sick-to-my-stomach feeling would reappear when reading the responses to the teacher survey. I didn't predict the shock or anger. I didn't know that I would hurt along with the kids. Yes, I knew I would learn, but I didn't know I would feel too—in such deep ways. I wanted to tear the surveys out of their hands to spare them from the anguish, yet I knew that they needed to see them and have the chance to rise up from them. I could not have predicted the sense of community I felt on our train trip to Washington, DC, or the joy I would feel in being invited to and attending one of the student's family parties.

I did not know at the time how life-changing this would be for me, not simply as a young scholar, but as an educator and a human being. I was learning from these students as part of my research, but they became my teachers in so many ways. Not only that, they became a support network for me as I completed the final phase of my dissertation. I was compelled to tell their stories; to share the ways in which they were talented, intelligent, insightful, creative, and worthy in ways that many of their teachers had never taken the time or had the access to see. I vividly remember typing in an interview quote from one of our students, Juliana, about how she never thought about college as 'a place for her.' I paused for a moment and considered myself at her age, just over a decade earlier. In the surroundings of a high school that never failed to reflect who I was—whether it was through the faculty and administrators, the curriculum, or the language heard throughout the classrooms and halls—I never thought about *not* attending college immediately after high school. Now, here, I was typing away late at night in my own personally designated "cubby space" in the campus library wearing comfortable sweats touting the university name—how much more at home could I possibly feel?

How might telling these students' stories help them and others like them to feel like college can be a place for them, or even a home? This question and the idea that my work—and more importantly, their work—could set this shift in motion kept me going. On nights when I felt I couldn't write another word, I saw their faces and heard their voices in my mind. I was not writing simply for my advisor or my committee or the academic community at large—I was writing for them.

REFERENCES

Cammarota, J., & Fine, M. (Eds.). 2008. *Revolutionizing education: Youth participatory action research in motion.* London, U.K.: Routledge.

Freire, P., & Macedo, D. (1987). *Literacy: Reading the word and the world.* South Hadley, MA: Bergin & Garvey.

CHAPTER 38

MY ALBATROSS: COMPLETING THE DISSERTATION AT LAST

JENNIFER A. BROWN, PhD

University of Massachusetts, Boston, MA, USA

It only took 18 years to finish my doctorate. I started in spring 1974, having persuaded the university to accept my BA Honors from the University of Reading.[1] This I completed in 1972, followed rapidly by marriage and immigration to the USA. It was indeed a lot more of a culture shock in so many dimensions of life than I had anticipated. One example, I was expected by my mother-in-law, with whom we were living, to make my husband's lunch to take to work each day. As requested, I made peanut butter and 'jelly' (jam) sandwiches, separately.

But being accepted into the PhD program in the Sociology Department at the University of Connecticut[2] brought friends, a familiar rural landscape, and an environment in which I was used to being successful and respected. It was about a year later that my husband told me he was leaving to "find himself," but not that he was leaving with the married woman next door. They left. Eventually, they returned and I realized that making it by myself had to be done! First, complete the master's credits, and exam, then the additional 24 credits, the proposal, and the dissertation. No problem.

There are a lot of stories from that time; a lot of life was lived. I would not have survived without the community of friends who surrounded me. To this day, I do not know where the voice came from that told my worried parents that I appreciated their invitation to return home with them, but that I would think about that after I had completed my PhD

---

[1] The University of Reading is located in Reading, Berkshire, United Kingdom. More information can be found at https://www.reading.ac.uk/.

[2] The University of Connecticut is located in Storrs, Connecticut, USA. More information can be found at http://uconn.edu/.

I failed the first time around to take my master's exam. I just could not complete it and had to withdraw from the attempt. It felt like a devastating failure. My major advisor even suggested that I consider trying the exam again and then quitting with the master's. That was also devastating. But I was determined not to fail a second time, and I kept going, taking the exam a year later and passing it, meanwhile accumulating credits toward the doctoral requirements. And I made it.

By 1979, I was really tired of food stamps and scrambling for jobs every summer and every academic year, so when my new major advisor told me about an opportunity for a new job in a nearby city planning department to assist with the 1980 census, I jumped at it. My dissertation data on the phenomenon of urban, rural turnaround migration was collected, thanks to my excellent major advisor. Among his many supportive and practical acts, this wonderful faculty member, a demographer, had hired me to manage the data collection for some grant-funded research, and had carved out for me a piece of the data. I was done with my coursework, and apart from a couple of incompletes, what could go wrong? I could finish up in a year or so.

I had a great time working for the city. One year stretched to two and three. The justification for a demographer on staff at city hall got weaker as the census results were out and available, and my life moved further and further away from the University. These changes were exacerbated after a bad house fire made the flat I had lived in since starting graduate school uninhabitable overnight. My home was gone. It happened the first evening the woman I had come to love came to dinner at my place. As a friend said later that night, "Hot date, huh?" Which is a lot funnier now than it was then. It took a long time to get over the trauma of the fire.

Together, my new love and I rented a flat, introduced our cats to each other, and started out on a happy new future. And along came the dissertation albatross; boxes of papers, piles of books, and my incredible guilt and sense of failure about my goal.

Thanks to an ad in the newspaper (remember those?) found by my partner (and now wife), I embarked on a new career about which I knew nothing, becoming an Associate for Institutional Research at a public university system office, working for a truly admirable and talented provost. I learned fast, it was a great fit, and it was intellectually challenging and brought a whole new set of colleagues, and learning and the satisfaction of making a difference in something important.

This, and ever-increasing political involvement with progressive and feminist organizations taking leadership roles, led to a renewed sense of competence and periodic efforts to get back to my dissertation with more and more elderly data. I tried rethinking the topic. We were active in the gay and lesbian civil rights movement, friends started getting diagnosed with HIV, getting sick, and began to die. At that time, it really seemed as if this awful epidemic would be unstoppable.

I started reading and reading the growing literature and research on AIDS and thinking and talking with colleagues in the sociology department. Gradually, I realized that I had already managed and completed complex projects bigger than many handled by the faculty in the department, and that the dissertation was 'just' a project, and not the impossible mountain it had become in my mind. So I went back, talked to my advisor about changing the topic to examining gender, social power, and safer sex practices. He thought that was good, but he did not have the expertise to chair it. He suggested another faculty member, and I talked to her.

She agreed to take me on. The university agreed that if I paid them for every semester I had missed, they would take me back. My dissertation advisor and I decided on two additional faculty members for the dissertation committee and a plan for completion. And I started writing proposals, one after another after another! The patience of that terrific woman, editing and returning, rereading and editing, and getting me to a doable, theoretically sound project that I could accomplish using available resources!

That is the hardest part of the work, particularly in social science and humanities disciplines: getting to the solid, clear proposal with hypotheses, and a sound method to test them. Find the faculty member who can do that with you, make them your committee chair, and you can do it!

I collected the data at four university campuses, each with different IRB requirements in spite of being in the same system. In those days, we used paper and scanners, so we actually exploded a pencil sharpener preparing those little golf pencils to hand out for respondents to use. It was the early days of computing, I generated miles of paper printing the statistical output (I had six null hypotheses) on dot matrix printers.

I had worked long enough to be eligible for a six-month sabbatical, so I applied and got the OK with the proviso that I spend two days a week keeping things going in my one full-time person (me), one co-op student (20 hours a week) office. I said OK! And I ran the stats and wrote and reran the stats and wrote and just kept going. I stuck to the minimum 15 minutes a day strategy, and if that was all I could do, I stopped there and walked the dog. I had a big cheering section, which was wonderful!

I had already learned that taking editorial advice is not destroying one's own voice. I had learned that persistence is the most important characteristic necessary once the proposal is approved. I had learned that the text formatting always seems to take longer than any of the writing.

I had also learned that intelligence is not the same as having a PhD, and I was determined to stop giving those who hire the perfect excuse for discrimination by not having a doctorate. And I wanted the albatross gone from around my shoulders.

So I kept writing and responding to the feedback. Until the feedback giver requested a return to the original text. We are all fallible! My advice is: never hand in fewer than three chapters at a time, get your committee chair to work with you until her/his needs are met before it goes to other committee members, select your committee very carefully, including their sabbatical schedules and their turnaround times, and have a timetable that you and your committee chair agree upon up front—and stick to it.

And then it was 1992, and my beloved, my parents, and my best friend from graduate school showed up and cheered, and I was hooded at the graduate ceremony celebrating 100 years of women enrolling at the University, by the head of the Women's Studies program, and the speaker was Ellen Peters, head of the state supreme court, and I stood there silently thanking all those women for all the years of fighting for our right to be there on that stage.

> And from my neck so free
> The Albatross fell off, and sank
> Like lead into the sea.
> The Rime of the Ancient Mariner (text of 1834)
> > —Samuel Taylor Coleridge

CHAPTER 39

A STORY OF THRIVING AND ARRIVING: MY ONLINE PhD JOURNEY

PATRICE JENKINS, PhD

Catskill, NY, USA

I completed a PhD program in Industrial and Organizational Psychology at an accredited online university. The degree requirements included three one-week residential colloquia. In total, I finished the program in four and a half years, having entered with a master's degree in counseling. Over the course of these years, there were many times that my motivation waned, and I struggled to write research papers and create insightful discussion posts. When I wanted to quit, well-meaning friends would say, "Do you wish you hadn't started?" My response, "No, I wish I didn't want it."

What did I want? I wanted something more for myself. I wanted a new challenge. I wanted the credibility that comes with three initials after my name, PhD. At the time I was developing a public speaking business and writing a book on the psychological and sociological sides of retirement. I believed the doctorate degree would place me on an even playing field with other consultants who address the nonfinancial side of retirement. How to go about getting what I wanted surfaced over lunch when a colleague told me about an online university that she was considering enrolling in for a doctorate degree. When I got back to my desk, I checked out the university's website. I sent an email to request more information, received a phone call within the hour, and was enrolled a month later.

Because I had never taken an online course before, I was hesitant to commit to a doctorate program through an online learning environment. To ease my concerns, I decided the first class would be an experiment. If I did not like this educational format, I could quit at the end of the quarter. Surprisingly, I also signed up for my first colloquium during the first 10 weeks of study. I am not sure why I did this so early in the program. Maybe there was a good deal on airfare then, or I needed a break from my three teenagers, or perhaps it was divine intervention. When I boarded the plane for the colloquium, I was five weeks into my first class, feeling isolated and overwhelmed. Quitting at the end of the quarter had begun to look more appealing than not. However, being at the colloquium and directly interacting with faculty and students gave me a greater sense of immediacy, that the university, though not brick-and-mortar, was "real." Now I could place a face to a name for some of my professors. In addition, meeting students attending their second or third colloquiums gave me hope: "If they can do it, I can do it." By the end of the week, I had been to the gift shop, bought a university coffee mug and baseball cap, and decided I was committing to finishing.

The first three years of my doctoral journey proceeded as planned. I had charted the required coursework over a three-year period so the path was clear: get through one class and register for the next, work hard, and repeat. Not that it was easy. As I said earlier, many times I felt like quitting. So, I taped a piece of paper to my computer with these words: "Everyone who doesn't quit, finishes." I wanted to be among the finishers. I also made a pact with myself that I could quit at the *end* of the 10-week quarter but not *during* the quarter. Almost every quarter had a trying time when I wanted to just give up. However, once I made it through the course, I no longer wanted to quit. Instead, the successful completion motivated me to enroll in the next class.

This method worked fairly well until I hit the most critical period in my doctoral journey: deciding on my research topic. I had completed all my course requirements and comprehensive exams, but as for going forward with the next steps of committing to a research topic, methodology, and research site, suddenly I felt discouraged, depleted, and just plain stuck. My self-confidence plummeted. For the previous couple years, I had thought I wanted to study retirement anxiety. During these two years, I had researched and written a small book on retirement anxiety and was presenting noncredit seminars at the local community college, where I worked as an assistant dean. Perhaps because I was already speaking and writing about retirement, I felt more driven to study something new and fresh for my dissertation. I wanted my topic to do something for me that I did not already have, including open doors to a corporate work environment. However, by changing my research topic, I was back to the start. I needed to come up with a dissertation topic, and soon. Fortunately, I had a very understanding mentor who encouraged me to "get in the literature" and find something that I was passionate about studying.

In a more traditional university, I likely would have selected my degree program based on a professor's area of expertise and, over the course of three or four years, would have contributed to this professor's research. Maybe my name would have been included on the list of published works. In contrast, at an online university, I did not have the opportunity to conduct research. I had to find an interest that was important to me, not merely latch onto my mentor's or professors' interests. I wanted to be excited about my research topic. I knew it would require more time, energy, and dedication than any of my previous educational pursuits. To find my way, I read numerous journals and books until one day my topic found me. I had been reading a chapter on the phenomenon of "thriving at work" (Spreitzer & Sutcliffe, 2007) and literally connected with this very positive phenomenon myself. *Thriving*—a psychological state of experiencing simultaneous feelings of vitality, energy, growth, and development—inspired me as an important topic, and I knew, "This is what I want to invest my time in researching." It struck me as potentially valuable to listen to and collect the personal stories of people who are thriving at what they do. Future research called for studies on collective thriving at work. I set out to find a company that represented collective thriving, a group, unit, or organization that is learning and growing as a whole (Spreitzer & Sutcliff, 2007). This proved to be a difficult undertaking as I learned organizations and businesses may not be agreeable to participating in a research study.

The company that I was most interested in studying was the Eileen Fisher (EF) Company,[3] a manufacturer of high-end women's apparel that is beautiful, stylish, and produced with a social conscience. EF was in its sixth year on the Great Place to Work list (Best Companies List, 2009). I read everything publicly available about EF and, thus, felt confident that it was a company that thrived at a collective level.

The university did not have ties to or previous studies with this company so I had to find my own way in. I started with an email to customer service and followed up with a phone call. It was a long shot. This department is expecting to hear from customers about their purchases, not a doctoral student requesting a research study. Fortunately, the customer service employee was kindhearted enough to put me through to the voicemail of the human resource (HR) director.

Over a seven-month period, I communicated with the HR director, answering her questions and addressing her concerns. My mentor helped me with this process, providing information on how much time my research would require of the HR department and how many onsite visits I would likely need to complete the interviews.

---

[3]Permission granted by the Eileen Fisher Company to identify the company in this narrative (S. Simberkoff, personal communication, January 6, 2017).

At one point, I was about to give up on getting my first choice to agree to the research study. Seven months is a long time to wait. During this time, I contacted another company on the Great Place to Work list. The director of this company's HR department informed me that the company policy was to allow no research projects. I also reached out to a smaller health-related company, a reference given me by a friend who was employed there and felt her work team represented collective thriving. However, my friend's supervisor did not approve the study. I got a little further with another company that rehabilitates individuals on society's margins by hiring them to bake brownies for a national ice cream company. Unfortunately, during the time this company's HR director and I were exploring the possibility of a study, a new chief executive officer came on board who did not view a research study as a priority. The seemingly unfruitful leads and the rejections by three companies were a new low point in my doctoral journey as I questioned whether I would ever find a company to study. Finally, in the spring of 2010, after over seven months of waiting, I learned through a conference call with four employees from EF's corporate headquarters that the company had agreed to my study. That was a happy day!

Once I had made it through the most critical period of my doctoral journey, defining a research topic and securing a research site, I dealt with nagging questions: Will I know how to do this? To conduct a case study? I had worked so hard to get my preferred company to say yes. Now it was time for me to come through. I suspect that second-guessing oneself—at least some of the time—is common among doctoral students. Fortunately, my mentor was there to encourage me, build up my confidence in research methods, and provide insightful scholarly support when I needed it.

Anticipating the challenge of making it through the dissertation process, at my third colloquium, I intentionally connected with three students who were at the same stage of their doctoral journey. During the research and writing period, we would hold "blockbuster" meetings—a designated time to work and check in hourly with each other via conference call. Knowing that my friends were working on their dissertations helped motivate me to put in the time. We were "study buddies," even though we lived across the country from one another. When any of my buddies expressed feelings of defeat, it did wonders for my own motivation to support them in their goal.

The research at EF turned out to be everything I had hoped it would be. The interviews with employees gave me fascinating information about thriving, even in high pressure, high-stakes situations. I relished the walk into the corporate headquarters and the design center, surrounded by beautiful clothing and people who were very happy with their jobs. While transcribing and coding the interviews, I decided to forfeit a vacation with my family so that I could interact with the material all day without interruptions. This self-imposed solitude for work was one of the best decisions I made. It was with great personal satisfaction that I realized how far I had come from the beginning of the critical phase: persisting and persevering to identify a topic I was passionate about, then researching and securing a site that I was excited about studying—and now writing and publishing the research. In the end, it was all worth it. I got what I wanted—something more, a challenge, and Patrice Jenkins, PhD.

REFERENCES

Best Companies List. (2009). Retrieved from: www.greatplacetowork.com/best/index.php.

Spreitzer, G., & Sutcliffe, K. (2007) Thriving in organizations. In D. L. Nelson & C. L. Cooper (Eds.). *Positive Organizational Behavior* (pp. 74-85). Thousand Oaks, CA: Sage.

CHAPTER 40

THE DOCTORAL STUDY: THE INTERTWINED PROFESSIONAL TRANSITION AND PERSONAL TRANSFORMATION

YING TANG, PhD

State University of New York at Oneonta, Oneonta, NY, USA

Being the first child in my immediate as well as among my extended family, including cousins and siblings, and so forth, allowed me the opportunity to experience many "firsts" in my life. I was a first-generation college student, the first one in my family who went overseas to pursue an advanced degree, and the only one who earned a PhD. I have always been very proud of being a strong and independent woman who defied some traditional beliefs about what a woman can or should do. In order to be independent, I have learned that I have to be courageous and quickly adapt or learn new skills to fit into a new environment. Traveling thousands of miles to a foreign land and learning a new way to live in the United States really put my adaptability to the test. The road I have traveled is not a common path for a woman from Taiwan leading a traditional Taiwanese lifestyle.

The last stage of my doctoral studies was quite eventful; however, I will start my narrative on one significant incident that kicked off this stage, my pregnancy. I have to admit, my husband and I were quite naïve and very optimistic when we decided to start a family before I finished my degree. In the perfect plan, I thought I would have my baby soon after I completed the degree. In reality, that perfect scenario didn't happen. Owing to the unexpected low return rate of my dissertation survey, I had to send out a second round of surveys to makeup the insufficient data for my research. Consequently, the amount of time it took for data collection was much longer than I had planned. While I waited again for the surveys to be returned, I had to take a break to have my baby. The pregnancy and a delay in collecting dissertation data resulted in almost a whole year delay in my graduation timeline. By this time, almost all my cohorts had finished their degrees and left either for home or for a job. I had to spend the last few months writing by myself, which was quite lonely without the peer support that I had often relied on during my doctoral studies. According to Protivnak & Foss (2009), peer support has been identified as one of the significant support systems for doctoral students. Ali & Kohun (2007) also assert that doctoral students who decided not to complete their degree often stated that the reason for non-completion was due to feelings of social isolation. I found myself often reaching out to my dissertation advisor whom I trusted and depended on not only for academic support but for moral and psychological support. We worked closely during that time, brainstorming ways to increase the survey return rate or suggestions on how I should write the last few chapters.

In fact, the departmental culture of my doctoral program was warm and welcoming in addition to the oft-mentioned "Southerners' hospitality." My professors were caring and friendly. I felt like I could go to them if ever I had any questions or concerns. Being the only Asian student in the program, I never felt left out or unwelcome on campus, which really helped me establish a sense of belonging to the program. Protivnak & Foss (2009) have identified departmental culture as one of the significant factors influencing doctoral students' experiences on campus, which accurately reflected my own experience on campus.

Eventually, as a first-time mom, having a baby to take care of posed many new challenges. Not only did I have to deal with diapers, bottles, and sleep deprivation, I also had resumed writing and tried to finish my dissertation within a few months. Again, in my perfect plan, I thought I could manage the tasks of being a mom while concurrently concentrating on finishing my degree. Research and data have shown that balancing a family and career goals have always been a challenge for professional women (Castaneda & Isgro, 2013; Castle & Woloshyn, 2003). Using my own experience tackling both childcare and a professional goal, I found myself more worried about completing my dissertation than enjoying the experience of being a new mom.

Furthermore, as if there was not enough anxiety to keep me on my toes, I also started the job search process, and a few schools had already contacted me for interviews. There were countless times that I had to stop writing to attend to my daughter's needs. In the meantime, my husband had an 8–5 job, and he could only help out when he was home. When he was home, he would walk around our apartment holding our colicky daughter for an extended time every evening. When I had to fly across the county for a job interview, he would stay at home with the baby. I remember calling home to check on them in the evening when I was away. My daughter's crying came through the phone so loudly, I could barely hear him. My last few months as a doctoral student were quite a challenging time for both of us.

As my husband and I knew very little about how to raise a baby, I often called my mother in Taiwan asking her questions or trying to find solutions to various baby-related issues. Moments like those made me realize that I couldn't continue without help. Needless to say, I was making very little progress with my dissertation and the deadline was fast approaching. I eventually faced my defeat and begged my parents to come to the United States and help me out, so I could finish writing. My parents obtained their visas and airplane tickets and came within a month and stayed with us to take care of my daughter so I could finally sit down for a decent amount of time and focus on writing the last few chapters of my dissertation. I am very grateful and feel very fortunate to have loving and supportive parents who would drop everything to come to my rescue. In conclusion, like I mentioned before, I didn't feel like I finished the degree all by myself. Along the journey, I had plenty of support from my peers, family, spouse, and my professors. If I could do it all over again, I would not do anything differently. Based on these personal experiences, I would recommend to women who are in the doctoral program to:

- Face the insecurity and fear, be open to new experiences, and be willing to take risks
- Have the courage to challenge some traditional beliefs about what a woman can achieve
- Reach out and build good relationships with professors and peers, because most likely they will become your strongest allies
- Be strong and feel in your heart that you can succeed, and
- Gracefully accept that you need help and do not be afraid to ask for help when you need it. I believe there should be a distinction between being stubborn and being self-aware.

REFERENCES

Castaneda, M., & Isgro, M. (Eds.). 2013. *Mothers in academia.* New York, NY: Columbia University Press.

Castle, J., & Woloshyn, V. (2003). Motherhood and academia: Learning from our lived experience. *Journal of the Association for Research on Mothering, 5*(2), 35–46.

Ali, A.; Kohun, F. (2007). Dealing with social isolation to minimize doctoral attrition—a four
stage framework. *International Journal of Doctoral Studies, 2,* 33–49. Retrieved from:
http://www.informingscience.org/Journals/IJDS/Articles?Volume=2–2007&Search.

Protivnak, J. J., & Foss, L. L. (2009). An exploration of themes that influence the counselor
education doctoral student experience. *Counselor Education & Supervision, 48,* 239–256.

CHAPTER 41

DEAR MILES: LETTERS FROM A GRATEFUL PhD STUDENT

KIT ANDERSON, PhD

University of Vermont, Burlington, VT, USA

Dear Miles,

I'm so sorry about the car exploding on the bridge yesterday. Well, not exactly exploding, but it was scary to be caught in that traffic with smoke pouring out from under the hood. Thank goodness we managed to get to the exit and find help. Blown head gasket, it turns out. At least we weren't too far from home.

Anyway, I hope we can plan another trip soon. Chasing down live oaks is great fun, and hearing peoples' stories about them even better. But there are definitely mysteries about why they are where they are and I'd love your help.

I'll let you know when my car is fixed or I can borrow one. And thanks again for your time. I know you're busy.

Dear Miles,

All right, I'm over that last round of despair. It did upset me, finding a book on live oaks by an anthropologist that seemed to have done what I thought was my idea. But you're right, hers was not a study of landscape and place and in fact, her book gives me more material to work with. This whole process of choosing a topic is fraught with worries.

At least I don't have to choose between live oaks in Louisiana and Ceibas in Guatemala. I'm so glad you suggested I do both. Long live comparative studies!

Dear Miles,

I'm glad you persuaded me to stay enrolled in one class this semester as I go through chemo. It helps a lot be in a classroom with others regularly. Do I really look a bit green around the edges? Last week I burst out laughing when I realized I was lying outside my apartment on blankets, too tired to sit up, reading Denial of Death for class. How tragic it must have looked.

Dear Miles,

Greetings from Guatemala. The time here has been amazing. You were right that no matter what I planned, things would likely change. Ceibas keep popping up in unexpected places, and at higher elevations than I expected. My Spanish teacher took me to see one in a village above Antigua. Now she wants to plant one in her yard. I was asked to give a talk on Ceibas at my Spanish school the other day. Nerve-wracking, but the teachers were kind and said they were glad to learn so much about their national tree.

Right now I'm tracking down famous Ceibas listed in an old book I found in a used bookstore. It's taking me all over the country. I also visited your black Christ in Esquipulas. I imagine you and Bill here, watching the pilgrims, listening, taking notes, joining them as they line up to touch the statue.

One of the Benedictine fathers took me out in a jeep to scout for more Ceibas. It was both odd and relaxing to speak English. I learned that the Ceiba with the whitewashed trunk in front of the cathedral (the one Bill photographed) was actually planted by one of the Louisiana Benedictines, not by a Guatemalan. He thought it was the right thing to do.

Before leaving, I found some Tierra del Santo tablets in the market. That reminded me of when I first met you, on my way back from Guatemala after 3 months of travel. Thought I'd better check out Louisiana State University (LSU) before starting my PhDs there. After Kathleen introduced us in your office, I burbled on about how I loved Guatemala. You understood immediately, then pulled open a file drawer, reached way into the back and brought out a carefully wrapped clay tablet and explained what it was. That was it. I knew you would be my advisor (even if you are an anthropologist, not a geographer).

Dear Miles,

Back for a few weeks now and totally overwhelmed. What to do with all these notes, images, maps, articles? It's chaos! I don't even know where to start. Need to talk.

Dear Miles,

You're very welcome. Considering what happened with my car, it's amazing you trusted me to drive the van with all those graduate students last weekend. Even when I drove over the parking curb and almost missed the first ramp, you stayed remarkably cheerful and encouraging. Did I tell you I actually hate driving? Only for you.

I can't remember being hotter and sweatier, except maybe on a bus in Guatemala. Too bad we got the van without air conditioning and a roof that banged. But somehow it was a great adventure, from archeological site to the monstrously huge dam trying to control the Mississippi tributary. You kept us laughing and made sure we had plenty of food and drink and thought-provoking questions. But my favorite scene was all of us gathered around on a sidewalk, listening to a scratchy recording of your beloved Hank Williams, as you stood there in your cowboy hat and boots, grinning.

I get the feeling all your students think you're the best professor ever. Especially the women. You take us seriously, and trust us to do well.

Now back to work.

Dear Miles,

The conference presentation at the Association of American Geographers (AAG) went well. The room was packed, and several other graduate students said they wished they had chosen something as interesting as my topic. Of course, they could have....

Although it drove the AV (audio-visual) people crazy, having two slide projectors and screens to show comparisons between live oaks and Ceibas side by side worked well. Thank you for all your help and encouragement to go ahead with this, difficult as it was, and for going through it with me before the meetings. It really did need trimming. Then again, this is all your fault. As you told me, comparative studies bring up all kinds of interesting and unexpected questions.

Dear Miles,

Sorry I haven't been in recently. I've thought about this long and hard. Seems to me this has been a wonderful experience, learning all about Ceibas and live oaks, about the culture, geography, and history of Louisiana and Guatemala, and about individual big trees that are so important to people. But honestly, it's enough now. I don't know what to do anymore. I may need to change topics or something.

Remember when Hurricane Andrew hit and you suggested an ethnography of a hurricane would be a great topic? Well, that week I was studying for comps, huddled next to a window because the power was out. Now I wish I'd chosen that for my research. It seems important, relevant, and has nice boundaries. Or how about I go back to flowers? You know, the role of flowers in landscapes, their symbolism, color, how they affect the experience of place, even when they are not blooming?

Or maybe I just need to find a job. Rethink my life. Go back to editing? It's also possible I'm in the wrong field. I'm wondering about Theology. Could I maybe switch now? This just isn't working.

Dear Miles,

Thanks for being there last week. You are so gracious, always ready to listen patiently to crazed students. I knock on your door, peer around to see you at your desk by the window, and then you stand up, give me a big smile and say, "Come in, sit down," and pull out a chair for me at the table. Time slows down.

How did you learn to be so patient when interrupted, to listen so intently, without laughing out loud when I come in with completely absurd ideas? You accepted all my woes, heard all the whining and misery, acknowledged how difficult this work can be, and then made a few simple suggestions. Patience, you said. A little rest. You also reminded me about some of the good things I've already completed. And now I'm fine, ready to go on. Flowers? Theology? What was I thinking?

Thank you, as always.

Dear Miles,

Teaching a class of 350, alone, for the first time this semester has made it difficult to get as much writing done as I'd hoped. It's frustrating. In two weeks, I'll leave for Vermont and before going I absolutely have to have some sort of draft done. I mean, this could go on forever. So here's the thing. I'm going to spend one week writing a chapter a day and whatever comes out you will have to agree to read or it's all over. Can you do that? Please? It might be a mess. But I need to get a sense of the whole instead of just little pieces.

Dear Miles,

Hello from Vermont. Made it, finally. Minus my computer, which was stolen from my trailer during the move. Fortunately, I had everything backed up on disks, so all is not lost. Will be back to work soon.

Thanks for reading the mess I left you. Now that I've had a little time away, I can see you're absolutely right. I have not yet "found my voice." What a kind way to put it.

You're absolutely right about the beginning. I just got so entranced by the evolution of trees that it seemed important to go into deep history. I'll start again with the sections that make the most sense and send you something in a few months. At least there is something on paper to work with. Still a bit hung up on how to do the comparisons, but I think your idea of natural and cultural history chapters with main sections on each tree within them, and a comparison at the end sounds good.

Dear Miles,

Again, teaching has taken up all my brain power. Another big class, this one on international environmental issues. It's depressing as hell. How students manage to go on in this field is beyond me. But I'm getting back to writing now and plan to be done by the end of the year. Will send each chapter as it's finished. I've included an outline to show you how it's shaping up.

Dear Miles,

Thanks for your comments. Things are coming together, finally. I had someone from geography read several chapters. He liked the natural history section. The rest he considered "discursive" and was surprised I was allowed to write like that. Not entirely sure what he means, though suspect it's too simple in style, not academic (i.e., stuffy) enough. Thanks for supporting readable English.

How soon do I have to have things in to the others so we're ready for the defense? I'm a bit worried about that since you're the only one who has been reading this stuff regularly. Received one objection to what I said about tree pruning styles. Completely unfounded, of course. I'm quoting people who work with trees every day. But what to do?

Dear Miles,

All right, yes, I can modify that section to suggest there are differences of opinion and style concerning live oak pruning. You're so diplomatic, allowing all points of view without judgment. I still get impatient, don't I? Let's see if this version works. I hope there aren't any surprises.

Looks like all is set for my defense next week. Now that I have something to wear, all is well at this end. It will be good to see you.

Dear Miles,

Thank you for a wonderful dinner. I bet you thought this day would never come. Seeing you and the rest of the faculty, especially Dr. West, and so many graduate students was a real treat.

I hope you were happy with the presentation. The question session was actually interesting, except for you-know-who. What drives some people to play such stupid games? I kept thinking you could stop him. But I guess that's not how it works. Just have to deal with it. The final suggestions from the committee were all valid and doable and I've done my best to incorporate them.

But I did finally blow up at the graduate office, I'm sorry to report. Honestly, the woman pulled out a ruler and announced that the margins of the final document, printed on very expensive acid-free paper, were a tad too deep at the BOTTOM! Who cares? I was so ready to be done, having had to convert the document from Mac to PC in order to print, and then having these embedded commands that were impossible to get rid of, and no way to go back. I screamed something about not getting a degree in margins and stormed out. And flew back to Vermont, furious and frustrated.

As far as I'm concerned, I earned my PhD fair and square. But maybe I'll never get the degree because of the damn margins.

Would you have lost your temper like that? I suspect not. A deep sigh, perhaps. Silence. Maybe a shrug before you left. Certainly, no furious words hurled at the poor woman wielding the ruler. Will I ever learn?

Dear Miles,

I have found a patient friend here who is exceptionally good at computer stuff and he has promised to help me convert the document and get it printed. It will take some time. But he is far more patient than I am and promises it can be done.

When it's done I'll send it along and plan to be there for graduation in the spring. You will do the hooding, whatever that entails, right? Can't wait.

In the meantime, I just found out that you submitted my work for best dissertation of the year at LSU. Wow. That is an incredible honor. Thank you. It doesn't really matter what happens next. To think you consider it worthy of that is more than enough.

Dear Miles,

Bad news first. I can't come to graduation. Back problems, can't sit on the plane that long. Maybe I'll never learn how a hood works.

Now the good news: Texas Press definitely wants to publish my dissertation. It will take some editing, but sometime in the next few years, you'll get a copy of the book Nature, Culture, and Big Old Trees!

Dear Miles,

I just learned you're gone.

We had such a wonderful visit when I was last in Baton Rouge. Hours at Highland Coffee hearing about your new research ideas, lunch across the street, and then you introduced me to the live oak you endowed on campus. I love the photo of you with the tree. You're still inspiring me, you know. Remember how you started reciting your poetry at professional meetings? Well, I tell stories now, and it's a lot more fun. But I'm still trying to learn your patience and acceptance of people just as they are.

Thank you, Miles. I was fortunate. And think of all the people who will smile as they read the plaque under your tree:

> *For family, students, and you*
> *Sing On!*
> *Miles Richardson*

Dr. Miles Richardson held the Fred B. Kniffen Professorship of Geography and Anthropology and the Doris Z. Stone Professorship of Latin American Studies at Louisiana State University. Dr. Richardson taught in all four fields of Anthropology: physical, cultural, linguistic, and archeological, and conducted fieldwork in Latin America and the American South. He was a founder of the Society for Humanistic Anthropology and edited the Anthropology and Humanism Quarterly.

PART V:
Postdoc, Completion, and Transition to Employment

This stage consists of transition into employment in the academy or other venues related to the student's field of study and includes a further acculturation period as the individual learns, for example, firsthand about the hierarchy within academic departments, as well as the relative emphasis on the three pillars of academic life—research, teaching, and service.

FINDING YOUR PROFESSIONAL FIT

So, now what? Perhaps you entered your doctoral program with a specific goal in mind. On the other hand, perhaps you were open to the unfolding of new possibilities. Now that you are finished or finishing, it is time to re-evaluate and assess whether your initial goal still fits if you have found your interest to be something different. Regardless, you now need to begin the research process again as you develop your job search. The key is professional fit.

Every institution, whether a college or another environment, has a culture with values, norms, ways of being and succeeding that are specific to that environment and your discipline. The research to undertake at this stage includes Internet information about employers, interviews, the work setting and activities, and expectations of potential employees. You will need to prepare to negotiate salary, benefits, and working conditions. You will also need to consider and determine your preferences and needs for relocation. The more open you are to relocation, the more opportunities you provide yourself.

You spent all that time in your doctoral program living in that cultural environment—do you remember what it was like to transition to the culture of your doctoral program? Now you have to do it all again as you move on to the next step in your professional journey.

A doctorate will open many doors for you, one of which is academia. If you choose the academic, and, particularly if you become a faculty member on tenure track, you will find that your continued employment, as well as opportunities for promotion, will be based on three aspects of your work: research, teaching, and service. The emphasis on each of these aspects will depend on the type of institution by which you are employed. Women are often called upon to provide more service and do more teaching than mens, which takes time away from conducting research. This becomes a catch-22, as research is typically the most-prized aspect in academia when presenting oneself for tenure and promotion. If you work in academia, protect your research time—always.

SECTION 5 NARRATIVES

Five of our contributors have shared their experiences with the transition to employment after completion of the doctorate. Four have found places in academia and one is a professional in private practice in her field. They share their experiences of continuing to use doctoral supports, networking a work-environment fit, endings of marriages, and switching the postdoc direction.

CHAPTER 42

WHY PERSEVERANCE WAS CRUCIAL

EILEEN CECILIONE, PT, DPT

C. O. R. E. Physical Therapy, Albany, NY, USA

The journey to acquire my doctorate was full of ups and downs. Thankfully, I was able to navigate through the winding road of graduate school and was soon off to conquer the world of physical therapy. After working for five years in the field, four of which were with my doctoral degree, I was faced with the excitement and fear of relocation. Was I going to find a job? Would I need to settle on a job that I didn't love? Would I be able to find something that would make me really happy? In the realm of physical therapy, the focus of most clinics is a traditional approach. Therapeutic exercise is what you are expected to do. Reimbursement is the highest, there especially when compared to manual therapy. Manual therapy is occasionally permitted, but typically frowned upon.

During the five years at my first job, I learned a great deal about therapeutic exercise. I also had a taste of manual therapy, and of course, I loved it. Knowing that I would be looking for a new job, I frequently daydreamed of the possibility of finding a clinic that would allow me to practice manual physical therapy. That little piece of exposure made me hungry for more.

My search for a new job led me to a clinic that actually focused on manual physical therapy. I was ecstatic. I was even familiar with the owner of the practice. She had given a presentation on a vibrational release technique at my school during the master's portion of my studies. I felt so fortunate. I could learn more about manual therapy and hopefully make an actual difference in people's lives. I just needed to get through the interview. I really wanted this job and was willing to make any concession necessary to get it. This, of course, was not the mindset I should have had going into it.

I was all decked out in my suit. I was ready. I walked in, introduced myself to the person at the front desk, sat down, and waited, and waited. I sat in the waiting room for an hour. My existence was barely noticed. I assumed that the owner was just backed up in her schedule, so I was willing to be patient, but an explanation of her tardiness would have been appreciated. Despite the confusion for the delay, I stayed optimistic. This job was going to be it. It was going to be amazing. Finally, the owner came out to get me. There was no apology for the delay. Her demeanor was indifferent and was as if I was causing her some great inconvenience. Her behavior and mannerisms were so confusing. It really caught me off guard. We finally went back into a room for the interview. She asked me some questions and I did my best to answer them. I let her know my background and experience. She was clearly not impressed with me. I kept thinking, "I have five years of experience and a doctorate. It must be worth something." She basically told me that I would be too much work for her to train and that she would be better off working with a new grad. I was shocked and devastated. Somehow, through that interview, she managed to belittle me to the level of a first-year student. I felt so worthless. To this very day, I have no idea why she felt so negatively toward me. It was awful. So awful, in fact, I was ready to quit physical therapy altogether. Somehow, she had gotten under my skin enough to derail my entire being.

Reality, however, soon set in. I was relocating. I needed a job. I still owned my home and carried the mortgage. My husband and I were hoping to buy a new home. There was no way that I could not have a job. It was so stressful. I decided that I would apply to every physical therapy job available. I just needed to get a job. I wasn't going to worry about it being my dream job. Once I had moved and gotten settled, I would try to find the perfect job. But for now, I needed work.

I was able to set up three interviews. The first was an outpatient orthopedic clinic. Everyone seemed nice. They were up-to-date on electronic documentation, which was new and exciting for me. During the discussion, I mentioned that I had some experience in manual therapy. I quickly learned that not all manual therapy is deemed the same. Shame on me for not understanding the difference. After mentioning that I was familiar with some "Barnes Techniques," I was curtly informed that, "We don't do that kind of manual therapy here." Needless to say, I never heard back from them. My second interview was at a skilled nursing facility. I had three years of experience working in that setting. I realized very quickly that I was extremely burned out from working in a nursing home and that no amount of desperation to get a job was worth feeling like that.

My last interview was at another outpatient clinic. The owner had advertised that manual therapy was part of the treatment process. I was hopeful, but so exhausted from the repeated rejection. My interview was at 7 am. I had driven three hours the night before. I was tired and feeling less than my best. The owner came out to greet me. He was so happy and easygoing. I felt immediately at ease. We spoke for a while. I was allowed to sit in on a treatment session. It was then that my mind was completely blown. I had no idea that a place like that existed. I had found it, my employment nirvana. It was a place that cared about its employees like family and valued good health care. Treatments were derived with the intention to heal pain and not just make it tolerable. People were actually being healed! And I was now going to be a part of it. I was offered the job and accepted it that day. That was eight years ago. I have never been happier.

The saddest part of this story is that it very well may not have happened. I could have given up and quit physical therapy altogether. I could have let the thoughts and opinions of others completely derail my life. It was such a difficult time. I knew that I didn't want to waste all of the time I had put into school. I liked being a physical therapist and I was proud of my doctorate.

It is important to not lose sight of your goals. There will always be challenges. If you can focus on the learning moments of those hard times, you might just be able to find your ultimate happiness. Thankfully, I was able to do just that. Good luck!

—Eileen Cecilione, PT, DPT

CHAPTER 43

"FINISH WISELY"

SEEMA RIVERA, PhD

Clarkson University—Capital Region Campus, Schenectady, NY, USA

E-mail: emailseema@gmail.com

During the dissertation period of my graduate work, I decided to take advantage of all of the opportunities I had as I was approaching the end of my time in graduate school (I hoped). There were many different factors that played a part in helping me finish my dissertation.

43.1 TAKE A CHANCE—THE SANDRA ABELL INSTITUTE

One of the most amazing experiences I had while working on my dissertation was attending the Sandra Abell Institute for Science Education Students, supported by the National Association for Research in Science Teaching (NARST). While in my graduate program, I joined the NARST organization and was kept up to date by the use of their Listserv. They posted about a program for graduate students, the Sandra K. Abell Institute for Doctoral Students, who were in the beginning or in the midst of their dissertation. I figured I might as well try and take advantage of every bit of help there was. I applied and got in, which meant spending a week at Biological Sciences Curriculum Study (BSCS) in Colorado Springs, Colorado. During my time there I learned about asking better research questions, how to improve upon my dissertation process, etc. But the most rewarding and long-lasting piece I took away from the institute was the bonds I created with several other female graduate students.

The four of us, nicknamed JAMSS because of our initials, bonded while we were at the institute, but this was only the beginning of our friendship. Upon leaving Colorado, we all returned to our respective states—New York, Texas, Georgia, and North Carolina. We kept in touch via e-mail and social media, worked with each other as a writing group on small parts of our dissertations, but most importantly, we continued to cultivate these bonds. This led to all of us graduating with our PhDs at the same time at our respective institutions. While this was maybe not the key factor in defending and finishing, it did have a large impact on my progress as a graduate student. Little did I know that this friendship would grow even closer after graduation.

As we looked for jobs, interviewed, negotiated, accepted and rejected work, I realized how valuable these friendships are. This time in my career path was a bit isolating; working on the dissertation is a bit isolating. While you may have friends and family around to support you, it is another level of friendship when your friend knows exactly what you are going through. Beyond this, I had few resources for navigating the job search. I truly believe I may not have turned down two jobs and then negotiated on my current job and contract had it not been for my JAMSS friendship. During graduate school the message I was given was, "If you want a job, you will have to move." This was a tough message to take to heart when my spouse was happy at his current job, our family was close by, and at the time I defended my dissertation, I was pregnant with my second child. Needless to say, the decision to move or not was not an easy one. I searched and ended up taking a job I was overqualified for. After about four months, when I realized I could not continue working there and be happy, again my JAMSS group was a strong support structure for me. Eventually, and maybe luckily, I came across a job that was local and seemed like a good fit...and so I applied. I was eventually interviewed and got the job, but the JAMSS group again played an integral role in this, from reviewing my proposed demonstration lesson, giving me constructive feedback, giving me points to consider during the negotiation for the job, and even guiding me in how to phrase more challenging communications—the kinds that require boldness to ask but still demonstrate zeal and interest for the job. These delicate and thoughtful communications, in my case, were only successful because of my JAMSS friendship.

We saw one another at the same one or two conferences that most students and junior faculty in our field attend. At one conference we decided to do a JAMSS trip, a non-working fun girls' trip, once a year. This summer will be our fourth girls' trip, hopefully a tradition that will continue every year. These trips and all the communications via technology throughout the year have brought our group together; we have been supportive of each other through several health and family crises, in balancing work with personal life, in managing motherhood and marriage, and so forth. I cannot imagine how different my school and career path might have played out had I not made these valuable and deep friendships.

43.2 THE FULCRUM

The balancing act between school and life was a challenging one during graduate school. I was pregnant when I started my PhD program and was working on my dissertation throughout most of my second pregnancy. In fact, toward the end it became sort of a race for myself to either defend and finish while pregnant or have this baby and who knows when I would finish. I knew the challenges of motherhood because my first was almost four years old at this point, and so I made the decision that I was going to work as much as possible to finish this and graduate before the arrival of the new baby. During my graduate program, I worked as a teaching assistant (TA) to help support myself and contribute financially to our family. My husband worked as a professional and has always been a truly supportive partner throughout my school and work. There were many weekends where he and my daughter went to her activities and to do errands while I went away to write for 6–7 hours in a day. Together we decided we would do whatever was deemed necessary and that we were able to do, so I could finish. We also had my mother nearby to help once in a while with our daughter. In addition to my family, I had several friends in the program with me who were also a support group.

I met one friend, Ally, through a moms' group and only then we realized that we were in the same graduate program. From there, our friendship flourished as we met with our children and new babies to talk about writing and keeping on track; we continue to be friends now that we both have finished our programs. Ally is a great friend because of her perspective on life; she helps me keep the 10,000-foot view of all that is happening so as to not stress about the smaller things. We were able to both celebrate each other's defense and graduation and continue to talk about potential work together. We hope to soon publish together!

Mary was another friend in my graduate program. She lived a bit farther away but we scheduled writing dates in coffee shops to help hold each other accountable for work. Mary and I had classes together; though I finished several years ago, Mary continues to work on her dissertation. We stay in touch and she will ask how I got through some parts of the writing or managing the relationship with her advisor. Another similar friend I had was Pam; as with Mary, Pam and I had classes together and also scheduled regular writing dates. While all of these relationships were rooted in some degree of friendship, they were also collegial and were a way to hold myself accountable and remind myself that I was not alone in this.

43.3 RESEARCH, CONFERENCES, AND MENTORS, OH MY!

While working on my dissertation, I stepped back from my role in some other projects that I was working on under my advisor. This was a decision that was hard to make because the research guided by my advisor had support, and we were already publishing from it. I knew that to finish my dissertation, though, I would have to make it a priority. Throughout this time, I did take advantage of being involved in some other projects, but with less commitment. I also made sure to attend and be present at conferences as often as possible to help further my career and help me grow as a young academic. One of the opportunities I applied for allowed me to travel to France to present my research paper. I also took advice from my advisor, the rest of my dissertation committee, and the senior faculty I met at conferences and institutes. My plan was to finish my dissertation but also make myself marketable. One piece of advice a mentor gave me early on was to not just rush, rush, rush and finish. Make sure to learn along the way, take opportunities to do research or teach, publish if you can or try to, so you can gain experience. While I didn't follow this perfectly, I tried to follow this advice as best as possible. I think that surrounding yourself with good mentors is one of the best ways to finish wisely. Sometimes, just finishing is the goal, but when you can stop and reflect on career goals, finishing with experience makes a big difference.

43.4 FINISHING

Some of the smaller, but significant pieces in helping me finish was working in a coffee shop, listening to instrumental music, using a website blocking app, and journaling about my work, as in where I left off and questions I had; that way I could pick up from that point on the next day. I figured out that these pieces helped me be most productive and I tried to stay with them. I have advised other friends since finishing to find what works for them and to stick with it. Not everyone has the same optimal writing time or the same habits. Find what works for you and finish!

CHAPTER 44

AND FOR YOU

TAMMY LYNN GARREN, PhD

Albany College of Pharmacy and Health Sciences, Albany, NY, USA

In my office, I have displayed items that bring me joy. There are pictures of my husband and my children, artwork and notes from them, thank you cards from colleagues, my first published articles, a sparkling frame proclaiming, "She believed she could so she did," my framed doctoral degree (evidence of the quotation), and the acknowledgement page from my dissertation. The acknowledgement reads:

> The culmination of this research came only with the tireless and generous support of a few special groups of people. At the university, Bob was a source of guidance, encouragement, and inspiration in my work. The tireless and patient assistance that he, Kristen, and Larry provided allowed me to finish with confidence at a time when I needed it most. I could not have asked for a better combination of brilliant minds and kind hearts. I want to also thank "Jack" and "Nick" and their students for allowing me to invade their classrooms. I count myself very lucky to have found such passion, enthusiasm, patience, and work ethic. I am also grateful to my peers in ETAP* and at ACRIDAT** who helped me in shaping my ideas. Finally, this day would not have come without my wonderful family. I am most grateful for my son, Jamie George, who learned from birth that the opening of a laptop meant the closing of playtime with Mommy, and accepted this with grace and patience beyond his years. He is the light at the end of my tunnel. For my mom, who was there for the first and last "homework" assignment and every one in between. And for you.

I tacked this up in my office right behind my chair because it reminds me that while I may struggle, if I have the right people at my back, I can do anything.

---

*ETAP: Educational Theory and Practice

**ACRIDAT: Albany Consortium for Research in Instructional Design and Theory

Thousands of days comprise the time between beginning the doctoral study and successfully defending a dissertation. Those are thousands of opportunities to wake up to challenges and run into roadblocks. Life goes on. The idea that women are urged not to have children or to set aside personal life while pursuing professional degrees is like asking us to perform miracles or control time. In the course of my doctoral study, I bought and remodeled a house; adopted a dog; had a child; wrote and ran part of a grant; worked as a tutor, a technical writer, and an adjunct instructor; got divorced; fell in love; put my house up for sale and moved; said final goodbyes to loved ones; and took an internship that would eventually lead to my dream job. But for every challenge I met in those five years, there was someone who was willing to reach out and help me as long as I was willing to accept their help.

Bob is actually a dean at the university and my former dissertation chair. I've never called him Bob in my life and I probably never will. I respect and admire him too much to be able to say it to his face. But in the acknowledgement, I wanted to show that real people, including Kristen and Larry, helped me but never judged me for needing that help; they pushed boxes of tissues across the desk but also never stopped pushing me to do my best. I have heard horror stories of dissertation committees where agendas, personalities, and pride clash to stall or completely end the dissertation process. One of the best decisions I made while finishing my doctorate was to form a committee that I knew would both challenge and support me. Toward the end of my data collection, my marriage fell apart, after which I wanted a pause. But in the act of finishing a PhD, a pause often turns into a stop. My committee did not even bat an eye when I cried my way through meetings. They handed me some tissues and then asked me how I planned to triangulate my data. It was as simple and as profound as that. The message they gave me as a whole, and individually in private conversations later, was that life was going to do some great and some awful things to me. They were there to support and guide me, but in the end I had to keep moving on, I had to finish what I'd started, and I had to do it well.

Jack and Nick are two teachers who participated in my study. I drove almost an hour and a half each way, several days a week, over two school years to collect data for my dissertation. They added extra work and sometimes extra stress to their daily routine so that I could collect my data and complete my study. They spent their free periods reviewing the progress of the day or planning for the next lesson. They didn't always agree with the methods but were willing to try things if it meant improving their students' learning experiences. It wasn't just gas money or the sheer force of will that got me through the years of data collection; it was the supportive, goofy, encouraging, sometimes cantankerous study participants who landed in my study. Amidst the chaos of all else, friendly faces made the journey a little easier.

Jamie George is now almost eight years old, but he was closer to forty while I was working on my dissertation. Born in my third semester of doctoral study, he was often lulled to sleep by the words of Vygotsky or the rough drafts of my own papers. He sensed when my stress level was high and would crawl into my lap for a snuggle. He gave me joyful respite from work and school with games and giggles and taught me to set things aside to enjoy the moment. I worked several part-time jobs in addition to attending school full-time (in addition to raising a child and running a household), and his nature was not to demand more than I could give. I wanted very much to be the kind of role model I had in my own mother, who worked while raising three children and pursuing her own college degree, often sitting next to me at the dining room table so we could do our homework together. In Jamie I found another kind of support, like the others, made pushing forward possible.

And the "for you" is a sentiment I added to the end of my acknowledgement as a placeholder for the reader to interpret. I like to think that the reader feels appreciated for reading my dissertation. I'm certainly happy that someone is willing to read it. It's for me. It's for the family that I can help support with the aid of a professional degree. It's for all others pursuing a PhD who need a light at the end of the tunnel. It's for all the people out there who do the simple things that help us get past the obstacles, and there will be obstacles. It's for the people who have our back.

CHAPTER 45

FINDING MY SCHOLARLY VOICE

MICHELLE C. STERK BARRETT, PhD

College of the Holy Cross, Worcester, MA, USA

My story is one of evolving developments as a scholar throughout the stages of my doctoral education. In particular, the greatest value I found in pursuing my PhD was gaining confidence in my own intellectual abilities and finding my academic voice.

Before I began doctoral work, the combination of my previous school environments and personal characteristics left me voiceless throughout much of the educational journey. I was a very shy child who had so little to say in my elementary school classrooms that a teacher once met with my parents to express concern about the fact that I never spoke. Though I was a bit less shy in high school, the large size of my school and classes left me feeling that I was just a number moving through the system—which did little to boost my academic confidence despite having earned very good grades. As an undergraduate, I participated in the honors program in order to have access to small seminars. However, I found myself intimidated by the articulateness, confidence, and expansive vocabulary of my classmates. The way in which classroom discussions were centered on critiquing the ideas of others also silenced me as I did not feel prepared to justify my perspectives if they were to come under attack. When I did speak in class, my heart often raced for many minutes beforehand and I had to convince myself with absolute certainty that my ideas were correct before opening my mouth. During my master's program in higher education administration, I continued to be relatively silent in comparison with my peers.

Despite this lack of verbal participation in post secondary education, I could write persuasively, study efficiently, and focus intensely when seeking answers to intellectual questions. But I did not see these strengths as clearly as I saw my deficiencies when comparing myself with others who seemed smarter, more confident, and more articulate. My early professional career furthered this perspective as I spent nearly a decade working in one of the most highly selective higher education institutions in our nation. In that context, I was exposed to many colleagues who had done doctoral work—all of whom seemed much more worthy of being called "doctor" than I felt I ever could be.

In the back of my mind, however, the possibility of further education lived for many years. Despite uncertainty about my own worthiness to be a doctoral student, I had a deep intellectual curiosity, a desire to grow, and a desire to challenge myself. Nearly two decades after beginning post secondary education, the possibility of seriously considering doctoral work moved from the back of my mind to the forefront for a number of reasons. First, I had been doing incredibly meaningful work for many years with the PULSE Program at Boston College. I had witnessed hundreds of students transformed by the PULSE service-learning experience, and I desired to share this with other higher education practitioners and scholars through empirical research—but I did not know how to do so. Second, my husband and I had become parents and I wanted increased flexibility in my schedule in order to be with our daughter in the daytime hours. Relatedly, my husband was enthusiastically supportive of my pursuing further education and was willing to make the sacrifices necessary for it to happen. Third, I had recently been introduced to the University of Massachusetts Amherst (UMASS), Boston's Higher Education Program, and it seemed to be an excellent fit with what I was seeking in a doctoral program. So, the combination of these forces incentivized me to move past my intimidation and submit an application to UMASS.

As I had hoped, the UMASS Boston program was a perfect fit for what I was seeking. Not only were there faculty members with expertise in my specific area of interest (Dr. Dwight Giles and Dr. John Saltmarsh), but the program's cohort model and focus on social justice were also aligned with my values. Most relevant to the development of my voice as a scholar is the program's emphasis on "serving as a means by which more individuals from underrepresented groups, including women and people of color, can become higher education leaders." In practical terms, this translated to classrooms that focused on students' assets rather than deficits and classroom discussions that were focused on constructing knowledge collaboratively rather than critiquing the ideas of others. This was exactly the formula I needed to find my voice in a classroom setting. My intellectual abilities were finally able to grow through practicing both my written and oral communication skills in classes.

In addition to practicing my communication skills, there were numerous other aspects of the doctoral experience that served to enhance the development of my scholarly voice. In an effort to find a more flexible work schedule, I chose to pursue a graduate research assistantship. I was fortunate to be hired by Dr. Tara Parker to support a Lumina-funded research study she was doing on state policies pertaining to developmental education. This unbelievable opportunity enabled me to experience many firsts in my academic career, including conducting research interviews independently (which was fascinating as I met many prominent educational leaders in the process), attending and presenting at academic conferences, submitting manuscripts to journals (and subsequently experiencing rejection), and coauthoring a book. Throughout it all, Dr. Parker continuously utilized an asset-based approach, and I never questioned whether she believed in my abilities. She was a cheerleader and an advocate throughout my development as a scholar. Dr. Dwight Giles, my dissertation chair, was also a constant cheerleader and advocate as I pursued researching the spiritual development of students who had participated in the PULSE Program. Again, he used an asset-based approach and helped me to see academic abilities I could not see in myself. His consistent encouragement to share my research through presenting at conferences, applying for (and receiving) two dissertation awards, and submitting journal manuscripts led me to do what I never would have imagined possible before beginning doctoral studies. Dr. John Saltmarsh and Dr. Alyssa Rockenbach also served on my dissertation committee. They offered incredibly helpful and thorough feedback on my dissertation drafts in a manner that left me feeling they believed in me and wanted to see me succeed—which was truly the feeling I had in interactions with all UMASS faculty throughout my doctoral education.

Developing my confidence as a scholar and believing I have something worth saying has been essential to my postdoctoral life. This confidence has led me to conduct formal presentations of my research in over 25 settings since finishing the coursework. It has enabled me to persist after facing rejection of my manuscripts to academic journals (two articles related to my dissertation research are now in press). It has enabled me to work effectively with faculty colleagues as the Director of Community-Based Learning at a highly selective higher education institution—the College of the Holy Cross. It is now leading me to pursue new lines of empirical research.

From the perspective of having completed doctoral studies and loving the process of doing so, it is now hard to believe that I could have let fear and intimidation stop me from pursuing further education in the first place. It was such a joy to study topics so deeply intertwined with my passions. It was so fulfilling to be challenged to learn and grow in directions I never would have imagined possible. It was so exciting to discover new talents and interests. It has been an incredible gift to gain the skills to serve profession-ally in an entirely new way—through research, publications, and conference presentations. Overall, I am deeply grateful to the UMASS faculty and students who finally helped me to find my academic voice in midlife. I feel incredibly fortunate that life circumstances (and my husband) incentivized me to overcome my fears and pursue my dreams.

CHAPTER 46

FINDING YOUR CAPE: DISCOVERING THE EDUCATOR INSIDE

SUSANNAH C. COASTON, EdD

Northern Kentucky University, Newport, KY, USA

E-mail: Susannah.Coaston@gmail.com

I did not intend to become a counselor educator. Really, I did not. When I started the doctoral program in counselor education, I intended to become a doctoral-level administrator with a nonprofit agency. My interest in supervising and providing mentorship to counselors for their growth and development was the hook, and pressure and encouragement from my faculty was the reel that drew me in. With this somewhat unconventional career aspiration within the program, my focus was more on clinical work and supervision rather than education. My first independent teaching opportunity was so terrible that without all of my colleagues' reassurances that the experience was completely atypical and without lots of support and mentoring, I probably would never have taught again. I can only imagine that my early doctoral program self (aka "2007 Me") would assume that some sort of head trauma or a dissociative fugue must have been involved if she heard, nearly a decade later, that I am working as a professor and loving it. How did I grow into this unexpected role? By jumping in with both feet. This essay represents a condensed version of what happened.

The first half of my doctoral journey taught me two things: I do not like administrative work and I thrive in a healthy, supportive environment with people who see in me what I cannot see in myself. My dissertation, on the other hand, taught me thriving is not always an easy thing to do when a short sprint becomes a grueling marathon. I remember driving home late in the evening after reading a disconcerting e-mail, sobbing to my significant other, and threatening to quit. At that point, I was rounding out my fifth year of doctoral work. My dissertation was taking much longer than I had antici-pated, due to unforeseen circumstances in my life as well as in the life of my dissertation chair. I had data collected and a dissertation relatively close to completion, but I was so tired, frustrated, and disillusioned that I could not see the point in continuing. My work as a counselor was challenging but rewarding, I was supervising interns and beginning to think I might enjoy the endeavor, and I was well respected in my workplace. I told myself I did not need "a stupid degree."

However, after a long conversation with a professional mentor, I begrudgingly agreed to keep going. Through my own stubbornness and determination, along with the support of those around me, I resolved to make my miserable experience worthwhile and get the degree anyway, even if I chose not to use it. Thus, I completed my dissertation, certain that while I may enjoy teaching a course here and there, I would never list "counselor educator" as my full-time job. I actually was learning to like teaching.

It took the loss of my marriage and a leap of faith for me to decide to apply for a professorship. Despite enjoying my role at the agency where I had been working, the options in terms of insurance benefits, salary, and the like were not enough to make payments on my student loans, mortgage, and car, and still eat regularly. I also realized that a full-time position as a counselor would likely have kept me from teaching, and crazily enough, I knew I would miss it terribly if I stopped. That said, I was completely terrified of what a full-time tenure-track position would entail. It took a good therapist to help me recognize that by accepting a position at a university, I was not necessarily committing the next 30 years of my life. My therapist asked if I could make a three-year commitment, and I agreed I could. My life was already turned upside down and I had no contingency plan. I figured three years was reasonable. I jokingly told myself I was "leaning in," but what I was really doing was leaping blindly into a profession in which success was not guaranteed. My research- and writing-related anxiety proved nearly paralyzing at times, and my "imposter" threatened to take over after any sort of critical feedback. Nevertheless, I applied, got interviewed, and accepted a position at the university where I had been an adjunct instructor for several years. This is not where the story ends.

When first asked to develop a teaching philosophy early in my doctoral program, I had not yet taught a graduate-level class. I gravitated toward educational theories that made sense to me, theories that seemed applicable to the realities of students pursuing a career, rather than simply an interesting major. I wanted to know how to reach adult learners, how to engage the whole learner, and find ways to help students truly interact with the course material. It turns out I knew myself as an educator before I had any confidence I could do the work of one.

That lack of confidence originated in the fear that I did not know enough. One of the most devastating experiences of my doctoral program involved hearing, "If you want to be a counselor educator, you clearly have a lot to learn." Those words have been ringing in my ears for the last nine years, though—thankfully—they have gotten quieter and quieter. Coming into my third year on the tenure track, I have finally figured out and accepted that I do not have to be the "expert"—I am now well aware that such an expectation would be unreasonable and mostly impossible. My teaching style does not involve the "sage on the stage" approach; instead, I prefer drawing upon my clinical experiences to enrich the discussions and activities that take place in my classroom. As it turns out, I do have a lot to contribute in the classroom.

As for research, I have never seen myself as a "big idea" person. Rather, I considered myself a good second-in-command, someone who can bring an idea to fruition or coordinate many moving parts to achieve a particular outcome. The tenure track, however, demanded I develop a cohesive research agenda of my own. The notion intimidated me (and that is putting it mildly). Ironically, my dissertation had been on burnout in counselor education, and after being so immersed in the world of burnout, I lost sight of other ideas and interests I had had throughout my doctoral and counseling careers. In an effort to reconnect with those concepts, I decided to get the burnout out of my head by putting all I had learned down on paper. Roughly a year later, that first article went out for review. You would not believe the tears and anguish that went into creating that document (although if you are reading this, perhaps you might). When I attended conferences or workshops that really inspired me, I would think, "I'd like to build upon this," only to stifle myself by saying, "But you can't do it until you get your first article out." It was agonizing. Fortunately, those ideas stuck with me (thanks to good note-taking and a "for future exploration" folder), and once I finally hit "send" on the manuscript submission, the ideas started bursting out. Suddenly, a geyser of research questions, extensions and expansions of old interests, and a few new potential projects began pouring out of me. Making sense of the sometimes discordant flow is a process, but it is one I am okay with. I am taking my time, examining each idea more closely, and considering its fit with the overall direction of my research agenda. I have learned that I do have unique ideas worth writing about and studying.

Combine the aforementioned lack of confidence with my preferred "second-in-command" mentality, and it probably will not surprise you to read that the notion of being evaluated by my peers, students, and other professionals in the field absolutely terrified me. I will confess to some measure of performance anxiety. I do not enjoy public speaking, presenting in front of large crowds, or doing much of anything that involves an audience. I tend to flush noticeably, my skin becomes blotchy and red, my hands get shaky, and I either talk too fast or lose the ability to properly enunciate. My critical voice has long told me this is not a promising recipe for an educator. Thankfully, I have learned differently.

When I applied for my faculty position, I had approximately 30 presentations to my name, ranging from talks at local and state gatherings to workshops at national counseling conferences. I presented whenever and wherever I could and, over time, found that it got easier. Professionals responded well to my ideas and materials, and I have yet to encounter the dreaded heckler I still fear might show up. However, if such a critic were to attend one of my sessions nowadays, I believe I would be okay. I might be red, my voice might shake, but as a counselor, I have de-escalated individuals wishing harm to themselves, calmed a 100-pound client who knocked a Marine unconscious with one punch, and adeptly addressed countless others who challenged me personally and professionally in a host of interesting ways. I have learned to respond with kindness, firmness, some humor, healthy boundaries, and a deep desire to help. Now, I have the confidence to know I could handle the situation should it arise. I have also discovered that thinking of the classroom (or conference presentation room) as an "audience" where I must "perform" increases my fear; however, thinking of the room as a place where conversation takes place reduces my fear and creates a climate where I am but a facilitator ensuring all voices are valued.

In other words, I have grown considerably as an educator, but it has taken time. It was not until the end of my first year on the tenure track (after approximately three years of teaching) that everything began to click. I attended a professional conference new to me and did so without any financial support, any presenting obligations, or familiar faces, hoping to find a potential theoretical home within the profession. It was this and more that I walked away with following two days of presentations and conversations. I attended all the sessions I could, not just to get my money's worth or because I thought I should, but because I was so engaged and so fascinated by the material that I simply could not get enough. The experience helped me realize I could be myself and be an educator at the same time.

This may not sound like inspired brilliance to many, but I had spent a good deal of time comparing my professional identity as a counselor to my identity as a counselor educator, and found the latter lacking. I did not know who I was or wanted to be as a counselor educator, and kept feeling as though I was pretending. I would receive feedback or compliments from colleagues or students, and would attribute these achievements to a good classroom, luck, or some other external source. I would smile and say thank you, because that is polite, but could still hear my imposter whispering, "If only they knew. ..." This conference experience showed me the characteristics that helped me be a good counselor are the same qualities that can help me be a good counselor educator. The biggest difference is that as a counselor educator, I wear a cape. Okay, not literally, but figuratively. The cape helps me to draw on my strengths, on the reserve of energy I principally use for engaging others, and on the knowledge and experiences that I have gathered over the years. I then share all that with my students. I share the good, the bad, and the sometimes ugly stories that contextualize the classroom material. I find that these self-disclosures, professional hints, and personal anecdotes create a collaborative environment that encourages others to share their own experiences and that allows everyone to walk away with something new. None of this seemed likely or even possible to the "2007 Me."

My cape has allowed me to stay afloat when I did not think I could. My cape has helped protect me from taking well-intended feedback too person-ally, and it has shielded me from the internal imposter set on sabotaging my fledgling confidence. I may not need my cape forever, as capes tend to wreak havoc for some (if you have seen *The Incredibles*, you know what I mean), but it has been a source of support and assurance throughout the start of my career. Now, some may argue that there is no cape and that the magic is inside; however, I never said the cape would be visible to the naked eye, and anyhow, I am not ready to hear that just yet.

In closing, my best advice for those new to graduate school, navigating the dissertation journey, or stepping/leaping into a faculty position is to surround yourself with others who see more of you than you can. When they compliment you, resist the temptation to brush them off with denials, defenses, or an eye roll, and ask yourself, "What if they are right?" (This is also good advice when sifting through course evaluations.) Consider the possibility that the positive, supportive words of your professors, classmates, colleagues, clients, students, or conference presentation attendees have actu-ally some truth in them. Next, remember you do not have to know everything, and that you did not get to where you are by not knowing anything. Finally, work to find a position or university that fits you (or craft a position to better suit yourself). My dissertation process taught me about more than just the necessity of persistence and the invaluable nature of caffeine; it taught me that fit is predictive of satisfaction in the workplace. Find someplace where you are able to be yourself, and be comfortable enough to take the risks necessary to discover the educator inside of you.

AUTHOR BIOGRAPHIES

Kit Anderson, PhD
Senior Lecturer (Retired), Environmental Sciences, University of Vermont, Burlington, VT, USA

At the age of 40, when her two sons were in college, the author quit her job as a garden magazine editor and director of a nonprofit in Vermont, and headed south to accept a PhD fellowship at Louisiana State University. After enjoying the warmth, food, music, and rich cultures of that region and Central America for five years, she made her way back north. Her dissertation research on live oaks and ceibas was published by University of Texas Press as *Nature, Culture and Big Old Trees*. Finding work in academia was challenging. Tenure-track positions tend to go to the young (and, until recently, males). But since 1997, as a lecturer and eventually senior lecturer at the University of Vermont, she has taught a wide range of courses in the Environmental Program: among them ethnobotany, traditional ecological knowledge, trees and culture, religion and ecology, and research methods. Publishing any research, unfortunately, has taken a back seat, although she has presented at national and international conferences. On the other hand, working with undergraduates on their senior theses was highly rewarding. Best of all is being able to continue living in Vermont.

Sherlene Ayala, MS, Doctoral Candidate
Clinical Specialist and Graduate Program Coordinator, Counseling and Educational Leadership, Montclair State University, Montclair, NJ, USA

Sherlene Ayala is a first-generation Latina cisgender woman born and raised in Spanish Harlem, NYC, USA. She attended public school throughout her academic career. After years of working in Higher Education Administration, she sought to pursue a doctoral degree in a Counselor Education program. At the start of her doctoral coursework, Sherlene noticed that she was one of four Latina women in a program of 60 PhD students. During her time in the program, she recognized that the racially underrepresented faculty members were teaching the multicultural counseling and social justice courses. That is how she met her advisor and now dissertation chair, an Indian-American woman who shares similar research interests. These research interests focus on systemic racism and cultural taxation of people of color in academia. At this stage of her doctoral journey, Sherlene is writing her dissertation proposal. In addition to being a doctoral student, Sherlene has 12 years of experience working in Student Affairs Administration in the capacity of Multicultural Affairs. She also serves as an adjunct lecturer in an Educational Leadership graduate program.

Michelle C. Sterk Barrett, PhD
Director, Donelan Office of Community-Based Learning, College of the Holy Cross, Worcester, MA, USA

Michelle is writing as a White, heterosexual, Catholic female. She was 37 when she began her doctoral work and 43 when it was completed. She is the mother of one child who was three when she began the program. Michelle's mother worked toward her college degree throughout Michelle's childhood, and her father completed his doctoral work when Michelle was six. Her father was a first-generation college student who eventually became a college professor. Michelle is currently the Director of the Donelan Office of Community-Based Learning at the College of the Holy Cross. She completed her PhD in Higher Education Administration at the University of Massachusetts (UMass) Boston. Her research has focused on spiritual development through service learning, developmental education, and the service-learning experiences of racially minoritized students. She previously worked with Boston College's PULSE Program for Service Learning, the Scott/Ross Center for Community Service at Simmons College, and City Year. She is co-author (with Tara L. Parker and Letitia Tomas Bustillos) of the book *The State of Developmental Education: Higher Education and Public Policy Priorities* (2014, Springer).

Jennifer A. Brown, PhD
Retired, Former Director of Institutional Research and Policy Studies, University of Massachusetts, Boston, Boston, MA, USA

Dr. Jennifer Brown left England in 1972 for an anticipated four years living in the United States. She entered the PhD program in Sociology at the University of Connecticut in January 1974. Her graduate student biography can be found in the essay in this book. In 1979, she began three years of service as city demographer for the City of Hartford, Connecticut, during the 1980 Census. It was a very interesting learning experience. In 1982, she began her career in institutional research (IR), a profession of which she had never heard. It turned out to be a good choice!

Dr. Brown spent 16 years building the institutional research function at the Connecticut State University system office, holding the position of executive officer for Academic Affairs and IR when she left. From 1999 to 2015, she served as Director of IR and Policy Studies at UMass Boston and is now retired. Jennifer very much enjoyed her steering committee roles in the Northeast Association for IR (www.neair.org) and her board roles in the Association for IR (www.airweb.org). She joyfully served terms as President in both associations. She also enjoyed her volunteer work with the Connecticut Women's Education and Legal Fund (www.cwealf.org), the Women's Issues Network Political Action Committee, and the Legislative and Electoral Action Program in Connecticut.

Jennifer became a U.S. citizen in 2002. In 2004, thanks to the Commonwealth of Massachusetts, she and her wife were able to marry, after 25 years of life together with limited legal protections. To sum it up, Jennifer identifies as an immigrant, naturalized American citizen, sociologist, big fan of higher education, White, married, lesbian, feminist, institutional researcher, avid reader, and quilter with a PhD. She is working on integrating into this list identities as a retired, Medicare eligible, senior, old-age pensioner, elder crone.

Beverly A. Burnell, PhD
Associate Professor, Counselor Education, State University of New York at Plattsburgh, Plattsburgh, NY, USA

Bev Burnell is a White, cisgender, heterosexual, spiritual, short, round woman who is blessed with loving family and friends, good health, and the best dog in the world. Ruby is a 14-year-old German Shepherd that Bev adopted as a three-month-old shelter pup. Ruby and Bev live in the woods, walk and play every day, and keep each other feeling young. Bev is from rural northern New York State and was a first-generation undergraduate student in secondary mathematics.

Bev has been a counselor for 35 years and a counselor educator for over 20 years. She was 38 years old when she started her doctorate in Counselor Education and Supervision at Syracuse University. In her master's program, she was trained as a generalist, having become a counselor when national credentialing (National Board for Certified Counselors, NBCC) and program accreditation (Council for Accreditation of Counseling and Related Educational Programs) were dawning in the early 1980s. She has been a counselor in school, college, and community settings. Her primary experiences and passions are for counselor education (career, ethics, skills, and cultural contexts of counseling) and college counseling. She is currently a counselor educator at the SUNY at Plattsburgh and also coordinates the college's Employee Assistance Program. She can be reached at burnelb@ plattsburgh.edu.

Hillary Hurst Bush, PhD
Postdoctoral Fellow, Department of Psychiatry, Massachusetts General Hospital, Boston, MA, USA

Hillary Hurst Bush, PhD, is a 2016 graduate of the UMass Boston Clinical Psychology Program and a 2006 graduate of Wellesley College. Hillary is a native of Malden, MA, and identifies as female, White, and Russian-American. For the four years in between finishing her undergraduate degree (at the age of 20) and entering a PhD program (at the age of 24), she worked multiple part-time and full-time jobs in marketing, human services, and research while completing continuing education coursework in psychology. She can be reached at hillary.hurst.bush@gmail.com.

Eileen Cecilione, PT, DPT
Physical Therapist, C. O. R. E. Physical Therapy, Albany, NY, USA

Eileen Cecilione completed her doctoral degree in physical therapy in 2005 from the Sage Graduate School in Albany, NY, USA. She identifies as White and Catholic, and grew up in rural New York in a low social economic household. When she started out on the career path for physical therapy, the doctoral degree was not an option. In 2003, she graduated from Russell Sage College in Troy, NY, with a combined bachelor's/master's degree in physical therapy. When the doctoral degree became available, Eileen immediately decided to complete the coursework. She knew that someday she would want to teach, and the doctoral degree would be vital. Eileen also knew that at 25 years old, it was the best time for her to get the coursework done. She wasn't tied down with a family or other responsibilities that would get in the way of her goal. The doctoral degree was important not only to her but to her family as well, as they grew up way out in the country and did not have much. Money was always very tight. Paying for college was a struggle for her family. Eileen watched her parents complete their degrees while she was a child. Getting through all of the coursework was a struggle for her. Donning the doctoral regalia and walking across the stage were the solidifying moments that perseverance was and is the answer.

Susannah C. Coaston, EdD
Assistant Professor, Counselor Education, Northern Kentucky University, Newport, KY, USA

A biracial Cincinnati native, Susannah earned her doctoral degree in Counselor Education and Supervision at the University of Cincinnati while concurrently completing her clinical licensure process, a combination she does not recommend. At present, she is an independently licensed professional counselor and supervisor specializing in clinical work with adults with severe and persistent mental illness. She is also an assistant professor at Northern Kentucky University and a certified wellness counselor in the state of Ohio. Her research interests focus on wellness, counselor development, and creative teaching and counseling interventions. If interested in learning more about Susannah's professional journey, please feel free to email her at Susannah.Coaston@gmail.com.

Nancy L. Elwess, PhD
Distinguished Teaching Professor, Biological Sciences, State University of New York at Plattsburgh, Plattsburgh, NY, USA

Dr. Elwess is a distinguished teaching professor in the Department of Biological Sciences at Plattsburgh State University, Plattsburgh, NY, USA. She has a BS in Zoology from Eastern Illinois University, an MA in Science Education from Governors State University, an MS in Molecular Biology from Purdue University, and a PhD in Molecular Biology from the University of Vermont. Following her undergraduate program, Elwess started her professional career as a middle school life science school educator in the public schools of Illinois. Once she completed her PhD, she became a research scientist at the Mayo Clinic in Rochester, MN, USA. Elwess decided she wanted to combine research and teaching; this is how she ended up at Plattsburgh State University. As a result, she has been awarded numerous national awards, including the 2015 Genetics Educator Award sponsored by the American Society of Human Genetics and the Genetics Society of America; the 2009 Presidential Award for Excellence in Science, Mathematics and Engineering Mentoring, presented by President Obama during a White House ceremony; the 2008–2009 Outstanding Undergraduate Science Teacher Award sponsored by the Society for College Science Teachers; and the 2007 National Association of Biology Teachers National Biotechnology Teaching Award. Dr. Elwess was part of the first generation in her family to go to college. She is a mixture of Native American, Hispanic, and Western European ancestry. In her free time, she enjoys competing in marathons (145 completed) and Ironman triathlons (11 completed).

Jody J. Fiorini, PhD
Department Head, Counseling, Educational Leadership, Educational and
School Psychology Department, Wichita State University, Wichita, KS, USA

Jody Fiorini, nee Luciani, is the granddaughter of Italian and Slovak
immigrants. Her father did not speak English until entering school at the
age of five. Her mother is the youngest of a family of nine children who
struggled to survive during the Great Depression. Her parents encouraged
her to pursue education as a means to ensure financial stability. At the age
of 36, Dr. Fiorini received her PhD in Counselor Education and Supervision
from Syracuse University in 2001. She worked as a counselor educator at the
SUNY at Oswego for 14 years where she also held positions as Department
Chair and Assistant Dean of the School of Education. She now works as the
Department Head of the Counseling, Educational Leadership, Educational
and School Psychology Department at Wichita State University. She is a
licensed clinical professional counselor (LCPC) in Kansas and a licensed
mental health counselor (LMHC) in New York State and has a thriving
private practice that largely serves individuals in poverty who would not
otherwise have access to mental health services. She was nominated for
a Women of Distinction Award for her pro bono work by Senator Kirstin
Gillibrand (D-NY). She is currently on the Executive Board of the Kansas
Association for Counselor Education and Supervision (KACES). Dr. Fiorini
has significant multicultural training and enjoys working with a diverse
clientele. Her book, *Counseling Children and Adolescents through Grief and
Loss* (2006, Research Press), co-authored with Dr. Jodi Mullen, received a
Book of the Year Award from the *American Journal of Nursing*. Dr. Fiorini's
areas of specialization in mental health practice include: counseling individuals with physical, emotional, and learning disabilities and their family
members; counseling individuals through grief and loss and relationship
issues; counseling individuals with anxiety and depression; and helping
clients cope with stressful life situations and transitions. She counsels both
children and adults in individual and group settings. She can be reached at
jody.fiorini@wichita.edu.

Tammy Lynn Garren, PhD
Instructional Designer, Center for Innovative Learning, Albany College of
Pharmacy and Health Sciences, Albany, NY, USA

Tammy Garren is a mom, a wife, an instructional designer, and a college
instructor who also happens to hold a doctorate. She has an Associate in
Arts degree in Liberal Arts, a combined Bachelor/Master of Arts degree in

American History, and a doctorate in Curriculum and Instruction. The transition from history to educational theory came when she taught her first college course and realized she knew a lot about American history but very little about how to teach it. Her doctoral work in the Department of Educational Theory and Practice at the University at Albany began in the fall of 2007 at the age of 24 and she successfully defended in the fall of 2012 at the age of 124.

Kim R. Harris, PhD

Visiting Professor, Theological Studies, Loyola Marymount University in Los Angeles, CA, USA

Kim R. Harris is visiting professor of Theological Studies at Loyola Marymount University in Los Angeles, CA, USA. She holds a PhD in Worship and the Arts from the Union Theological Seminary in the City of New York. Kim is a member of the Black Catholic Theological Symposium and the North American Academy of Liturgy. As a founding teaching artist in the John F. Kennedy Center for the Performing Arts' "Changing Education through the Arts" program, Kim is a committed teacher and advocate for arts integration in learning.

Allison M. Hrovat, MEd, Doctoral Candidate

Assistant Professor and Department Co-chair, Human Services Department, Holyoke Community College, Holyoke, MA, USA

Allison M. Hrovat, MEd, is a mental health counselor, doctoral candidate, and department co-chair of the Human Services Department at Holyoke Community College. Ms. Hrovat's clinical work has focused on the treatment of trauma and chronic mental illness and has spanned across community settings including family violence projects, sexual assault centers, and community mental health agencies. Ms. Hrovat is active in regional and national professional organizations for counselors and has experience teaching and supervising counselors-in-training at the master's level and, in her current role, working with students training for positions in human services and supervisory roles. Ms. Hrovat's professional identity as a counselor, educator, and scholar is continuously evolving while rooted in a strong belief in the importance of compassion in understanding the lived experiences, strengths, and barriers of others.

Ms. Hrovat was raised in a middle-class family and attended an urban high school in Euclid, OH, a near suburb of Cleveland. The intersection of Ms. Hrovat's middle-class upbringing and her experiences in an economically and racially diverse community continue to inform her decisions to work in diverse, urban environments and to consistently wrestle with questions of identity and privilege. Ms. Hrovat identifies as a White, English-speaking, documented, cisgender, heterosexual, able-bodied female. Ms. Hrovat speaks Spanish as a second language and has provided services in several Spanish-speaking communities, during which she has negotiated her linguistic and documentation status privileges. Ms. Hrovat identifies as an ally and is engaged in community groups focused on racial, immigrant, and LGBTQI+ justice. At the age of 21, Ms. Hrovat lost her mother to cancer and then, just 14 months later, lost her father to cancer. Her experiences as a young caregiver to her parents during their illnesses and to her younger sister during her high school years had a profound impact on Ms. Hrovat's development and perspective, and in fact, caused her to change professional paths toward counseling.

At the time of the writing of the piece in this volume, Ms. Hrovat was early in her doctoral program. She subsequently completed her coursework, passed her comprehensive exams, and defended her dissertation proposal. Ms. Hrovat was then diagnosed with two chronic health conditions that completely changed her daily life. At the time of this submission, Ms. Hrovat's health has stabilized and she has been slowly working to complete her dissertation. The biggest challenges to do so have been emotional—struggling through the self-talk of failing to complete on time and not meeting others' expectations; the imagined embarrassment of defending a dissertation several years after initially planned; and somehow allowing self-compassion for the impacts of life-changing events. For that reason, the timing of the publication of this volume feels significant. Ms. Hrovat can be contacted at ahrovat@hcc.edu.

Patrice Jenkins, PhD
Self-employed, Catskill, NY, USA

Patrice Jenkins is an organizational psychologist, consultant, and frequent speaker on topics related to career and retirement transitions. She is the author of *What Will I Do All Day? Wisdom to Get You over Retirement and on with Living!* (2011, Patrice Jenkins).

Patrice started her doctorate studies in industrial and organizational psychology at the age of 47. After her first year of part-time study, she chose to leave her position as an Assistant Academic Dean so that she could be more available to her family and still meet her academic goals. The flexibility of an online university contributed to her success. You can learn more about Dr. Jenkins' work at www.patricejenkins.com.

Nadja C. Johnson, PhD
Assistant Dean of Students, Clark University, Worcester, MA, USA

Dr. Nadja Johnson currently serves as Assistant Dean of Students at Clark University in Worcester, MA, USA. In this role, she has oversight of the Office of Multicultural and First-Generation Student Support. Additionally, she provides generalist expertise in the Dean of Students office, coordinating resources with departments across the institution, primarily supporting students facing academic, social, and personal challenges and working with special student populations. Prior to joining Clark University, Dr. Johnson was Director of diversity and student success at Valley City State University. She also previously held leadership roles in multicultural programming and international student services and served as an adjunct professor of sociology and psychology at Florida Atlantic University and the University of Central Florida.

Dr. Johnson worked as a community mental health therapist before launching her career in higher education. She holds a BA degree in Psychology from Fisk University, MA degree in Clinical Psychology from University of Central Florida, and a doctorate in Comparative Studies from Florida Atlantic University.

A native of Jamaica, born of African descent, Dr. Johnson received all her tertiary education in the United States and completed her doctorate degree as an international student. She is the only member of her immediate family to study and live in the United States. Her dissertation research focused on identity negotiation of immigrant populations and social activism of diaspora communities. She has also published her work on the social organization of immigrant communities in the *Journal of International and Global Studies*. In her "spare" time, she enjoys sports, music, food (lots of it) and dancing, and spending time with family and friends. She is always happy to hear from others with similar experiences or those who simply want to connect: nadjajohnson@yahoo.com.

Signe M. Kastberg, PhD
Private Therapist; Retired Associate Professor and Director of the MS Program in Mental Health Counseling, St. John Fisher College in Rochester, NY, USA.

Signe M. Kastberg is a first-generation high school graduate American (daughter of an immigrant). Dr. Kastberg has spent the last three years providing direct service to individuals and groups as a therapist. She was previously associate professor and Director of the MS Program in Mental

Health Counseling at St. John Fisher College in Rochester, NY, USA. She earned an AAS degree from the SUNY at Cobleskill and a BA from Skidmore College. She completed a master's degree in Education at Harvard University and was subsequently awarded a Fulbright scholarship for independent research in Denmark. Upon returning to the United States, she worked as a Director of Continuing Education for a number of colleges and universities and in private business. She completed a PhD in Human Development in 1998 at the University of Rochester and a Graduate Certificate in Gender and Women's Studies. During her doctoral studies, she was designated as a Scandling Scholar, May Eddy Butler Walker Scholar, and Jack K. Miller Memorial Scholar. The National Association for Women in Education recognized Dr. Kastberg's dissertation research with the Ruth Strang Research Award. Upon completion of her doctoral degree, Dr. Kastberg served as assistant professor of Counseling and Human Development at the University of Rochester and subsequently held a joint appointment as assistant professor of Counselor Education and college counselor at SUNY Brockport. She has served as a counselor at Cornell University and as assistant professor at Ithaca College. She is a LMHC in New York, Virginia, and Florida.

Dr. Kastberg's research interests focus on the intersection of social class with gender, education, and mental health services. She has been a frequent presenter on the ways in which talented girls and women from lower social-class backgrounds are discouraged from upward career and social mobility, and particularly the ways in which both teachers and counselors participate in this process of social reproduction. She is currently writing about therapeutic applications of traditional West African drumming. Dr. Kastberg can be reached at signe.jag@gmail.com.

Jelane A. Kennedy, EdD
Associate Professor, Student Development and Higher Education Program, Counselor Education and Family Therapy, Central Connecticut State University, New Britain, CT, USA

Jelane A. Kennedy, is a first-generation college student of European American heritage, who is cisgender, spiritually eclectic, and identifies as a lesbian feminist who was raised in the Midwest. She grew up in a single-parent home after her father passed away when she was seven. Her mother, having graduated high school and gone on for a cosmetology certificate, was at a loss at first raising her two girls on her own as a single-parent. Her mom always encouraged Jelane and her sister to get an education because "you never knew what life will surprise you with." Jelane currently is an associate professor in the Department of Counselor Education and Family Therapy at Central Connecticut State University. Prior to moving to Connecticut, she taught for over 20 years at The College of Saint Rose in Albany, NY, having obtained the rank of full professor. She also received the Thomas Manion Distinguished Teacher Award for her work at The College of Saint Rose. Her doctorate in counseling is from The College of William and Mary in Virginia, which she completed at the age of 33. Jelane received the Ruth Strang Research Award for her dissertation from the National Association for Women in Education (NAWE). Her master's is from The Ohio State University in Ohio and bachelor's degree from Alma College in Michigan. She holds certification from NBCC and is licensed as a counselor in Virginia and New York. Prior to becoming a college professor, she worked in student affairs for 10 years at 4-year public, private, and community colleges. Dr. Kennedy has experience as a private practice counselor while living in Virginia, most of her clients identified as lesbian and military. Her research interests have centered on diversity issues.

Dr. Kennedy also identifies as an outdoorswoman and artist who believes time in nature to be an integral part of a healthy lifestyle. She sees, in nature, the power to restore, heal, and inspire us to step outside our comfort zone. She combines this with a love of travel, which she shares with her partner, Eileen. She believes travel can help us to be more open to diversity. She blogs about her experiences using both photography and prose to encourage others to find inspiration in even the smallest adventures we take, www. travelsinabbey.wordpress.com.

Cherie L. King, ScD

Associate Professor, Program Coordinator, Clinical Professional Counseling Program, and Chair of the Department of Counselor Education and Family Therapy, Central Connecticut State University, New Britain, CT, USA

Dr. Cherie King, CRC CDMS, is presently an associate professor and program coordinator for the Clinical Professional Counseling program and Chair of the Department of Counselor Education and Family Therapy at Central Connecticut State University in New Britain, CT. After a 16-year career as a rehabilitation counselor, vocational expert, and disability management consultant, she entered her doctoral program in Sargent College of Rehabilitation Sciences at Boston University when she was 38 years old and graduated with a Doctor of Science (ScD) degree in Rehabilitation Counselor Education in 2009. She is a certified rehabilitation counselor (CRC) and certified disability management specialist (CDMS). She lives in Connecticut with her husband of 28 years, Kevin. Her three children are well-adjusted young adults in college and/or starting their careers. She is happy to say that she and Kevin are enjoying the empty nest.

As a teacher of clinical counseling skills, Dr. King strives to facilitate student self-discovery of what it means to be a counselor. She focuses on helping students to find answers from within and to explore and understand their own reactions as they progress through the program and work with clients. Her goal is to help students to appropriately and effectively apply theory to real-world practice and continue to develop the technical skills necessary to be an effective counselor. She encourages a thorough understanding of counseling theory and technical skills and development of a theoretical perspective so that when students graduate, they are well-equipped to serve the counseling needs of persons with disabilities and other challenges. She strives to create an atmosphere of mutual respect, openness, and teamwork. Above all, she challenges students to be critical thinkers and to explore their own frame of reference, values, and attitudes and the influence of these factors on their ability to counsel objectively and nonjudgmentally. Disability awareness and rehabilitation values are the cornerstones of her teaching philosophy. As a rehabilitation counselor educator, she makes it her priority is to infuse the rehabilitation philosophy of ability, inclusion, self-determination, and self-sufficiency into her teaching. As she prepares students to work with individuals with disabilities, it is important that she challenges them to examine their attitudes, biases, and feelings surrounding the construct of disability. Disability means different things to different people, and many times disability is identified only as physical. However, disability includes psychiatric, cognitive, developmental, and sensory challenges. She sees her job as a rehabilitation counseling educator to create an environment within the classroom that allows honest exploration and discussion of fears, beliefs, and attitudes. Dr. King can be reached at kingche@ccsu.edu.

Aja E. LaDuke, PhD
Assistant Professor, Literacy Studies and Elementary Education, Sonoma State University, Rohnert Park, CA, USA

Aja E. LaDuke is an assistant professor of Literacy Studies and Elementary Education at Sonoma State University (SSU) in Rohnert Park, CA. Prior to joining the SSU faculty, Aja was a member of the Teacher Education Department at The College of Saint Rose in Albany, NY. She completed her PhD in Curriculum and Instruction at a large public university in New

England, where she also earned her BS and MA degrees through the university's teacher preparation program. Aja taught third grade before returning to graduate school initially to pursue an additional certificate as a reading specialist. In taking a literacy course taught by one of the department's female professors, Aja was inspired to expand her studies in reading education to include critical literacy, language diversity, critical pedagogy, and multicultural education and earn her doctorate. As a teacher educator and an individual who mirrors the shared identity groups of roughly 80% of the K-12 teacher population (i.e., a White, female, American, native English speaker from a middle-class background), Aja is committed both to shifting those numbers and to helping all teacher education students discover ways to cross cultural borders that will enrich both their teaching and their lives. Aja teaches literacy methods, educational foundations, and multicultural education courses from a critical lens to undergraduate and graduate students in the field of education. Her professional interests include integrating critical literacy and social justice into K-12 curricula as well as recruiting and retaining teacher candidates from diverse identity groups and backgrounds.

Delmy M. Lendof, EdD
Director for Residential Staff and Programs, New York University, New York City, NY, USA, and Adjunct Assistant Professor, Higher and Postsecondary Education Program, New York University and Teachers College Columbia University, New York City, NY, USA

Dr. Lendof is a Director for Residential Staff and Programs at New York University; adjunct assistant professor in the Higher and Postsecondary Education Program at New York University and Teachers College Columbia University. Dr. Lendof has a Doctor of Education degree from Teachers College, Columbia University; a Master of Science in College Student Development from Long Island University, C.W. Post, and a Bachelor of Arts in Politics, Economics and Society from SUNY, College at Old Westbury.

Dr. Lendof is a student affairs professional with 20 years of experience working in higher education and serving students at public and private universities. She currently serves as the Director for Residential Staff and Programs at New York University, and prior to that worked as Assistant Director for Residential Life at Rutgers University New Brunswick, and Teachers College, Columbia University.

Dr. Lendof is highly involved in regional and national organizations and has presented at a number of conferences. She is currently a member of the National Association of Student Personnel Administrators (NASPA) Region

II Conference Planning Committee, the co-chair for the NASPA Latina/o Knowledge Community (LKC) Preconference, and chair for the Region II LKC. She served as a faculty member for the 2014 James Grimm National Housing Training Institute and the 2013 NEACUHO/ACUHO Regional Entry Level Institute.

Dr. Lendof was born in the Dominican Republic and moved to the United States at the time when she was 13 years old. She first lived in the South Bronx and learned to speak English while attending New York City Public High Schools. She attributes her success to the outstanding support from family members, friends, teachers, and mentors. She is happily married and has two sons, Alejandro (the age of 16) and Michael-Gabriel (two years old).

Margaret Leone, PhD
Lecturer, Department of Foreign Languages, State University of New York at Plattsburgh, Plattsburgh, NY, USA

Margaret Leone taught ESL in France prior to obtaining a master's in French from the University of Rochester. She worked for 15 years as a middle-school/high school French teacher in northern New York before entering the doctoral program in Second Language Education at McGill University in Montreal, Canada. She is currently working as a French lecturer in Upstate New York. She can be reached at margaret.leone719@gmail.com.

Melissa Luke, PhD
Professor, Counseling and Human Services, Syracuse University, Syracuse, NY, USA

Melissa Luke is a Dean's professor in the Department of Counseling and Human Services at Syracuse University, where she also coordinates the doctoral program in Counseling and Counselor Education and the master's program in School Counseling. She is a nationally certified counselor, an approved clinical supervisor, and a LMHC in the State of New York. Dr. Luke is a member of the American Counseling Association, the Association for Specialists in Group Work, and Counselors for Social Justice. She is a member of and currently serving as a Research Trustee in the Association for Lesbian, Gay, Bisexual, and Transgender Issues in Counseling and the President-elect of the Association for Counselor Education and Supervision (ACES). Dr. Luke is also a member of Chi Sigma Iota and serves as the editor of the *Journal of Counselor Leadership and Advocacy*.

Dr. Luke's scholarship focuses on counselor preparation and practice to more effectively respond to the needs of underserved persons, particularly

LGBTIQ+ youth. Having fifteen years of experience in the P-12 educational context, Dr. Luke's scholarship has a specific focus on school counselors, and she has published extensively in the area of counselor supervision and group work. Toward that end, Dr. Luke is involved in a number of interdisciplinary research projects, including the design and implementation of training simulations that use actors as standardized school stakeholders (administrators, teachers, students, family members), the professional identity development and ethical decision-making of school counselors across global settings, as well as the role of mentorship in leadership and research development in counselors-in-training.

Dr. Luke negotiates her privileged and historically marginalized identities as a White, able-bodied, English-speaking, female ally born at the end of the baby boom generation. Although Dr. Luke is currently highly educated and living in an upper-middle-class community in the northeastern region of the United States, she grew up in a low-income, working-class Jewish family and was a first-generation college student. Rooted in her relational and growth-oriented values, Dr. Luke worked as a secondary English and social studies teacher upon graduating college, before retraining as a school counselor. After more than a decade of professional experience in P-12 schools, Dr. Luke entered a doctoral program in Counselor Education, during which she continued to work full-time in the schools. Dr. Luke can be contacted at mmluke@syr.edu.

Karen L. Mackie, PhD
Clinical Assistant Professor and Clinical Coordinator, Mental Health Counseling Program, Counseling and Human Development, Warner School of Education, Rochester University, Rochester, NY, USA

Karen L. Mackie is a counselor educator at the University of Rochester's Warner Graduate School of Education and Human Development. She lives with her husband, 13-year-old daughter, and a cat in Fairport, New York. She began her graduate studies in her late 20s, after first attaining credentials to practice as a professional counselor in college and agency settings before embarking on the PhD journey. Her doctoral program was centered in counseling and human development. As a teenaged immigrant to the United States from the United Kingdom and first-generation college student, she subsequently completed her undergraduate and graduate degrees at universities in New York. Currently, she studies and teaches courses related to integrating aesthetic theories and expressive arts into counselor training; collaborative language and feminist family systems counseling; reflective counselor supervision; and issues of social class and aging in counseling practice.

Yettieve A. Marquez-Santana, EdD
Assistant Director, Office of Residence Life and Housing Services, New York University, New York City, NY, USA

Yettieve (Yetty) Marquez-Santana was born and raised in the South Bronx and is a first-generation college student. Her mother is Puerto Rican, her father is Guatemalan, and she identifies as Latina. She earned her bachelor's in 2006 in Business Management with a minor in Black Studies at SUNY New Paltz, and her master's in 2008 in Organizational Leadership with a concentration in Higher Education at Rider University. She achieved one of her biggest lifetime goals of becoming "doctor before 30" when she completed her four-year doctoral journey (2010–2014) and earned her EdD in Educational Leadership and Policy at Fordham University. Her dissertation topic was on exploring the career trajectories of women Senior Student Affairs Officers at four-year public institutions. She currently works at New York University as an Assistant Director for the Office of Residence Life and Housing Services. Yetty believes in the importance of seeking and embracing professional development opportunities that challenge her to explore critical pedagogy, while giving back to the field through her mentorship, professional association involvement, research, publications, and presentations. Her professional passions are student leadership, women empowerment, promoting inclusive excellence, and professional recruitment. She can be reached at yettieve.marquez@gmail.com.

Kate Bresonis McKee, MAT, MSEd, Doctoral Candidate
Assistant Dean, School of Arts and Sciences, Massachusetts College of Pharmacy and Health Sciences, Boston, MA, USA

Kate Bresonis McKee is Assistant Dean of the School of Arts and Sciences at Massachusetts College of Pharmacy and Health Sciences University and a PhD candidate in Higher Education at the UMass Boston. Her in-progress dissertation entitled *The Entanglement of Gender, Science, and Interdisciplinarity: Standpoints of Women PhD Students in the Sciences* draws from a set of research interests that include (a) how the public good is conceptualized in Science, Technology, Engineering and Mathematics (STEM) education and careers, (b) the success and advancement of women and underrepresented minorities in higher education and STEM, (c) interdisciplinary approaches and structures in higher education, and (d) the role of strategic planning in organizational learning and cultural change.

Kate credits her educational experiences—good and not so good—for compelling her to pursue a PhD in Higher Education. Two transformational graduate school experiences equipped her with an enormous amount of insight into unresolved negative feelings, including an overall sadness, that characterized her undergraduate experience. In the paraphrased words of Paulo Freire in Pedagogy of the Oppressed (1968, Continuum), her graduate courses and community offered the tools, language, and conceptual lenses to "name" the problem that underpinned these feelings—a patriarchal culture, a dearth of women professors, etc. This was a powerful and freeing experience through which she shed years of guilt and self-blame for feeling that she must have done something wrong. She realized quickly that she wanted to do the complex work of helping to create welcoming campus cultures and an enhanced sense of belonging for students, faculty, and staff. Compelled by a desire for a deep and multilevel understanding of the complex organization and functioning of higher education, she began her PhD in June 2009 at the age of 35. This rigorous scholar-practitioner experience and the welcoming community in which it occurred helped her uncover a strong voice grounded in advocacy. She strives each day to raise awareness and to work against structural and cultural forces that can isolate, marginalize, or make students, faculty, and staff feel wholly invisible or unwelcome in a college or university community.

Kate received her master's degree in secondary-level teaching from The College of New Jersey in Ewing, NJ, her master's degree in College Student Service Administration from The College of Saint Rose in Albany, NY, and her Bachelor of Arts degree in English from Boston College. She lives in Reading, MA, with her husband, John, her seven-month-old daughter, Lily, and big loving black cat, Panther.

Silvia Mejía, PhD
Associate Professor, Spanish and Latin American Literature and Film, The College of Saint Rose, Albany, NY, USA

Silvia Mejía, a first-generation college student, is currently an associate professor of Spanish and Latin American Literature and Film at The College of Saint Rose (Albany, NY). In 2007, she graduated as a PhD in Comparative Literature from University of Maryland (College Park). Five years earlier, she had obtained an MA in Latin American Literature from the same university. Silvia's areas of academic specialization are film theory and criticism, immigration studies, and comparative studies of contemporary Latin American and Latina/o narrative production.

Before coming to the United States to pursue graduate studies, Silvia received her BA in Social Communication from Universidad Central del Ecuador (Quito). Between 1992 and 2002, she worked as a reporter, correspondent, and editor for the national daily newspapers *Hoy* (Ecuador) and *La Prensa Gráfica* (El Salvador), as well as the magazines *Europ-Magazine* (France) and *Cash* (Ecuador). Silvia was 29 years old when she began graduate school, leaving behind what she calls her "first life" as a full-time journalist.

Silvia lives in Albany, NY, with her husband, David, and their daughter, Zoe. She may be contacted at mejias@strose.edu.

Markesha Miller, PhD

Clinical Coordinator, Clinical Mental Health Counseling, South University, Savannah, GA, USA; Owner and Director of Holistic Psychological Associates in Columbia, SC, USA

Accomplished, humble, and "marked" for success, Dr. Markesha Miller has made her life's work to empower women and enrich families. As a licensed professional counselor (North and South Carolina), motivational speaker, and certified family court mediator, Dr. Miller is committed to making sure our families are healthy, happy and strong. As a fifteen-year court-appointed special advocate and frequent lecturer and presenter at conferences, universities, and expert to various media outlets, Dr. Miller answers the call daily to provide her expertise across numerous platforms.

As the first in her family to pursue a terminal degree, she is a 2000 graduate of the University of South Carolina with a BA in English and Psychology, with additional degrees in Counselor Education (2003) and a Doctor of Philosophy degree in Counselor Education and Supervision (2010). Qualified and committed, Dr. Miller is the Owner and Director of Holistic Psychological Associates in Columbia, SC, Vice President/Clinical Director of The Center for Emotional and Behavioral Change, and serves as the clinical coordinator of South University's Clinical Mental Health Counseling program. You can catch Dr. Miller every Thursday on WACH-Fox 57 for "Therapy Thursday."

Over the past 15 years, Dr. Miller has provided hundreds of private counseling sessions, and has participated in national, regional, and state-wide presentations on topics ranging from multicultural education issues (undergraduate and graduate students) to examining the various educational, cultural, and environmental issues that are unique to women of color. She is committed! Committed to her profession, community, and the fabric of our communities ... family.

When not changing the world through counseling, lecturing, and serving, Dr. Miller is volunteering, shopping, and writing. Originally from Pageland, SC, Miller currently resides in Columbia, SC. Dr. Markesha Miller can be reached at markmiller@southuniversity.edu or drmiller@thecebc.com.

Wanda I. Montañez EdD

Director of College Success for the Massachusetts Charter Public School Association, Hudson, MA, USA

Dr. Wanda I. Montañez is the Director of College Success for the Massachusetts Charter Public School Association (MCPSA). Born in Puerto Rico, she and her family arrived in the United States in the early 1980s. As a low-income, first-generation, bilingual Latina college student, Wanda earned her Bachelor of Arts degree in Psychology from Framingham State University. After graduation, she began her work in the college-access field working at a Latino organization, providing college counseling services at two public high schools in Boston, and coordinated an afterschool program for young girls that focused on better understanding their Latina identities. In 2004, Wanda earned her Master of Education degree from Boston University with a focus in Community Counseling. She continued her college access and success work at the college- and university-level, working with students, educators, and administrators within private, public, and community colleges. At the age of 32, Wanda entered the Higher Education Administration program at the UMass Boston with cohort 2009 and subsequently earned her Doctor of Education degree in 2014. Her dissertation topic, "The Role of Multiethnic Latino Students' Sense of Belonging in College", was fueled, in part, by her work with underrepresented students over the course of her professional career in the K-16 pipeline. In her role with MCPSA, Wanda works to design and implement systems and programs to support the statewide charter school community in boosting college attendance and completion rates. If you'd like to reach Wanda, email her at montanez_w@yahoo.com.

Anna W. Nolan, PhD

2016 Doctoral Graduate and current stay-at-home mom with three children, Menands, NY, USA

Anna W. Nolan earned her PhD in Curriculum and Instruction from the University at Albany in 2016. She started her doctoral journey as a former elementary school teacher who was then employed as a staff development specialist and ended it as a stay- at- home mom of three young children. Anna is excited to start her postdoctoral career.

Cinzia Pica-Smith, EdD
Assistant Professor, Human Services and Rehabilitation Studies, Assumption College, Worcester, MA, USA

Cinzia is a 46-year-old White, cisgender woman. She was born in Napoli, a large metropolitan city in Southern Italy, and first came to the United States as an international undergraduate student. After earning her bachelor's, she traveled to Nicaragua to work in a feminist women's cooperative—an experience that cemented her political consciousness—and then to the People's Republic of China to work as a teacher for two years. She returned to the United States and pursued her first graduate degree (a master's in Counseling from The College of Saint Rose in Albany, NY) and practiced as a clinician for three years before going back to graduate school (another master's from Harvard's Graduate School of Education in Risk and Prevention and a doctorate in Child and Family Studies from the UMass Amherst). She was 34 when she entered the doctoral program, and she is grateful to have had both a counseling and self-reflective practice and process before entering the program. This orientation was key in her ability to analyze, make meaning, and build resilience while in the program.

Emily Phillips, PhD
Adjunct Lecturer and Retired Professor, Educational Psychology, Counseling, and Special Education, State University of New York at Oneonta, Oneonta, NY, USA

Emily grew up in the tenements of the lower East Side of Manhattan. Her mother, who was raised as an Orthodox Jew, attended vocational high school for sewing. Her dad only completed 6th grade before being sent to work in the coal mines of Kentucky. Her mother insisted Emily would not only go to college but also excel. She did her bachelor's as a dual secondary English and English major while being newly married to her childhood sweetheart and having her daughter. Then she did her master's in Education/School Counseling while pregnant and having her son, followed by a Certificate of Advanced Study for permanent school counseling certification. She did not, however, begin work right away as a school counselor.

She has worked in related fields for the American Red Cross (ARC), as a social worker at a day treatment center, mental health clinician, long-term psychiatric patient case management, elementary school counselor, and counselor educator. She has taught parenting classes, child abuse prevention and treatment, and play as specialty areas. At the age of 44, she began her doctorate and was 47 when she completed it. As an ABD, she was hired by the college where she completed her master's degree to fill in for someone on leave for a medical emergency. She spent a crazy year as a new counselor educator while completing her doctoral dissertation. After the professor she was hired to replace died, the college did a national search. Seven people competed for a faculty line, and they hired Emily. She was over 50. She moved as quickly as she could since she was advancing toward retirement. She was promoted to associate and then finally full professor. She could never have done this without the total support of her husband (who has since died). They were at the best point ever in their then 25-year marriage. He was willing to find a better paying job in their small rural town, become a virtual single parent of a high school senior with attention deficit disorder and a learning disability, and hold down the fort while she lived in two cities, got up at 5am to type for hours, and ranted and raved at the archaic doctoral system.

She has published several critical incidents in the field of counselor education and created activity guides for the state school counseling organization, matched to the national standards for School Counseling Programs. In retirement, she has taught as an adjunct instructor in counselor education. Her mother would have been very proud of her. Her mother died a few years before Emily completed her doctorate.

Seema Rivera, PhD
Assistant Professor, STEM Education, Clarkson University, Capital Region Campus, Schenectady, NY, USA

Seema is the daughter of immigrants. Her parents moved to the United States from India, and she grew up in Upstate New York. While her extended family was Lutheran, she was not raised in a religious household but did convert to Catholicism when she married. After college, Seema was unsure of her career path and decided to try teaching science for one year in the Bronx at a magnet school. This year of teaching was challenging; not only was the job tough, but Seema's brother also died that year. It was a difficult time; however, Seema found that education was a place she could make a difference. She then completed her master's and then taught chemistry for several years in New York State. She was going to take one class at a time at a Curriculum and Instruction doctoral program while teaching, but was then offered a full-time teaching assistantship position, meaning her doctoral program would be paid for if she was teaching and researching at the university. Being that it was a good offer and it allowed her to focus more specifically on science education, she decided to leave public school teaching and become a full-time doctoral student at the age of 30. She was also pregnant with her first child at this time. She finished her doctorate in a little over four years, when she was pregnant with her second child. You may contact Seema at emailseema@gmail.com.

Anne Toolan Rowley, PhD

Associate Professor, Communication Sciences and Disorders, The College of Saint Rose, Albany, NY, USA

Anne Toolan Rowley, is a college professor and licensed speech language pathologist in New York State. She enjoyed her professional career but sought academic promotion and the challenge of an advanced degree. She had been a lifelong learner, and as such, she saw the doctoral degree as the way to achieve her aspirations. Her desire was to select a doctoral program that would complement her profession as a speech-language pathologist. A degree in reading and literacy would do just that.

The challenge of full-time work, family needs, and personal commitments did not deter Dr. Rowley from seeking the degree later in life than your typical doctoral student. The completion of the degree spanned nine years of part-time study. She felt that the journey, though arduous at times, was worth it to receive promotion and enhance her undergraduate and graduate courses with the knowledge that bridged the areas of language and literacy for individuals across the lifespan.

Deborah J. Smith, EdD

Professor, Health Sciences, Empire State College, Saratoga Springs, NY, USA

Dr. Smith writes as a first-generation college student. She obtained her bachelor's degree in English, a master's degree in Counseling and the Bachelor of Science in Nursing degree before returning in her forties to pursue doctoral work. Dr. Smith earned her EdD in Educational Technology in 2000 from the Graduate School of Education and Psychology at Pepperdine University in California, commuting from New York. The frequent flyer miles were tremendous, and she enjoyed using each one. She still flies around the world and writes for travel magazines and public radio. Dr. Smith is an ANA-certified clinical nurse specialist in Adult Psychiatric–Mental Health Nursing. She taught in area schools of nursing and worked in a hospital and outpatient adult psychiatric settings, including an APA-recognized interdisciplinary horticultural therapy program. Dr. Smith is now professor of Health Services at SUNY Empire State College in Saratoga Springs, New York, and may be reached at Deborah.Smith@esc.edu.

Maureen E. Squires, EdD

Associate Professor and Program Coordinator, MSEd Program, Teacher Education, State University of New York at Plattsburgh, Plattsburgh, NY, USA

Dr. Squires writes as a White, middle-class Catholic woman who grew up in rural Central New York. She is the first person in her family to pursue doctoral studies. At the age of 27, after teaching high school English for five years, she began the doctoral program in the Graduate School of Education at a SUNY University. Five years later, at the age of 32, she graduated with a CAS in Educational Leadership and an EdD in Educational Theory and Practice. She now teaches graduate courses in Special Education and Adolescence Education in the Teacher Education Unit at SUNY Plattsburgh. Please direct email correspondence to msqui001@plattsburgh.edu.

Jamie S. Switzer, EdD

Associate Professor, Department of Journalism and Technical Communication, Colorado State University, Fort Collins, CO, USA

Dr. Jamie S. Switzer is an associate professor in the Department of Journalism and Technical Communication at Colorado State University (CSU). She received her doctorate in Educational Technology from Pepperdine University and also holds degrees in Technical Communication from CSU and Radio/TV/Film from Texas Christian University. She has over 26 years of experience in new media technologies.

Dr. Switzer conducts research on computer-mediated communication, new media technologies, virtual environments, and educational technology. She has published in *the Journal of Virtual Worlds Research;* the *Handbook on 3D3C Platforms: Applications and Tools for Three Dimensional Systems for Communication, Creation, and Commerce; The Handbook of Research on Virtual Workplaces and the New Nature of Business Practices;* the *Journal of Media Education; Mass Communication and Society;* the *Journal of Media Education; Feedback; Computers and Education; Teaching and Learning with Technology: Beyond Constructivism;* The *Encyclopedia of Distance Learning, Teaching, Technologies, and Applications; Interactive Educational Multimedia; Innovative Higher Education; THE Journal; the Journal of Educational Technology Systems, The Internet Encyclopedia; The Encyclopedia of Multimedia Technology and Networking; The Encyclopedia of E-Collaboration; E-Collaboration: Concepts, Methodologies, Tools, and Applications;* and *The Handbook of Research in Computer-Mediated Communication.* Dr. Switzer is the founder and Director of the Online Mentoring Program in the Journalism Department at CSU. She also founded the Center for Innovation in Learning Technologies in the CSU College of Business.

Liza A. Talusan, PhD
Educational Consultant and Speaker, Brockton, MA, USA

Liza Talusan graduated with her PhD from the UMass Boston. She began her doctoral journey at the age of 36 when her children were of the ages two, five, and eight. She engaged in her doctoral study full-time while also working as a Director of a multicultural center; served in three graduate assistantships during her doctoral studies; and held leadership positions on a number of national committees. She is the daughter of Filipino immigrants and the middle child among five siblings. She is a practicing Catholic committed to LGBTQ inclusion, a fierce educator, and unapologetic about fighting for the rights of all people. Liza can be reached via her website at www.lizatalusan.com.

Ying Tang, PhD
Associate Professor, School Counseling, State University of New York at Oneonta, Oneonta, NY, USA

Ying Tang is a first-generation Asian American and a counselor educator specialized in school counseling. She started her doctoral study in the United States at the age of 28. Within several years of her doctoral study, she had been through many significant life events, from living in a foreign country for the first time, to getting a doctoral degree, and also becoming a mother while completing her dissertation. The pathway she took may not be a unique one, but the transformational journey from a shy Asian student to a strong and independent professional woman has definitely been phenomenal.

Terri Ward, EdD
Associate Professor, Special Education, The College of Saint Rose, Albany, NY, USA

Terri Ward is an associate professor of Special Education at The College of Saint Rose in Albany, New York. She lives with her wife, Hope, and two adopted children from foster care. Her research interests focus on the ability to create and sustain inclusive educational environments for all children. Current collaborative research projects focus on the assessment of learning, differentiated instruction in K-12 settings, and the relationship between positive experiences in foster care and adult life outcomes. She continues to keep in contact with her doctoral colleagues even 20 years later.

Wendy Neifeld Wheeler, PhD
Dean of Students, Albany College of Pharmacy and Health Sciences, Albany, NY, USA

Wendy is a straight, White, Jewish female, and first-generation college student who began her doctorate at the late age of 41 after completing a bachelor's degree and two master's degrees. It took her five years to complete the doctorate, while working both a full-time and part-time job. Her commitment to her terminal degree was motivated by her desire to be the best educator she was capable of being. The degrees that she has amassed are in the disciplines of psychology, college student personnel, community psychology/chemical dependency, and curriculum and instruction. This broad-based academic foundation has been instrumental in mattering to the students with whom she has the privilege to work in higher education as an administrator and as an adjunct faculty member. You are welcome to contact her at wnwheeler1991@gmail.com.

GLOSSARY

APA/MLA/Chicago Format: Formal writing style guidelines used for academic writing. **APA** (American Psychological Association: used in psychology and education fields); **MLA** (Modern Language Association: Used in liberal arts and humanities fields); **Chicago format**: Used in humanities fields.

Academia/Academe: A place and community of individuals in pursuit of research, learning, and scholarship.

Candidate/Candidacy/ABD: A student who has completed all required coursework and has passed her comprehensive or qualifying exams, but has not yet completed her dissertation, is a doctoral candidate and is said to have achieved candidacy. ABD (all but dissertation) is not a formal degree status, but many graduate students use the term informally.

Cohort: A group of students who start a degree program at the same time and lockstep take classes together (generally full time) with the idea of creating a community that travels through the degree program together. A doctoral cohort may persist through the period of required coursework (generally the first two years), but then begin to proceed through the remainder of the program at different speeds toward the completion of comprehensive exams and the dissertation.

Colloquium/Colloquia: An academic gathering at which specialists deliver an address on a topic and then answer questions related to the topic. "Colloquia" is plural.

Comprehensive or Qualifying Examinations: Examinations in which the student is asked to demonstrate comprehensive knowledge of the discipline; these exams are used to qualify the student to go forward to complete the dissertation.

Degrees: Doctorate/Doctoral Degree/Advanced Degree/Terminal Degree

PhD: Doctor of Philosophy, highest degree that can be earned in almost any field. It requires graduate students to complete a dissertation of original research.

EdD: Doctor of Education, highest degree earned in a school of education, graduate studies are usually focused on the application of knowledge to benefit the community. It requires completion of a dissertation of original research.

ScD: Doctor of Science is an academic research doctorate, awarded in fields of science at research institutions. Dissertation of original research is required.

Psy D: Doctor of Psychology, with a primary focus on assessing and treating clients. Research is considered secondary. Dissertation consisting of original research may still be required.

DPT: Doctorate of Physical Therapy, a post-bachelor's professional doctorate earned by physical therapists; usually takes three years to complete; students study many areas of rehabilitation and complete several internships. The DPT has been the required entry-level degree for physical therapy practitioners since 2015.

EdS: Education Specialist degree may be earned after completion of a master's degree. For some, it may be the in-between degree before completion of a doctorate. This is common in the field of education.

CAS: Certificate of Advanced Study, a post-master's degree certificate for students seeking advanced studies but who may not want to complete a doctorate.

Dissertation/Thesis: Dissertation is a long written essay required for the completion of a doctoral degree. The dissertation generally consists of several required components that demonstrate that the doctoral candidate has reviewed extensive literature on a given topic, has identified an area of inquiry within the topic, has developed a method for exploring the area of inquiry, has collected and analyzed data related to the area of inquiry, and has used the analysis to draw conclusions that contribute to overall knowledge of the area of inquiry.

Dissertation/Thesis (Chapters): A completed dissertation consists of five or more chapters that present the research questions or problems to be studied, a review of the literature, methodology for gathering and analyzing data, results/findings, and discussion of findings, conclusions, and recommendations.

Dissertation/Thesis Advisor: A university faculty member, generally within a doctoral candidate's academic department, who has agreed to serve as an advisor/mentor and guide the candidate's process of completion of the dissertation; may sometimes be assigned but is most often chosen by the candidate after careful consideration of the candidate's needs and interests and the needs and interests of potential advisors. This person may be the same or distinct from the academic advisor who helps the student select courses and typically possesses content expertise related to the doctoral candidate's research topic.

Dissertation Committee: A group, can be two or more, of university faculty members who, like the dissertation advisor, have agreed to provide guidance for a doctoral candidate in completion of the dissertation. The dissertation advisor is the chair of the dissertation committee and is a member of the committee with whom the candidate works most closely. The committee consists of 3–4 members, two of whom must be in the doctoral candidate's field of study. Dissertation committee members may also be referred to as "readers."

Dissertation Defense: The dissertation process culminates in the candidate's presentation of her research to her committee readers and one or two "outside readers." The readers may ask the candidate questions about any aspect of the research on which the dissertation is based, as well as on related speculative areas of inquiry. The doctoral candidate "defends" her methods and findings, demonstrating knowledge and understanding of the parameters and limitations of research processes. A successful defense results in completion of the doctorate.

Dissertation Proposal/Prospectus: The dissertation begins with a proposal, generally consisting of the first three chapters: statement of the problem, review of the literature, and methodology. The proposal is a plan, a road map that identifies the problem/topic to be studied, what is known and is not known about the topic, and how the researcher (doctoral candidate) will gather and analyze data to address the problem or answer the research questions.

Dissertation Proposal Defense: The dissertation proposal must be approved by the dissertation committee before the doctoral candidate can go ahead with the proposed research, thus the candidate defends her proposed road map, demonstrating that she has a viable method for addressing the research questions.

Doctoral Graduate Assistantships (GA)/Teaching Assistantships (TA)/ Research Assistantships (RA): These are generally part-time employment positions on campus that may be paid as a stipend and/or as tuition waivers or some combination of stipend and tuition waiver. The positions generally require 10–20 hours of work per week, but, in reality, may result in a greater time commitment.

Executive Programs: Programs usually created for students who have multiple years of experience in their field. Many times these are part-time programs not requiring full-time study on campus.

External/Outside Dissertation Reviewers: Someone not in a student's department who is willing to be on the dissertation committee, this person usually has a doctorate and has special expertise in the field. In some cases, one or two external reviewers, beyond those on the dissertation committee, are required at the dissertation defense stage.

Funding: Refers to how one pays for the doctoral program; can consist of full or partial monies from personal assets, grants, fellowships, assistant-ships (teaching, research, or administrative), and/or loans.

Heterosexual Privilege: This is the assumption that all people identify as heterosexual and people are treated as though this is a fact.

Hidden Curriculum: This is a set of unspoken expectations about what should or should not happen in the classroom or education work setting that a person learns through trial and error about the values, beliefs, and norms.

Hooding/Hooding Ceremony: Hooding is the act of placing the academic hood (part of the academic regalia) over the head and shoulders of a candidate to symbolize completion of the degree. This can take place at graduation or at a separate smaller ceremony prior to graduation, for doctoral graduates within a school or college of a university (e.g., all doctoral candidates in a school of education would attend a common hooding ceremony distinct from the graduation ceremony).

Institutional Review Board (IRB): This board consists of a variety of university faculty representatives of the academic disciplines in the university, whose job is to review the proposed research to be sure that it protects the rights and welfare of human research subjects. IRBs at colleges and universities have the authority to ask for modifications in research, and can disapprove or approve research. Ethically, research cannot be conducted without the IRB approval.

Imposter Syndrome: A persistent fear of being exposed as a fraud even though the person has demonstrated the skills and knowledge to be successful. This, many times, impacts high-achieving individuals.

Matriculation/Nonmatriculated Student: Matriculation means that a student has been accepted into a degree program for formal study. A nonmatriculated student is the one who has not applied or has not yet been accepted into a degree program but who may be taking classes from a degree program with or without the intent for the credits to count toward a degree.

Mentor/Mentorship: A mentor is someone who is more experienced in an academic endeavor or profession and who guides and supports a less experienced person in their area of expertise.

Macroaggressions: Large-scale or overt actions made by people in privileged positions toward those not in a privileged position (i.e., race, religion, sexual orientation, age, etc.).

Microaggressions: Small everyday acts and assumptions that people in privileged positions act upon those not in a privilege position (i.e., race, religion, sexual orientation, age, etc.).

Postdoc: Employment or internship/fellowship after the completion of doctoral studies.

Professional Identity: The identity that a person gains through the education and professional training that is connected to one's profession.

Program Completion Rates: Indicates the percentage of students who complete a degree from among those who started that degree program.

"Publish or Perish": In academia, a professor is expected to publish in order to gain tenure and/or rank. Each college or university has guidelines as to how a scholarship is defined and what "counts" toward tenure and promotion.

Qualitative/Quantitative/Mixed Methods Research: The forms of research methodology characterized by how data is collected, analyzed, reported, and interpreted.

Regalia: Regalia refer to the clothing worn as part of the graduation ceremony and at other formal events in the academy, that is, cap, gown, and hood. The term dates back to the early English times. There are different kinds of regalia for bachelor's, master's, and doctorate degree candidates. Each varies in the design of the robe and symbolism created by the length of sleeves, piping, and colors, and designs depend both on one's school (i.e., School of Business, School of Education, etc.), as well as the college/university where one completes the degree. Wearing of regalia is a symbol of membership.

Research Agenda: The area of research that a faculty member is interested in pursuing. An individual's research agenda may be formal or organic in nature as those areas develop over the career of the faculty member.

Residency Requirement: Degree programs may require students to complete a certain number of credit hours in a semester, for a certain number of semesters (e.g., residency might require one to be a full-time student taking nine credits a semester for two consecutive semesters.).

Scholar/Scholarship: A scholar is someone with an academic interest and body of research work in a particular specialty; scholarship usually refers to a scholar's publications, books, and/or peer-reviewed articles and presentations at regional, national, and international conferences.

SPSS: A statistical computer software package or a set of tools used in quantitative research.

Study Carrel: A small cubicle with a desk for the use of a reader or student in a library; some carrels are actually small offices and can be reserved for a semester. Because the number of carrels is limited, doctoral students typically have priority.

Tenure/Tenure Track/Professorial Rank: A faculty member is a probationary employee of a college/university for five or six years, at which point he/she must apply for tenure. During those years she is usually employed at the rank of assistant professor, and he/she must accumulate a course of publications, presentations, service activities, and student evaluations that demonstrate a commitment to the profession for which she studied, the college she works for, and to the students she teaches. Tenure must be applied for, based on criteria set by the institution, and is determined by review of peers and administrators. Professorial ranks above assistant professor are also applied for, based on institutional criteria, and consist of associate professor and professor (also known as full professor). Adjunct instructors and lecturers are faculty members who do not participate in the "tenure-track" process.

Time for Completion: This refers to the longest amount of time the university or college allows a student to complete the degree he/she has been accepted into; for doctoral degrees this might range from seven to ten years.

TWI: Traditionally White institution; a college or university that has over many years had a student body consisting of individuals who primarily identify as White/European American. It is sometimes also referred to as PWI, that is, predominately White institution.